BLESSINGS &
BALDERDASH

Commentaries from The Christian Index,
America's Oldest Religious Publication

J. GERALD HARRIS

TRUSTHOUSE
PUBLISHERS

Copyright © 2018, J. Gerald Harris

Blessings and Balderdash
Commentaries from The Christian Index, America's Oldest Religious Publication

ISBN: 978-1-945774-28-7

Trust House Publishers
P.O.Box 3181
Taos, NM 87571

www.trusthousepublishers.com

Ordering Information: Special discounts are available on quantity purchases by churches, associations, and retailers. For details, contact the publisher at the address above or call toll-free 1-844-321-4202.

1 2 3 4 5 6 7 8 9

Bobby,

May our great God forever smile upon you with His loving favor.

Gerald Harris

Ps. 84:11

Table of Contents

FOREWORD

Why would I call a book Blessings and Balderdash? I am assuming you know what the word "blessings" means. The word "balderdash" may be a bit more unfamiliar. "Balderdash" means "hogwash," "poppycock," "twaddle" or "nonsense."

Now that you understand the words in the title of this collection of editorials, let me explain the reason for choosing the name of this book. As a pastor for forty-one years I became accustomed to having my sermons critiqued from time to time. The comments ranged all the way from, "Pastor, that was an inspired and inspiring sermon" to "How am I supposed to apply your sermon to my daily life?"

Those sermon evaluations were intermittent and mild compared to the comments I received from the more than 400 editorials I wrote for The Christian Index over a period of fifteen years. Social media has certainly contributed to the frequency and the ability of people to register their comments and opinions. Furthermore, I have discovered that Baptists and Christians in general have no hesitancy about expressing their opinions and everyone seems to have one about most subjects.

Consequently, some have expressed their opinion that certain editorials were a blessing and an encouragement to them. However, others seemed to delight in letting me know that my editorials were nothing but balderdash, tripe, hogwash or nonsense. I can honestly say that I was happy with receiving all comments whether complimentary or denigrating. I resolved early on that a difference of opinion is never a cause for withdrawing from a friend.

I have also learned that if one passes the words of praise he receives on to Calvary, he can also pass the criticism that comes his way on to Calvary as well. Jesus, our Savior, is worthy of all praise anyway and if criticism comes our way as a result of our efforts to serve Him, He is also fully capable of taking our criticism, thus giving us the freedom to continue our service to Him unabated.

DEDICATION

I have always had great admiration for David Robinson, who made the National Basketball Association All-Star team ten times. His testimony is that he became a Christian at age 26 after someone encouraged him to read the Bible. He was an extraordinary student, an honored athlete, and an American patriot, graduating from the U. S. Naval Academy and serving in the U. S. Navy prior to his NBA career. Robinson founded and funded the Carver School in San Antonio, a non-profit private school named to provide more opportunities for inner-city children. He married Valerie Hoggatt in 1991 and they have three sons, all of whom are following in the train of their successful and honorable father.

Why would I give a synopsis of David Robinson's life in this dedication? Simply because of a quote from "The Admiral" as he was affectionately called as a member of the San Antonio Spurs. Robinson stated, "I know I will leave my work unfinished. I just hope I planted enough seeds in my children and grandchildren that they will continue (that work)."

Billy Graham, America's evangelist, said something similar: "The greatest legacy one can pass on to one's children and grandchildren is not money or other material things accumulated in one's life, but rather a legacy of character and faith."

With that being said I would like to dedicate this book to my fourteen grandchildren (including our oldest granddaughter's husband). The fabulous fourteen are Billy and Miriam Godwin's children: Hayley Godwin Echols and her husband Taylor, Harris and Hope; Jerry and Andrea Harris' children: Hudson, Brinley, Alden and Maleah; and John and Karen Harris' children: Grace, Luke, Mark, Austin, Ashley Grace and Steele.

The Genius of The
Southern Baptist Convention

As a Southern Baptist you are making a remarkable impact upon our world for the cause of Christ. Most of you couldn't possibly know what God is doing in and through our denomination. Though I had been a pastor for many years, it was not until I sat on the Cooperative Program Subcommittee of the Executive Committee of the SBC that I began to get a clear picture of the scope of our mission outreach and the expansive ministry we have as Southern Baptists.

I wish every Southern Baptist had the privilege of serving on that subcommittee and hearing the presidents of our agencies tell about what God is doing through our denomination. It was exciting to see their passion as they cast their specific vision for the future. I was captivated every time I heard their report and grieved that we never had all the funds necessary to meet all the needs.

I had the same experience when I was a member of the Administration Committee of the Georgia Baptist Convention. I was always blessed at the ministries and mission endeavors taking place in our state. You have heard all the statistics, but the truth is that Southern Baptists are making a difference in our world.

Yet, there is so much more we could do if the resources were available. I feel a powerful urgency about the work of the Lord. I serve on the SBC Funding Study Committee and we are prayerfully trying to find how we can provide more money for our burgeoning seminary enrollments without dipping into money allocated for other agencies. The method of funding our divine cause is the envy of just about every denomination on the planet.

The Cooperative Program is what makes it all possible. It is the golden cord that binds us together and gives us an effectiveness that is matchless among other denominations. It is the genius of the SBC.

The Cooperative Program was established in 1925 for the purpose of funding the work of Southern Baptists around the world. At that time the financial needs of the denomination were great and the God-given vision of the convention's leadership was compelling.

On the front page of the May 21, 1925 edition of The Christian Index an article appeared entitled "Our Great Task." The Commission on the Co-Operative Program crafted the article. The second paragraph reads: "Difficulties, burdens and crises are no new thing in the history of the Kingdom of God. The past is a record of triumphs over difficulties by conquering faith and united effort. The difficulties we face are more than matched by the ability of our people to meet them if we approach them in faith, prayer, courage and sacrifice. The success of the future depends upon the heroic spirit shown by our people at this time."

Len G. Broughton of Jacksonville, Florida (later pastor of Baptist Tabernacle in Atlanta) brought the convention sermon in 1925 to the annual meeting of the SBC in Memphis. He proclaimed: "...unless a miracle of giving is performed at once, there is nothing ahead of us but retrenchment that will set us back in all lines of our work for many decades to come. Pathetic and heartrending appeals are coming from every source; never were the fields so white, and never was the harvest so plenteous.

"Never was our wealth so general, and never was our extravagance so extravagant. And yet our denominational machinery is almost padlocked, while the work rushes on in its madness without a thought of its steward-ship to God…No, we are not going to lower our standard; we are going away from this Convention with our goal higher along all lines that ever, realizing that the altitude of our goal today will mark the attitude of our going tomorrow."

I would echo the same appeal today. We can certainly do more together than we can do separately; and a part of Empowering Kingdom Growth is pooling our resources to accomplish our purpose of reaching the lost, edifying the saints and building heathy kingdom families and churches.

When I was a student at Mercer University I read a short story in a literature class. I think Guy de Maupassant wrote the story, but I haven't been able to confirm it. It's a story about a kingdom that decided to honor their sovereign. Someone suggested that everyone bring the best bottle of wine he possessed and each one would pour his wine into a large vat, which would become a gift to the king.

One individual decided that he would substitute water for wine and that if all the others brought their finest wine no one would ever know that he diluted the wine with water. It was a sinister thought that was not his exclusively.

Amazingly, everyone had the same idea and the vat was filled with nothing but water. When the king's chalice was dipped into the vat and presented to him as a most delicious wine supposedly given by his adoring subjects he tasted the liquid and frowned in dismay. "This is nothing but water," he thought.

As the people of God, we must be sure that we give to our Sovereign the very best that we have. We certainly can't water down the gospel when we preach. We can't dilute our convictions with the empty philosophies of this world. We can't offer to God the leftover moments of our time; nor can we afford to give Him a tricking trifle from our treasures.

As you give to your local church and as your church gives to the Cooperative Program we are able to keep our lifeline of faith and ministry open to a world that is so much in need of the hope we have in Christ. The faithful support of the CP by all of us is the finest and most practical way of providing for the continuation of all our Christian enterprises.

Can one be Politically Correct and True to the Bible?

Today's society places a premium upon being politically correct. Proper terminology must be used so as not to be offensive to anyone. For example, obese people are now referred to as the gravitationally challenged. An old person is gerontologically advanced. A meter maid is a parking enforcement adjudicator.

Someone who is blind is photonically non-receptive. Political correctness first defined the deaf person as hearing impaired, but more recently has suggested that such an individual is visually oriented. The man with a receding hairline is not balding, but is in follicle regression.

Political correctness refuses to call anyone who tarries long at the wine a drunk, but simply suggests that such a person may be intemperate. The embezzler has only misappropriated funds; and the sexually promiscuous person is only guilty of an indiscretion. Consequently, those who call for PC refuse to call anyone a sinner, but at best regard him or her as spiritually challenged.

We now have politically correct Bibles that are gender neutral and hymnals that have translated what is referred to as offensive language into something more palatable to our modern society. To me all of this sugar sweet, easy-to-digest, don't upset-anyone kind of gospel is a long way from repentance. It is almost certain that this kind of "Christianity" does not result in the kind of life change needed to impact the world for God and for good.

Actually, those who insist on political correctness are interested in far more than terminology. They are proponents of a philosophy that embraces a way of life that is foreign to the biblical principles we hold dear. Their buzzwords are toleration and inclusivism. They want to reduce our beliefs and convictions to the lowest common denominator so that no one is offended by anything that is said or done.

As a result of a humanistic, secular world's vigilance and the church's indifference we are becoming an antinomian society – a society without regard for the law of God.

Scripture verses have been removed from National Parks; the Ten Commandments have been taken down from courthouse walls, and nativity scenes have been removed from town squares because they are supposedly a violation of First Amendment rights. In other words, they are not politically correct.

Therefore, for a preacher to be politically correct he must no longer ring the bell on sin; and he must suppress any thought that might prompt him to mention the "h" word. He must avoid all Biblical references to theological definiteness and exclusivity lest he be regarded as narrow-minded or bigoted.

However, Jesus never seemed to be interested in political correctness. He dared to drive the moneychangers out of the temple, challenged the dead religion of his day and called the religious leaders 'hypocrites, blind guides and fools" (Matthew 3:7).

Furthermore, Jesus made exclusive claims, He said, "I am the way, the truth and the life: no man cometh unto the Father, but by me" (John

14:6). In fact, the Word of God unflinchingly and unapologetically and without any pseudo-intellectual mumbo-jumbo attests to the uniqueness of Jesus as the only way to be saved and avows that Christianity cannot accord moral equivalence to any other religion.

This unyielding exclusivism incites hostility from the politically correct crowd because it contradicts the "enlightened" tenets of secular humanism, which are incompatible with the absolute truth found in Holy Scripture.

In a society where everything seems to be tolerated but the pure, uncompromising preaching of the Word of God we must remember that Jesus said, "The disciple is not above his master, nor the servant above his lord. It is enough for the disciple that he be as his master, and the servant as his lord. If they have called the master of the house Beelzebub, how much more shall they call them of his household?" (Matthew 10:24-25).

Dare to have an unswerving allegiance to the truth. It may get you maligned by the world, but it will win you the favor of heaven.

From Religious Belief to Atheist Hubris

I have fond memories of my home church as a child. The worship center of the church was constructed in 1926. Across the front of the church there was a very large mural that stretched from one side of the church to the other. The painting depicted a number of biblical scenes including: the return of the prodigal son to his father, Jesus blessing the children, as well as the baptism of Jesus.

The stained-glass windows in the church were absolutely beautiful. When I became bored with the pastor's sermon I could be blessed by just looking at the windows. When the sun shone through a certain way the variegated colors of the windows were cast upon the people in the church. I was fascinated by the light, the shadows and the colors.

This is the church where I first saw the light, was saved, baptized, and nurtured in the faith. This is where my early Christian walk was encouraged by faithful Sunday School teachers and Royal Ambassador leaders.

After I got married and while I was away in the seminary my home church relocated to a beautiful, new campus. It was the right decision and I rejoiced in the progress being made by the church, but the old church facility was sold to someone who chose to redesign the building and turn it into an apartment complex. Now, almost 40 years later it is still an apartment complex, but it has not been well kept. In fact, it is an eyesore – so dilapidated and an apparent contradiction to its location on Church Street.

Is America becoming spiritually dilapidated and a contradiction to the term "Christian nation"? We may not be able to see it clearly because we tend to become absorbed by our culture. However, since Jonathan Edwards preached his sermon, "Sinners in the Hands of an Angry God" in 1741, America has moved from religious belief to atheist hubris. What we at first abhor, we begin to tolerate and ultimately embrace if we are not careful.

Ask our missionaries – those who have been away from the United State for a while. Ask them if they have observed any changes in our culture. Wayne Jenkins, who has served for 21 years as one of our missionaries in Germany recently told me on a brief visit to Georgia that he likened America to a seventeen-year-old boy who is 50% muscle and 50% hormones. He said, "The focus in this country is upon the temporal, not the eternal, upon instant gratification and being entertained."

Jenkins declared, "I am shocked at the influence of MTV and the proliferation of television programs that promote the homosexual agenda. In view of the shocking trends I am still convinced that the only thing that can affect change is the church. We need to recapture our lost vision of the Kingdom and work together to bring about the changes that are so desperately needed."

Ken Ellison, who spent more than 30 years as a missionary in Indonesia expressed astonishment and grief upon his return to America at the high divorce rate and the gambling craze in the land. He also cited his disbelief that a high school would be opened in New York for gay and lesbian youths.

The evangelical church is becoming a sub-culture in a pagan society. Don Wildmon, president of the American Family Association, recently indicated in a special commentary that Federal Judge Myron Thompson in Alabama answered a pivotal question for this country when he ruled that the display of the stone containing the Ten Commandments in the Alabama Courthouse was illegal. He said the pivotal question was, "Can the state acknowledge God?"

The judge's answer was "No"!

Things are changing rapidly in America. It is past time for God's people to stand up and be counted. If we don't rally to the cause of righteousness and if the pulpits of this country don't become ablaze with the truth of God's word we are not going to be able to prevent the decline and fall of the American republic. To our grandchildren the faith of their forefathers will become only a wistful memory – rather much like the old church building in my hometown.

Anything Christian Looks Unlawful

Some "John Doe" who prudently wishes to maintain his or her anonymity, notified the ACLU (American Civil Liberties Union) that the Ten Commandments are posted in a breezeway outside the Courthouse in Winder in Barrow County. Since the ACLU (Anything Christian Looks Unlawful*) seems to thrive on attempting to strip away all vestiges of Christianity in America, they jumped at the opportunity to flex their corporate legal muscle in Georgia just as they did in Alabama recently.

Eddie Elder, chairman of the Barrow County commissioners, and his six colleagues dismissed the first notice from the ACLU and gave little thought to the matter until a second letter was received threatening a lawsuit unless the Decalogue was removed.

It appears that we are being stripped of all insignia of our faith.

I remember when the Bible was read each morning in the public schools and prayer was offered by the teacher or perhaps by the principal over the intercom system. Our school assemblies were often chapel services with local pastors called upon to preach a sermon. A school principal permitting such an expression of religion today would face the risk of retribution or removal, or both.

For all intents and purposes prayer has been removed from the schools. Nativity scenes have been removed from public view. Efforts have been made to remove "In God We Trust" from our coins and currency. Schools no longer have "Christmas Holidays" but "Winter Holidays," and "Easter Holidays" have been replaced with "Spring Break."

I heard Herb Revis, pastor of North Jacksonville Baptist Church in Jacksonville, Florida, say, "It is no wonder that having removed the Ten Commandments from our schools we now must pass out condoms." The elimination of the law of God will pave the way for anarchy in our land. The Ten Commandments remind us that we are fallen creatures. The Bible says that the law is our "schoolmaster," designed to reveal our sinfulness and help us see our need for Christ (Galatians 3:24).

Today's philosophy has man, not God at the center of the universe. Modern man does not want to be reminded that he is a sinner, that he is not self-sufficient. So, he says, "Away with the Ten Commandments. I don't want anything that can remind me of my failures and frailties. I will base my religion on my understandings and observation, not some archaic set of rules."

Actually, Friedrich Schleiermacher, known as the father of modern liberalism, may have been the one who gave birth to the insidious philosophy that is rampant today and which has now become full grown. He propagated his teachings at the beginning of the 19th century and purported that religion is not so much a matter of doctrine, but of feeling, intuition and experience. When Schleiermacher opened that door, he cast great aspersion upon the fundamentals of the faith.

Why? Men would rather rely upon their own experience or feelings than "the faith that was once delivered to the saints" (Jude 3). Sinful creatures would rather attempt to eliminate the truth than have to be confronted by it.

The trend today is to eliminate the Ten Commandments, disavow the inerrancy of the Scripture, deify man, humanize God and ultimately dismantle Christianity.

The gradual, cunning fashion with which we were once being stripped of our religious freedom is now happening openly and blatantly. A society that has adopted the post-modern philosophy refuses to accept absolute truth. Sometimes even professing believers unknowingly influenced by the prevailing culture stressing "felt needs" will "adjust" the teachings of Scripture to accommodate their own misdirected whims.

We can retreat into our Christian "communes" and live unobtrusive lives or we can stand up for Christ. Some say that there is nothing we can do, that we are victims of a secular culture that rules the day. But if the early disciples living in a corrupt society could turn their world upside down for the cause of Christ (Acts 17:6) can we attempt to do less?

*The editor's interpretation of the acronym.

Mother Teresa on the Path to Recognition as a Saint

I was privileged to attend the National Prayer Breakfast on February 3, 1994 in Washington, D.C. The occasion attracted a "Who's Who" list of America's most notable government and civic leaders. The primary speaker for the occasion was Mother Teresa of Calcutta, India.

The diminutive nun was born Agnes Gonxha Bojaxhiu in Skopje (now in Macedonia) to Albanian parents on August 26, 1910. By the time she was twelve she had developed a special interest in international missions and knew that her ministry was to be to the poor, downtrodden people of this world. Known as "The Saint of the Gutters" this Roman Catholic nun spent most of her life caring for the sick, the outcast, the helpless people of India who were in her words "nothing less than Christ in distressing disguise".

In 1979 Mother Teresa accepted the Nobel Peace Prize in the name of the "unwanted, unloved and uncared for". On one occasion Pope Paul VI gave her a Lincoln Continental and she auctioned it off and used the proceeds to establish a leper colony in West Bengal. It would be difficult for anyone to question the selfless spirit of this woman who cared for the impoverished with reckless abandon.

Mother Teresa died in 1997 at the age of 87 after a long life of faithful and magnanimous service to the destitute people of this world. On Sunday, October 19th, six years after her death, hundreds of thousands of Roman Catholic pilgrims gathered in St. Peter's Square at the Vatican in Rome to observe the ceremony to mark the beatification of Mother Teresa.

Typically, the road to sainthood in the Roman Catholic Church is a long and arduous process stipulating that one miracle must be attributed to the candidate before beatification and a second miracle attributed to the candidate after beatification. The ceremony at the Vatican on October 19th marked the fastest ever process of beatification in the Catholic Church.

I will never forget what this missionary to the poorest of the poor said at the National Prayer Breakfast. She lamented, "I feel the greatest destroyer of peace today is abortion, because it is a war against the child, a direct killing of the innocent child, murder by the mother herself. Any county that accepts abortion is not teaching its people to love, but to use any violence to get what they want. This is why the greatest destroyer of love and peace is abortion."

So, I have a great deal of admiration for Mother Teresa, but I vehemently disagree with the Roman Catholic pathway to sainthood. I believe that anyone who has come to faith in Jesus Christ is a saint. In fact, the New Testament refutes a special class of "saints". Unger's Bible Dictionary says, "While it is true that in experience some believers are more "holy" than others, yet in their position before God, all believers are sanctified, thus saints by virtue of what they are "in Christ".

Adrian Rogers says that there are two classes of people: the saints and the "aints". When the Apostle Paul wrote his first epistle to the church in Corinth he penned, "Unto the church of God which is at Corinth, to them that are sanctified in Christ Jesus, called to be saints, with all that in every place call upon the name of Jesus Christ our lord, both theirs and ours: grace be unto you ..." (I Corinthians 1: 2-3a).

Every saved Georgia Baptist is a saint. We are the children of God, heirs of God and joint heirs with Jesus Christ (Romans 8: 17). "We are a chosen generation, a royal priesthood, a holy nation, a peculiar people (and) called ...out of darkness into his marvelous light" (I Peter 2: 9). The redeemed have become new creations, have new names written down in glory, have a new citizenship (heaven) and already made to sit in heavenly places in Christ Jesus. Christians are children of the King - royal bluebloods.

The way to sainthood is not through St. Peter's Square, but through Calvary's cross. Since those of us who have been redeemed by the blood of the Lamb have become "saints" we must remember to live like who we are.

Christmas Victor: Bethlehem Over Babel

Katharine Hepburn, an academy award winning actress, died at age 96 on June 29th. She professed to be an atheist and once said on a TV talk show, "I don't believe in a god and as far as when I die, I'm looking forward to a nice, long rest in the ground."

In another interview done in 1990 as she was growing more aware of her own mortality she declared, "I don't fear the next world, or anything. I don't fear hell, and I don't look forward to heaven."

I believe Hepburn's position on death and eternity is an anomaly. Yes, there are people who claim to believe in annihilation or who refuse to admit that there is more to life than what we experience between the cradle and the grave, but it has been wisely stated that there are no atheists in foxholes. Likewise, there are probably extremely few atheists lying at death's door.

Thomas Paine, a noted American atheist and author, declared in the face of death, "I would give worlds if I had them, that The Age of Reason had never been published. O Lord, help me! Christ, help me! O God what have I done to suffer so much? But there is no God! But if there should be, what will become of me hereafter?"

Mirabeau, the noted French statesman said, "Give me more laudanum, that I may not think of eternity. O Christ! O Jesus Christ!"

You see, the Bible says that God has set eternity in our hearts (Ecclesiastes 3:11). Man, in his depravity often denies the existence of God and refuses to embrace the truth that we were made for eternity, but still cannot escape the haunting truth of Solomon's wisdom. Something within us bears witness to the reality that there is more to life than this present world offers.

In the first pages of Genesis it becomes obvious that the men of earth longed for eternity or heaven or something beyond their mere earthly existence. In Genesis 11 we discover that the people of the earth gathered in the plain of Shinar and proposed to construct a tower, a ziggurat that would reach into the heavens.

They thought they could make a name for themselves by building a stairway to the stars or a skyscraper with an elevator that would take them all the way up to God's penthouse.

In fact, when God saw this ridiculous project concocted by the irrational minds of finite men, He brought the building program to an abrupt halt. He confused the language of the builders so that they could not understand one another, called the place Babel and scattered them over the face of the whole earth.

It is impossible for any man to work his way into the presence of God. Mortal man, obviously shrouded in definable limits, through his little self-help projects or major man-made religions cannot bridge the gap that has been eroded by centuries of sin and work his way into heaven or elevate himself into the presence of God. Therefore, the tower of Babel stands as a monument to the foolish notion of mankind trying to work his way into the realm of God's favor.

Conversely, Bethlehem is a monument to God's successful effort to enter man's world of confusion and wickedness with the answer that provides hope and life and joy. Since man could not reach up into God's arena, God decided to reach down into man's arena with love and grace.

At Bethlehem we observe act one and scene one in God's drama of redemption. This is where God expressed His love in the "unspeakable gift" of His only begotten Son. In this obscure village the Son of God became the Son of Man so that the sons of men might become the sons of God. At Bethlehem "The Word was made flesh, and dwelt among us, (and we beheld his glory, the glory as of the only begotten of the Father,) full of grace and truth" (John 1: 14).

We can look for happiness in one direction and search for life in another direction. We can build first one tower and then another, but they are all Babels.

Oh, the vanity of man's Babel and the victory of God's Bethlehem. The wisdom of Bethlehem is to the wisdom of Babel as the depth of an ocean is to the depth of a mud puddle.

Come then and let us join the endless procession of the ages and make our way in humility and hopefulness, not to Babel, but to Bethlehem, to the place where God bestowed upon mankind His most precious gift. "O, come let us adore Him, Christ, the King."

Bride for a Day - or Two

I prayed for Britney Spears today. I don't know her personally. I have never met her and probably never will, but I was prompted to pray for her today. She has become an extremely visible (no pun intended) personality in the world of entertainment and consequently has considerable influence on life in America. Teen idols such as Spears have helped shape fashion and pop culture for decades not only in our country, but also around the world.

Spears was born in Kentwood, La., on December 2, 1981 to Jamie and Lynn Spears. She comes from a Southern Baptist background and has frequently spoken of her faith. She got her start in music by singing in church as a child.

She has continued to do some good things by using her fame and influence to establish the Britney Spears Foundation, which provides fun-filled playrooms for sick children on extended hospital stays.

However, it must be difficult to walk circumspectly in the environment in which she lives. Reports indicate that her songs have become racier, her videos more provocative, and her photo-shoots more sexually oriented.

At last year's Video Music Awards television program Spears kissed another female singer, Madonna, and remarked, "I don't understand what the big deal is … Hasn't America seen two girls kiss before?"

Then on January 3 Spears and Jason Alexander, a childhood friend from her hometown, had been partying at a local bar and spontaneously decided to get married. Alexander said, "We were just looking at each other and said, 'Let's do something wild, crazy. Let's go get married, just for the h--- of it.'"

So, dressed in tattered jeans and wearing a baseball cap, Spears and Alexander got married at 5:30 a.m. on that Saturday morning at the Little White Chapel in Las Vegas. Her Palms Casino Hotel limousine driver escorted her down the aisle. If you are astonished that they got married at such an early hour, many of the more than 50 wedding chapels in Vegas are open 24 hours a day. In fact, if you want a "quickie" wedding in this city that never sleeps you can pull up to the "I Do" drive-through window at the Chapel of Love and for less than $100 drive off as husband and wife with an order of wedding cake to go.

Hours after the Spears-Alexander wedding the couple concluded that they had "taken a joke too far" and quickly arranged for an annulment. The 55-hour marriage ended at 12:24 p.m. on Monday, Jan. 5. David Chesnoff, Spears' attorney who orchestrated the annulment, said, "Plaintiff Spears lacked understanding of her actions to the extent that she was incapable of agreeing to the marriage."

Marriage is not something to be engaged in on a whim. It is not a joke. It is to be entered into "advisedly, discreetly, and in the fear of God." The devil would love to undermine the home, which is the first institution established for the welfare of the human race and the very foundation of our social order.

The gay/lesbian coalition that persistently pushes for the public to accept same sex marriages militates against the beauty of the marriage relationship as God intended it to be. The Hollywood exaltation of infidelity and cohabitation also drives a stake into the heart of the sanctity of marriage. The rampant polygamy that is prevalent in some Mormon communities is an affront to the marriage relationship as God designed it. The serial brides of Hollywood, such as Elizabeth Taylor, Joan Collins, and Zsa Zsa Gabor, who have been married a combined 22 times, cast a negative influence upon the institution of marriage.

In fact, statistics show that the United States has more divorces annually than any other monogamous country. In a recent year 19.4 million Americans, or 9.8 percent of all adults, ended their marriage relationship.

But the Spears/Alexander debacle has perhaps done more to diminish the Biblical ideal of marriage than anything that has happened in recent years. Our youth need a better example. Hopefully, they can find it in you.

Who is the Fugitive?

On 9/11, 1963, The Fugitive began its four-year run on television. The mystery thriller starred David Janssen as Dr. Richard Kimble, a man who had been falsely accused and arrested for killing his wife. Lt. Sam Gerard doggedly pursued the innocent doctor for four years as Kimble valiantly sought to find the one-armed man who was responsible for his wife's death. The final two-part episode was the highest rated television program at that time.

Every week the American television audience was captivated by Kimble's ingenious methods of living incognito and narrowly escaping the unabating pursuit of the determined Gerard, whose scowl was enough to curdle the milk of human kindness in the warmest heart. In more recent years a movie based on the theme of the old television program has been widely distributed and shown throughout the nation.

The FBI regularly publishes a list of their most wanted criminals. We are familiar with the concept of what it means to be a fugitive. The most recent and most infamous fugitives on record have been hiding somewhere in the Middle East.

And just when our hopes for the capture of one of those fugitives were growing abysmally dim, he was miraculously discovered in what was described as a "spider hole." When Saddam Hussein was found near his hometown of Tikrit he was disheveled, unkempt – in a word, "filthy." Newsweek reported that he had in his possession a couple of Mars candy bars and a can of roach spray.

The point was even more brought home as Paul Bremer, the United States administrator in Iraq said, "Ladies and gentlemen, we got him!"

Now, the search for Osama bin Laden intensifies. He has successfully eluded his pursuers in this international "hide and seek" escapade for much too long. His hiding place could be in any one of thousands of caves in the desolate mountains of Pakistan or Afghanistan.

Furthermore, he has instructed his followers to plant explosives around his hideout whenever he stops to make sure that he dies as a martyr in the "Holy War" he wages, rather than be captured by soldiers from the United States.

Bin Laden is a fugitive. Millions of people want to see him captured and brought to justice. But this leader of the Taliban is not the only fugitive in the world today. In fact, history is replete with fugitives. They are everywhere.

The Garden of Eden had some fugitives – Adam and Eve. After they had disobeyed God and eaten of the fruit of the tree of the knowledge of good and evil, they hid from God. They were fugitives and God came looking for them.

Jonah was a fugitive. He had been commanded by God to go to Nineveh to preach to the people of that great city. The reluctant prophet headed out in the other direction, became a fugitive, and found his "spider hole" in the belly of a whale.

The Apostle Paul was a fugitive. Although he didn't realize it, he was running from God. The Lord pursued him and found him on the road to

Damascus. In a rather amazing encounter he was captured by the Lord, made accountable for his rebellious past, and changed for eternity.

There have been times when I have been a fugitive, running from God and trying to escape accountability or evade His will or pursue lesser gods. Have you ever been a fugitive? It might just be worth your time to check it out.

It is entirely possible that we are happy that the media has turned the world's attention on the Bully of Baghdad and the Tyrant of the Taliban, because it makes our sins look a little more respectable and we assume it takes us off the "Most Wanted" list. But there is no little sin, because there is no little God to sin against; and while it is true that one step closer to God may make us more of a follower, one step away from him makes us more of a fugitive.

The Secular Worldview is Bold, Brazen, Unashamed

I never thought I would see the day when "Christian" America would have to specify that marriage should be between a man and a woman. In fact, it has been said, "If God doesn't judge America, He will have to apologize to Sodom and Gomorrah."

On March 13, 2003 the U.S. Census Bureau released its newest profile on the home, family, and marriage. Its surveys have shown that the homosexual population is not as large as the homosexual activists have claimed. In fact, of all couples in the United States, 90% are heterosexual and married, 9% heterosexual and unmarried, and 1% homosexual.

Yet the gay/lesbian contingent of our population pushes its agenda with fervency and reckless abandon. Its agenda includes the implementation of homosexual curriculum at all school levels, homosexual adoption of children (including access to foster care programs), supervisory access to all youth groups (homosexuals are now engaged in a legal battle with the Boy Scouts of America over this issue), the lowering of the age of consent for sex between children and adults, inclusion of sex-change operations in all universal health plans, as well as open homosexuality in the military.

Now the prevailing issue that looms so enormously over America is the homosexual effort to redefine the nature of the family. Canada has already sanctioned same sex marriages. Earlier this month the Massachusetts Supreme Court ruled that the state cannot discriminate against gays and lesbians in marriage.

San Francisco's Mayor Gavin Newsom, in an act of municipal disobedience, opened Pandora's box two weeks ago by allowing marriage licenses to be issued to same sex couples. Now lesbians and gays are getting married by the thousands in the city by the Golden Gate.

Although homosexuals are much in the minority, they are assertive and vocal. Just recently Representative Karla Drenner, the only openly gay member of the Georgia Assembly, voiced her criticism of pastor Richard Walker of Macland Church in Powder Springs in regard to his prayer before the Georgia House when he expressed his belief in marriage being "between one man and one woman only for life."

Television has produced several sit-coms in recent years that seem to suggest that homosexuality is a normal rather than an aberrant lifestyle. Twenty years ago, John Ritter pretended to be gay as Jack Tripper on Three's Company in order to get the apartment landlord to permit him to live with two young women. Since then the entertainment industry's effort to present homosexuality as normal is legion. Queer Eye for the Straight Guy, The L Word, and Will and Grace are examples of current TV fare attempting to win approval for the homosexual lifestyle.

Several Christian denominations have accepted homosexual memberships and have church leaders who are gay. These churches never condemn homosexuality but pride themselves in tolerating and accepting it. They refer to it as an "alternate lifestyle" or a "sexual preference."

However, Richard Eldredge's Valentine's Day "Peach Buzz" column in the *Atlanta Journal-Constitution* takes the cake. He writes about Ken and Barbie, the Mattel Toy Company's premier dolls for more than four decades. He writes, "After 43 years, Barbie has finally discovered that Ken, her longtime beau, isn't exactly anatomically correct ... Barbie and Ken have drifted apart."

Then Eldredge announced that Mattel recently introduced Blaine, a new doll, at the annual American International Toy Fair in New York. He then added, "Judging by the pictures we saw, it could not be immediately determined whether Blaine would be romantically interested in Barbie or Ken."

Now, the attempt is being made to insure the sanctity of marriage through a constitutional marriage amendment the homosexual lobbyists are decrying as discriminatory. As a result, they have recognized the advantage of hitching their wagon to the civil rights star. By asserting that their goal is to achieve their rights as citizens, and invoking the rhetoric of the 1960's, they touch a nerve in American society.

Any nation that allows rights to rule over reason, responsibility and righteousness is headed for anarchy. Judges 17:6 declares: "In those days there was no king in Israel, but every man did that which was right in his own eyes." No one was in control. No one gave the orders. No one was responsible to anyone.

The book of Judges gives the brutal, ugly, wretched accounts of the natural outcome of people doing what is right in their eyes. They can always justify what they do. This is the hallmark of a permissive society; but there is no way to equate permissiveness with the Christian faith.

The church has a responsibility to reach out to the homosexual in love and compassion, and to share the hope of the gospel, which can produce remarkable change and a new life. However, the church also has the responsibility of lifting up the banner of truth. The truth is that God defined marriage in the book of Genesis when he created Eve to be Adam's helpmate and life partner.

When the Georgia Senate voted on the marriage amendment I am told that the gallery had five times more people opposed to the amendment than those who were in favor of the amendment. If the church was as enthusiastic about the cause of Christ as the homosexuals are about their cause, we would have won the world to Christ long ago.

The World's Greatest Comeback

History has recorded some spectacular comebacks. Several years ago, news came from the Atlanta Braves training camp that Andres Galarraga had been diagnosed with non-Hodgkin's lymphoma in his lower back.

He missed the entire 1999 season, but the cancer was eradicated, and the process of recovery and rehabilitation was initiated. Doctors were uncertain as to how the torque of his powerful swing would affect the area in his lower back, which had been weakened by the cancer.

But on April 3, 2000 the Braves were playing the Colorado Rockies. Greg Maddux and Pedro Astacio were in a pitching duel. Astacio carried a no hitter into the fifth inning. In the seventh inning the game was tied 0 to 0.

After getting Brian Jordan to fly out to centerfield, Astacio threw a low fastball to Galarraga and with a mighty swing he hit the ball out of the park for a long homerun. Skip Carey, the Braves announcer said, "It's amazing that a year ago today he wasn't sure he'd be alive today. What a great comeback. If Hollywood wasn't watching, it should get the tapes."

In 1978 the Chrysler Corporation was plagued with management and sales problems. The company was heavily indebted and near bankruptcy. Chrysler stock was reduced to $2 a share.

Then President Lee Iacocca of the Ford Motor Company, who had introduced the sporty Mustang, the popular Mercury Cougar and the luxurious Lincoln Mark III, was immediately hired as president and chief executive officer of the Chrysler Corporation.

The first thing Iacocca did was reduce his own salary to $1 a year. Then, with his business savvy and forceful personality, Iacocca obtained U.S. government loan assistance, cut costs, introduced the popular K-cars, repaid all loans within 5 years and turned the company around. His Chrysler minivan, introduced in 1984, became one of the best-selling vehicles in North America.

Chrysler products were soon coming off the assembly line in record numbers. On July 15, 1983, The New York Times carried this headline: "Chrysler's Sharp Turnaround." It's hard to overstate the magnitude of the turnaround. It was an amazing corporate comeback.

On June 2, 1996 Captain Scott O'Grady was flying a mission over Bosnia. Suddenly a surface-to-air missile hit his plane and sheared it in two. Intuitively, he pulled the ejection rod and within seconds was going down in his parachute over hostile territory.

For six days Captain O'Grady valiantly survived off the land and evaded the belligerent Bosnians. By the fifth day he was out of water and eating ants and leaves in order to sustain his life. What he didn't know was that the United States military was making plans and preparations for a gigantic rescue operation.

The recovery of Captain O'Grady was scheduled for the early morning. As the fog lifted he heard the hollow, chopping sound of helicopters and within moments the rescue was complete.

However, the three remarkable comebacks mentioned above pale in comparison to the miraculous comeback of Jesus Christ. He was mercilessly scourged and died a cruel, ignominious death upon a cross – a horrible instrument of torture. He was then placed in a borrowed tomb where his body began to decompose and deteriorate.

But, go to the tomb of Jesus Christ! Men and angels shout, "He is not here, for He is risen. Come, see, the place where the Lord lay!"

Accept the literal, bodily resurrection of Jesus as a fact and you will never doubt that He created the heavens and earth, that He fed the multitudes, walked on the waters, read the thoughts of the hearts of men, gave the blind their sight, the deaf their hearing, and the mad their reason.

He lived before He was born. He lived after He died. He always was. He is. He always will be. Hallelujah, what a Savior!

Riding into the Sunset to the
Shining City on a Hill

Ronald Reagan was a man of indomitable courage, profound convictions, unflappable optimism and personal charisma. He stood like a giant sequoia on the American landscape, but Alzheimer's disease, a foe he could not defeat, ultimately took his life on June 5, 2004.

Prior to his death his beloved Nancy said, "Ronnie's long journey has finally taken him to a distant place, where I can no longer reach him." Such is the tragic fate of those who succumb to the ruthless thief that steals both the mind and body of its victim; and blessed are those who care for loved ones who are debilitated by the villainous culprit.

I had the enviable privilege of meeting Mr. Reagan at a National Affairs Seminar in Washington, D. C. in 1979. He addressed our gathering and said, "I have believed for a long time that God put this land here, between the two oceans, to be found by people from every corner of the world who had a spark, a love of freedom, a courage to uproot themselves and come here, and because of that, this new breed we call America, which as the result of a great melting pot has a mission in the world.

"John Winthrop, standing on the deck of the Arbella off the coast of Massachusetts hundreds of years ago, gathered the pilgrims around him and told them before they went ashore that we could be a shining city upon a hill – that the eyes of all mankind were upon us and that if we failed God in this undertaking we would be a byword throughout the world and for all time to come.

"And today, I believe the people of this country are more ready than they have ever been, more disturbed at the feeling they have lost something, more ready for a spiritual revival and to stand up once again and see America become the hope of the world whatever the price may be."

After hearing Mr. Reagan, I sensed that he was a Christian man, a man of integrity and faith. Adrian Rogers, former SBC Convention president, recounted that he first met Reagan in 1980 when he was a candidate for president. Rogers said, "Someone asked him, 'Governor … do you know Jesus Christ? Not do you know about Him, but do you know Him?'"

"He said, 'Oh, yes, He is very real to me. I have trusted Him as my personal Lord and Savior, and I pray every day. But I don't wear my religion on my sleeves.'"

A new book, *Hand of Providence: The Strong and Quiet Faith of Ronald Reagan*, declares that the secret to Reagan's astonishingly successful presidency was his deep Christian faith."

Reagan was also a man of integrity. Peggy Noonan's book, *When Character Was King*, points to his courage, kindness, persistence, honesty and almost heroic patience as the key to his success as president.

He was also a man of great courage. He boldly called the Soviet Union the "evil empire." Paul Kengor, author of God and Ronald Reagan says that Reagan defeated the "evil empire" with his faith. Kengor says, "When Reagan went to Moscow and shocked the atheist establishment in that country by his public pronouncements of faith, he knew exactly what he was doing."

Reagan was a leader. He said in December of 1990, "A leader, once convinced a particular course of action is the right one, must have the determination to stick with it and be undaunted when the going gets rough."

The 40th president was a man of humility. He said, "… there is no limit to what a man can do or where he can go if he doesn't mind who gets the credit."

Reagan's sense of humor is legendary. He said, "I have left orders to be awakened at any time in case of national emergency – even if I am in a cabinet meeting." He also declared, "The nine most terrifying words in the English language are, 'I'm from the government and I'm here to help.'"

President George W. Bush remarked concerning Reagan's death: "(He) won America's respect with his greatness and won its love with his goodness. He had the confidence that comes with conviction, the strength that comes with character, the grace that comes with humility, and the humor that comes with wisdom.

"He always told us, that for America, the best is yet to come. We comfort ourselves in the knowledge that this is true for him, too. His work is done. And now a shining city awaits him."

The Confession of a
Flag Waving American

It was a Saturday evening in September of 1983 in Jackson, Miss. The sun was casting long shadows over War Memorial Stadium and a gentle breeze, a refreshing zephyr, provided the ideal climate for an autumn clash on the gridiron.

The two combatants, the U.S. Naval Academy and Mississippi State University, had completed their pre-game rituals on the beautifully manicured turf and the maroon and white MSU band was poised to play the national anthem.

To the expected pageantry of a college football game was the added excitement of having one of our nation's service academies represented on the field. American flags were given to every ticket holder as a favor and an air of patriotism swept across the 60,000 spectators.

Over the public address system, the announcer informed the amassed throng that four TA-4J Skyhawk Navy jet fighter planes were about to leave the Naval air station in Meridian and would be flying over the stadium in eight minutes. The Mississippi State marching band moved in perfect cadence and formed with precision the three letters: U-S-A. The drum major lifted his baton and the band played the National Anthem.

I was positioned on about the 30-yard line near the top of the stadium. With my right hand over my heart I was looking at the band and singing *The Star-Spangled Banner* and at the same time glancing at the eastern sky to see if I could see the Navy jets approaching the stadium.

I didn't see them until they suddenly appeared in a flash of glory and thundered over the crowd. They seemed to be almost at eye level as they zoomed past right as we got to the "bombs bursting in air" part of the song. I got goose bumps and teary eyed in that dramatic and exciting moment.

I must confess to you that I am a red-blooded, flag-waving, patriotic American. I have never gotten over the fact that by God's grace I was born in America and have lived all my life in "the land of the free and the home of the brave." I cherish our freedoms and live in profound gratitude for those who have fought to preserve our lives and liberty.

As we approach our Independence Day 2004 I share the sentiments of the English novelist and poet, Sir Walter Scott, who said, "Breathes there a man with soul so dead, who never to himself hath said, 'This is my own, my native land!'"

We have a rich and wonderful heritage. One of the first official acts of America's first Congress, the 1774 Provincial Congress, was to open in prayer. Most students of our nation's heritage, particularly those unmoved by the revisionist historians, contend that the aforementioned prayer meeting was not some shallow "to-whom-it-may-concern" prayer. In fact, some writings indicate that it might have lasted several hours.

The nation was birthed in prayer, nurtured by devotees of the cross and kept in the traces by those who refused to let America wander too far from God.

In 1798 President John Adams said, "We have no government armed with power capable of contending with human passions unbridled by morality and religion. Our Constitution was made for a moral and religious people. It is wholly inadequate to the government of any other."

Patrick Henry, great patriot and one of the founding fathers of our country, declared, "It cannot be emphasized too strongly or too often that this great nation was founded not by religionists, but by Christians, not on religions, but on the gospel of Jesus Christ."

John Jay, the very first Supreme Court justice, said, "Americans should select and prefer Christians as their rulers."

We must not forget the rock from whence we were hewn. Upon coming to America in 1831 the Frenchman, Alexis de Tocqueville, said, "Not until I went into the churches of America and heard her pulpits aflame with righteousness did I understand the secret of her genius and power. America is great because America is good, and if America ever ceases to be good, America will cease to be great."

The best way for all of us to celebrate the birthday of our great nation is to remember our heritage, repent of our sins and return to the faith of our founding fathers. Only then can we legitimately sing with expectant faith, "God Bless America."

Four Things Every Church Needs

There are four things the church desperately needs if it is to make an impact upon our age: fervent prayer, anointed preaching, genuine persecution and divine power.

First of all, there is the need for fervent prayer. Read the history of the revivals on record and you will discover that, without exception, when genuine revival occurred it was ushered in on the wings of prayer. What our churches need is persistent, penitent, passionate prayers.

We have many men and women in our convention who know how to grasp the horns of the altar and pray heaven down to earth, but no one inspires me to want to be a man of prayer more than Fayiz Saknini.

This dear man of God worked in our language mission's ministry with Arabic speaking people at the Georgia Baptist Convention. I have had the privilege of being his pastor. His life is a testimony of the power of God to answer prayer. When he prays I believe God must stop what He is doing to listen to Pastor Saknini.

When we pray, we link ourselves to an omnipotent God with whom nothing is impossible. We will never accomplish what God has commissioned us to do unless we pray. We often walk around like spiritual paupers when God has the resources of heaven to bestow upon those who know how to pray.

We also need anointed preaching, the kind that characterized Jonathan Edwards when he preached "Sinners in the Hands of an Angry God." Edwards had not slept for three days and nights. He had spent his time fasting and praying before he preached that epochal sermon and history records that the power of God was upon Edwards when he preached that message.

Preachers must preach as dying men to dying men never sure to preach again. Preaching must never be reduced to a profession. It is a calling; a divine calling and those who stand behind the sacred desk to proclaim the unsearchable riches of Christ must seek the fullness of God's Spirit and preach as God's emissary from heaven.

Thirdly, today's church needs persecution. Some of you will greet that suggestion with questions or perhaps even scorn. However, we have been told that the blood of the martyrs is the seed of the church. Typically, the church has had greater success in times of adversity than in times of prosperity.

It is time for God's people to get out of their cocoons of isolation or comfort zones and risk something for the cause of Christ. Quit playing it safe. Timothy Sangster, a pastor in Savannah, spoke in chapel at the Baptist Center last spring and quoted a motto of the Hell's Angels motorcycle gang. He said, "If you are not living on the edge you are just taking up space." We've got lots of Georgia Baptists just taking up space.

Knock on the door of the most gospel-hardened soul you know. Enter the pro-life fight. Stand up against the evolutionists, the humanists, and the secularists. Stand up for righteousness in the marketplace. Demand that the Ten Commandments be displayed in the public square.

Stand up for truth. Become a bold witness for Christ and you will put yourself at risk. You may get ridiculed or persecuted. If you do, just praise the Lord! But "beware when all men speak well of you."

Finally, we need divine power. We have become so well-organized. We have the finest communication skills. We have developed the most attractive ministry resource kits. We have polished seminars and "How to Minister" conferences. We have trained soloists and professional instrumentalists and slick media presentations. We have well-educated ministers and impressive buildings, but lack the power of God upon our lives.

We need a visitation of the Holy Spirit upon our churches. We have seen what eloquence, training, education, personality, publicity, promotion and programming can do, but we need to see what God can do. We must remember that it is "not by might, nor by power, but by my Spirit saith the Lord of hosts."

The songwriter said it best: "All is vain unless the power of the Holy One come down."

I believe this year can be Georgia Baptists' best year ever, but not without fervent prayer, anointed preaching, perhaps genuine persecution and certainly not without divine power.

Do we Have More in the Show Window than the Storeroom?

Catherine Zeta Jones, one of Hollywood's most celebrated stars, is often seen wearing a cross of gold and diamonds. Jennifer Anniston, the darling of the television series Friends and estranged wife of Brad Pitt, wears a cross of platinum and diamonds. Fashion model Naomi Campbell is reported to have a collection of enormous, jewel-studded crosses. Italian fashion stylist Giuliana Cella has more than four hundred of them.

Sammy Sosa, the home run hitting outfielder, formerly of the Chicago Cubs and now with the Baltimore Orioles, typically hits his chest, throws a kiss heavenward and points to the sky after hitting a home run. Other athletes have been seen making the sign of the cross, kneeling in the posture of prayer or kissing their rosary necklace prior to or immediately after some strategic juncture in an athletic contest.

Candidates for public office have been known to invoke the name of the Lord in their campaign speeches or political rallies. While conservatives often accuse liberals of using religion to pander and liberals paint conservatives as closed-minded fanatics, both have typically claimed belief in a higher power.

What is the meaning of all these outward expressions of religions or faiths? Surely, we would be remiss to categorically renounce those who give external evidences of religion and label all those who wear Christian jewelry, make pious gestures, and utter sanctimonious shibboleths as superficial.

But here is the question for the average, Bible-believing, Sunday-go-to-meeting Baptist: What evidences of your faith would you have left if you didn't go to church on Sunday?

Church going can be very superficial if there is no other evidence to substantiate one's faith. In fact, church attendance may be much like an accessory or an addendum tacked on to what one may consider life's more essential features.

Recent statistics reveal that the church in America is experiencing significant attrition; and it may be due to the fact that many church members are vainly attempting to give expression to a make-believe faith. The Apostle Paul declared that in the last days there would be those who would have only a "form of godliness, but deny the power thereof." Their faith is only a pretense, a charade. Many are guilty of an easy believism that is void of repentance and a genuinely transformed life.

Leonard Ravenhill, the evangelist and revivalist, said, "You may belittle experiences and speak of the dangers of emotion, but we are suffering from a species of Christianity as dry as dust, as cold as ice, as pale as a corpse and as dead as old King Tut. We are suffering, not from a lack of correct heads, but from a lack of consumed hearts."

The church that was once a force for evangelism is now a field for evangelism. Hopefully, the wave revivals that are presently beginning to sweep across our state will not only bring brand new converts into the church, but cause church members to heed the admonition of Paul who said to the church at Corinth: "Examine yourselves, whether ye be in the faith; prove your own selves" (II Corinthians 13:5).

The incident that convinced me to write this editorial happened last week when I was going into a neighborhood restaurant. A twenty-something fellow came out of the restaurant shouting obscenities and taking the Lord's name in vain. On his t-shirt was a picture of two tablets of stone seemingly embossed with Roman numerals from I to X superimposed over an American flag. Above the picture were the words "Honor God's Word It's Carved in Stone" and under the picture were the words "Keep the Ten Commandments".

The poor man with the vile tongue seemed to be unaware that he was wearing the Ten Commandments on his shirt and violating one of them with his words. It is hypocritical to insist on the Ten Commandments being displayed in the public square and not have them inscribed in your heart. Maybe we have more in the show window than we have in the storeroom.

The One-Eyed Monster

Television! It's almost impossible to find anything on television worth watching. It hasn't always been that way. I remember the first television set I ever saw. The year was 1948. The TV set was in the show window of a department store in Washington, D.C.

There were at least a dozen people standing outside the store gazing at the "test pattern" on the television screen. As I reflect on that long ago experience I recall that we were all fairly mesmerized by what we saw on display.

It was two more years before I ever really saw anything of substance on television. The Western Auto Store in my hometown was televising the 1950 World Series between the New York Yankees and the Philadelphia Phillies. I stopped by the store on the way home from school just long enough to see Joe DiMaggio and Richie Ashburn come to the plate for their respective teams.

It was not until 1952 that we got a television set in our home, but we were captivated by such shows as *The Adventures of Ozzie and Harriett, Father Knows Best, Leave it to Beaver, I love Lucy* and *Beat the Clock.*

During those years I don't remember those pristine programs being anything other than family friendly and sometimes even having moral value. They were certainly not laced with lewdness and saturated with sex like much of television programming today.

However, as early as 1961 Newton Minow, head of the Federal Communications Commission, addressed the National Association of Broadcasters and declared television a "vast wasteland."

Minow added, "The power of instantaneous sight and sound is without precedent in man's history. This is an awesome power. It has limitless capabilities for good and for evil. And it carries with it awesome responsibilities which you and I cannot escape."

After declaring television a "vast wasteland" Minow banned TV on school nights in his own home. His daughter, Nell, was 9 at that time. Now Nell has two children, ages 9 and 12, and they are not allowed to watch TV at all. "When we were growing up TV was not as treacherous as it is today," Nell remarked. "Today TV isn't a vast wasteland. It is a toxic waste dump."

Ozzie and Harriett has been replaced by *The Osbournes*. *Father Knows Best* disintegrated into *Married with Children*. *Beat the Clock* has devolved into *Fear Factor*. And the latest fare includes such entertainment drivel as *Desperate Housewives* and *The Simple Life*, another reality show that started as a perversion of the old program *Green Acres*.

According to research conducted by the Parents Television Council the amount of violence, vulgarity and profanity in supposed "family-hour" programming has skyrocketed in recent years. Additionally, television is constantly pushing the envelope with programs presenting hypersexual behavior and casual sexual encounters without consequences.

It is apparent that much of Hollywood under-values the home. Television's perverted portraits of the family and attempts to normalize homosexuality, co-habitation and extramarital affairs are breaching the defenses of wholesome family life.

Not all television is bad, but too much watching - even benign TV programs - stifles creativity, impedes imagination, curbs productivity and limits physical activity, making "couch potatoes" of its victims.

Al Vecchione, former president of MacNeil/Lehrer Productions said, "In the roughly fifty years since it was introduced, television has evolved as a menace to our society's mental and even physical health. Increasingly, we see the world only through its lens. TV has transformed everything it has touched - politics, the justice system and the presidency, to name a few."

Vecchione continues, "TV has distorted our values and standards and shaped the minds of two generations of children. Its influence on our mores ... may surpass that of our religious institutions, its capacity to mold public policy may be greater than our political institutions, its reach into our children's minds may be stronger than our educational system."

I might well pray for you the prayer that the Apostle Paul prayed for the church at Thessalonica: "And the very God of peace sanctify you wholly; and I pray God your whole spirit and soul and body be preserved blameless unto the coming of our Lord Jesus Christ" (I Thessalonians 5:23). I doubt if God would be allowed to use much television programming as a refining tool to answer that prayer.

Psychiatric Association Supports Same Sex Marriage

God only had one Son without sin, but He never had a son without trials and tribulations. Human beings are creatures of emotion. God gave us the capacity to laugh, cry, fear, mourn, rejoice, worry, get angry, etc. These are the normal and natural experiences of life. However, these emotions or feelings may become overwhelming at times and so help is needed.

Counseling is a legitimate service and ministry, and many people are genuinely helped by pastors or skilled therapists gifted in providing the guidance and advice needed to overcome the stress and strain of emotionally traumatic seasons of life.

As a pastor, I frequently referred church members to Christian counselors for guidance and therapy, but I am suspicious of modern psychiatry. We must carefully discern the theories and philosophies of those who practice in this field of medicine before we recommend them to the people of God.

It appears that psychiatry is based upon two false assumptions: the belief in evolution and the belief in secular humanism. These principles seem to be fundamental in all their current theories about the mind and how it functions. Genesis 1 tells us that God created man in His own image. We did not evolve from some lower form of life. Humanism teaches that man is the highest reality (not God) and determines for himself what is good or evil.

However, the Bible says, "It is better to trust in the Lord than to put confidence in man." (Psalm 118:8)

The truth is that some of the psychiatric theories and practices being imported into Christianity dangerously distort important biblical doctrines and potentially pervert the mission and ministry of the church.

I do not want to demonize or reject modern psychiatry/psychology, but it appears that there are elements of this discipline that are a threat to the basic truths of the gospel of Jesus Christ.

Counseling that focuses on the mind and body and omits the spirit is faulty from the beginning, because man was created with a body, mind and spirit. Therefore, counseling that neglects the spirit is basically humanistic in nature and highly suspect.

Unfortunately, the American Psychiatric Association has come under increasing scrutiny in recent years among Bible believing Christians because of their philosophy and methods of counseling. While there are splendid Christian psychiatrists who have sound, holistic practices that treat people as triune creations of God, it appears that such counseling is no longer the norm.

Sigmund Freud is generally called the father of modern psychiatry/psychology. He called himself "a completely godless Jew" and "a hopeless pagan." He believed that Christianity was a delusion to be dispelled, that religion generally was invented to fulfill man's needs, and that when one comes of age, he no longer needs religion.

Exactly fifty years ago the APA held a symposium on "Progress in Psychiatry." In their report they stated: "Psychotherapy is today in a state of disarray almost exactly as it was 200 years ago."

The next year Percival Bailey addressed the APA and made the following pronouncement: "The great revolution in psychiatry has solved few problems ... One wonders how long the hoary errors of Freud will continue to plague psychiatry."

Indeed, there are multiplicities of therapies, and it is difficult to critique them all. Nevertheless, the one underlying theme is that man is basically good and needs to reach his highest potential. Psychiatrists typically say that this can be accomplished by teaching self-esteem, self-worth, and self-love - anything to make one feel good about oneself.

The word "sin" is often replaced with words such a "disease," "dysfunction" or "addiction." While these words have some legitimacy, they often tend to release a person from any responsibility for his/her actions. The Bible speaks of sin as a real problem and gives the answer.

Therefore, it is not surprising that the APA at their recent 158th annual convention in Atlanta voted to approve a proclamation to support legalizing same sex marriage. The decision marked the first time a major medical association had registered support for such unions and immediately won the praise of gay and lesbian activist groups across the nation.

The landmark decision was made on a Sunday, and interestingly enough, Sigmund Freud, for whom every action had significance, hung his shingle out on a Sunday, an Easter Sunday to be exact. Some have thought that this action of Freud was symbolic in nature and have interpreted it as an overt way to mock Christianity.

There are wonderful God-fearing Christian psychiatrists who stand against the current flow of the APA. We thank God for them. Make sure that your counselor is a committed Christian who is firmly grounded in the Word of God. Psalm 1: 1 says, "Blessed is the man that walketh not in the counsel of the ungodly..." Colossians 2:8 declares, "Beware lest any man spoil you through philosophy and vain deceit, after the traditions of men, after the rudiments of the world, and not after Christ."

Do Something that Produces Big Dividends - Memorize God's Word

Angel Martinez memorized the entire New Testament and could quote it without any reservation, qualification or hesitation. I was privileged to know the noted evangelist and had him preach in several of the churches I served as pastor.

Martinez, who referred to himself as a little shoeshine boy, was converted in a Baptist mission in San Antonio in July 1935 at the age of 13 and preached his first sermon in September of that same year. At the conclusion of that message, every member of his family except his father was converted to Christ.

During the course of his illustrious sixty-year ministry as an evangelist, Martinez saw more than 500,000 come to faith in Christ. He was known for his colorful attire, his simple but powerful messages, and his memorization of Scripture.

He once told me that he began the memorization process by listing some of the better-known verses of Scripture and committing them to memory. He then selected some of the well-known chapters of the New Testament, such as I Corinthians 13, Romans 8 and John 14, and memorized them. From the more familiar chapters to some of the shorter epistles, Martinez continued his memorization process.

When he started memorizing the New Testament he confessed that it was a long and laborious process as he rehearsed the verses of Scripture over and over again. After months of disciplining himself to learn the Scripture, the memorization process became easier and easier until he could memorize a whole chapter in a relatively short period of time.

I will never forget his response when I asked him why he took on such an enormous project. He responded by quoting Psalm 1:2: "But his delight is in the law of the Lord and in his law doth he meditate day and night." He also referenced Psalm 119:11 which says, "Thy word have I hid in mine heart that I might not sin against Thee."

Many people today do not have access to the Bible. In April 1997 thousands of Bibles were confiscated in Uzbekistan. In this country known for its authoritarian presidential rule, the law forbids the distribution of Bibles.

In November 2003 a village was ransacked, Christians were beaten and arrested, and Bibles were confiscated at H'le and O Village in la Bang Province in Vietnam. Unidentified police officers entered the village in vehicles and began threatening the villagers, warning them about holding unofficial prayer meetings before taking away the Bibles found in the houses.

Recently, Cybercast News Service reported that in Saudi Arabia it is a matter of official policy "to either incinerate or destroy Bibles, crosses and other Christian paraphernalia." God forbid we should ever be restricted from having a copy of the Bible, but what if that were the case? How much of God's Word have you hidden in your heart and mind?

In January 1968 North Korea seized the intelligence-collecting ship USS Pueblo, an incident that came close to igniting a second Korean War. The 83 crew members were imprisoned and, in some cases, tortured mercilessly. In order to maintain their sanity in a horrific situation, they called to memory as many verses of Scripture as possible and combined their knowledge of the Word of God to create what came to be known as "The Pueblo Bible."

I recently came across a website: Bible Memorization - Benefits and Methods. Here are some of the benefits of Bible memorization listed on this website:

It multiplies the effect of God's Word in our lives.

It conditions the thought life, the secret of success.

It gives the Holy Spirit wide access to us.

It keeps us alert for spiritual battle.

It facilitates and transforms our personal Bible study.

It makes group worship more meaningful.

It can give spiritual authority.

It gives freedom in teaching and preaching.

It is indispensable for our evangelism.

It helps you pray in public.

Consider the words of Joshua 1:8: "The book of the law shall not depart out of thy mouth (he is quoting it); but thou shalt meditate therein day and night (he is rehearsing it continuously), that thou mayest observe to do according to all that is written therein: for then thou shalt make thy way prosperous, and then thou shalt have good success."

How far is the Courthouse from the Church House?

S enior United States District Judge William C. O'Kelly rendered his decision in the Civil Action Case of John Doe v. Barrow County (Georgia) on July 18. He ruled that the defendant (the Barrow County Commissioners) must "immediately remove the Ten Commandments picture currently hanging on the wall of the breezeway connecting the Barrow County Courthouse and the Courthouse annex."

Interestingly, the plaintiff in the case was some spineless, pusillanimous character who insisted on identifying himself as "John Doe." Ironically, the judge concluded his verdict with the statement: " ... it is finally ordered that this matter is dismissed with prejudice." The use of the word "prejudice" has never been used with a more sinister ring to it.

To exacerbate the whole situation the surreptitious plaintiff was awarded $1.00 in damages and the County Commissioners were ordered to fork over $150,000 for the plaintiff's attorneys' fees and expenses.

What happened in Barrow Country last month is just one of a multiplicity of incidents that illustrate that Christians are being discriminated against in America and that we are losing our religious freedom.

We are well aware of the decision of the 11th U. S. Circuit Court of Appeals on July 5, 2003 when they ruled that Alabama Chief Justice Roy Moore's 5,300-pound Ten Commandments monument was an unconstitutional state establishment of religion.

Earlier this year a King James Version of the Bible was removed from the 48-year-old, four-foot-tall monument in front of the Harris County Civil Courts building in Houston, Texas following a suit filed by a real estate broker, who claimed the display offended non-Christians. A judge ruled that displaying the Bible on county property represented an unconstitutional promotion of Christianity by the county.

In an Oakland, CA. office a flier was posted promoting a gay and lesbian employee association, but a federal court ruled that a flier promoting family values could not be posted on the same bulletin board because it was "homophobic in nature" and labeled it as "sexual orientation-based harassment."

Agape Press reported in February "A student columnist at North Carolina State University says there's a climate of anti-Christian bigotry on campus." Junior chemistry major Daniel Underwood, says, "There's a marginalization of anyone who holds any sort of religious views firmly." He recalled an incident in which a professor asked a guest speaker not to mention the name of "Jesus" while addressing his "Social Deviance" class. Underwood contended that most of the university's professors are uncomfortable with born-again Christians, but seem open to embrace other religions - particularly Islam.

Also, at this years' Academy Awards ceremony, host Chris Rock lauded Michael Moore's film *Fahrenheit 9-11* as positive and creative, and yet decried Mel Gibson's *The Passion of the Christ* as divisive and discriminatory. This is typical of the leftist ideology, liberal worldview and godless secularism of "Hellywood."

We are also familiar with the exploits of Michael Newdow, who did not want his daughter exposed to the words "under God" in the Pledge of Allegiance. After his valiant, but vain attempt to rewrite the Pledge of Allegiance, he filed another suit to ban prayer from the inauguration of George W. Bush.

The latest fiery dart hurled at Christianity has come from Annie Laurie Gaylor of the Freedom From Religion Foundation, who registered her complaint against those who memorialize victims of vehicle accidents by placing a cross by the side of the road. She commented, "There's this tendency to litter our landscape with crosses without considering whether this is the best way to memorialize your loved one. We can all feel sorrow about a roadside accident, but do we have to be preached at every time we drive by?"

Do you see what is happening? The ACLU, the People for the American Way, the Freedom From Religion Foundation, MoveOn.org, the Gay and Lesbian Task Force and a plethora of other organizations are chipping away at our religious freedom. Once prayer and Bible reading are taken out of the public schools, nativity scenes are taken out of the public square, the Ten Commandments are taken from the courthouses of America and crosses are removed from the highways and intersections of life, what is next?

The voices from the pulpits of America may one day be monitored, governed or perhaps even silenced. Beware, it may not be all that far from the courthouse to the church house.

Let the Pulpits be Aflame with the Bold Proclamation of the Gospel

Early one Sunday morning before going to church I was surfing through the channels on the television set to find some good gospel music and happened to pause at *The Hour of Power* from the Crystal Cathedral. They were having a patriotic service with beautiful music appropriate for the occasion. I was captivated by the pageantry and music presented in that televised service.

Then the younger Dr. Schuller announced that he was going to offer a prayer for our country and our military. I stopped what I was doing to join him in the prayer. He said, "God has given us a wonderful promise in prayer in II Chronicles 7:14: 'If my people, which are called by my name will ... pray then I will hear from heaven, and forgive their sin, and will heal their land'."

He left out the conditional part of the promise. Maybe he forgot that part or inadvertently left it out, but he omitted the part about "humbling ourselves, seeking God's face and turning from our wicked ways." I would really like to give Schuller the benefit of the doubt, but there seems to be a trend toward leaving out the concept of repentance in favor of a "feel good" religion.

Then on a recent *Larry King Live* interview, Joel Osteen was so nebulous in answering some of King's questions that he felt it necessary to write a letter of explanation about his comments, but he repeatedly sidestepped questions about whether Jews, Muslims and even atheists would go to heaven. King then alluded to the fact that some people thought he preached a "cotton candy theology" with no spiritual nourishment.

Whether church styles are contemporary, traditional, classic, avant-garde, modern, old fashioned or blended, the gospel must be proclaimed and the saved must be called to submit to the Lordship of Christ. We must never be satisfied with compromising the Scripture; we must preach the whole counsel of God.

Vance Havner used to say that the man of God should preach to "comfort the afflicted and afflict the comfortable." In practically every congregation there are forlorn people with heavy burdens. These people need to know that there is help and hope in the Lord. They need messages that encourage their heavy hearts, lighten their burdensome load and brighten their darkened pathway.

But then there is the clan of the comfortable. They need to be motivated, stirred, challenged, shaken, pried from their complacency. They don't need "feel good" sermons. They already feel good. In fact, they are anesthetized so much so that they do not feel any sense of burden for souls lost in the darkness of sin or churches that are floundering in an increasingly secular society.

In this day of instant gratification, trial marriages, quick divorces, government-funded abortions, lewd movies, coarse language, vulgar jokes, mindless television, frivolous pursuits, political shenanigans, crusaders for tolerance, easy believism and indolent church members the pulpit must not give an uncertain sound.

It is true that people like to be made to feel good and, simply put, human nature recoils at the idea of being corrected or convicted. Therefore, many modern-day pastors avoid preaching any kind of message that would be offensive or controversial.

The gospel doesn't need to be exclusively repackaged as the answer for low self-esteem, the fear of failure, the pathway to success, the solution to career problems, psychological distress, etc. And unbelievers do not need to be perceived as lonely singles, bored executives, victims of dysfunctional families or aimless sojourners, but as sinners in need of salvation.

Charles Spurgeon, the great English preacher, said, "The preacher's work is to throw sinners down into utter helplessness that they may be compelled to look up to Him Who alone can help them. Preach not calmly and quietly as though you were asleep, but preach with fire and pathos and passion."

Desperate times call for demonstrative preaching. The degree of our fervor and passion should be commensurate with the situation that exists in our churches and in our society. I am certainly not advocating sermons that are "full of sound and fury signifying nothing," but sermons that inspire and motivate.

George Whitefield proclaimed, "Would (to God that) ministers preach for eternity! They would then act the part of true Christian orators, and not only calmly and coolly inform the understanding, but by persuasive, pathetic address, endeavor to move the affections and warm the heart."

Adrian P. Rogers: A Man of God

"FAREWELL" was the lone word unfurled across the top of the front page of *The Commercial Appeal* on Friday, November 18, 2005. That was the word used by the Memphis, Tenn. newspaper to say goodbye to Adrian Pierce Rogers, the beloved pastor emeritus of Bellevue Baptist Church and one of America's most notable and powerful preachers.

The memorial services for the only man in recent history to be elected as president of the Southern Baptist Convention three times was held at the 29,000-member church near Memphis at 6 o'clock on Thursday evening November 17th. The Memphis paper stated that more than 10,000 multiracial and multigenerational mourners gathered to show their respect and admiration for Rogers, many of them spilling over into rooms converted into viewing areas where large screens broadcasted the service.

The two-hour worship experience celebrating Roger's life was broadcast on local radio and television stations, as well as by the International Daystar Christian Television Network. It was also available on the Internet.

Adrian Rogers was a peerless preacher with a golden voice. At the memorial service, Jerry Vines, pastor of First Baptist Church in Jacksonville, Fla., said, "You haven't preached until you have preached an Adrian Rogers sermon. Adrian and I would talk on the phone and sermonize, and I must confess that I have cleverly disguised some of his outlines. Haven't we all?"

Adrian Rogers was a dynamic leader. Vines stated, "He was the acknowledged leader of the conservative resurgence." Many contend that Southern Baptists would not have experienced the historic return to the faith of our fathers without the leadership of the Bellevue pastor.

In an interview with The Florida Baptist Witness in October Rogers stated, "I look back on my life and there are a lot of things that have happened. I have written books, pastored churches, and preached on radio and television around the world. But I think the part that God allowed me to have in the turning of the SBC may have the longest-lasting effect and be the most significant."

Adrian Rogers was the epitome of a loving pastor-shepherd. The wooden shepherds' staff leaning against the casket during the memorial service beautifully illustrated this strategic role. The shepherd feeds and protects his sheep. Underscoring this role, Ken Whitten, pastor of Idlewild Baptist Church in Tampa, Fla. and former Bellevue staff member, commented, "I felt safe knowing that he (Rogers) was alive. I felt that our denomination was safe knowing that he was alive."

James Dobson, founder and chairman of the board of Focus on the Family commented, "Adrian Rogers was the wisest and most gifted human being I know. He was like a great oak tree and many little creatures find shelter in its branches, and when it falls everything is disoriented."

Adrian Rogers was phenomenally wise and had sanctified common sense that transcended anything this world offers.

Peter Lord, longtime friend and colleague in ministry, commented, "He could take either side of any argument and win."

Adrian Rogers was incredibly personable and upon occasion I visited with him. He knew how to make a simple, plain vanilla preacher like me feel like I was someone of genuine worth. Through the years he got to know our family and although he primarily only saw our identical twin sons at Southern Baptist Convention meetings he had the remarkable ability to differentiate between the two boys when their own grandparents had trouble telling them apart.

The last time I had a chance to talk with him at length was at the inauguration of George W. Bush earlier this year. We talked about his plans to train and equip young pastors and his desire to mentor those who wished to draw from his knowledge and experience. He was excited about the future. But cancer came on sandaled feet and attacked our hero, our knight in shining armor.

As I saw my hero lying in the casket, the feeling was surreal, hard to believe, almost impossible to accept. I had figured him to be immortal, invincible, and incorruptible. And of course, he is all that, but now he belongs not just to us, but he belongs to the ages. He is no doubt rejoicing in his celestial home and undoubtedly "kicking up gold dust on the streets of glory."

Let it be "Merry Christmas" Now and Forever

Last year Target stores became the Scrooge of 2004 and told the Salvation Army that they could no longer have their red kettles available to collect money for benevolent purposes. Consequently, the Salvation Army indicated that Target's decision was a devastating blow to their "Sharing is Caring" campaign because Target locations produced an estimated $9 million in donations the previous year.

This Christmas season Wal-Mart got off to a bad start with the Catholic League and a multitude of others when a woman complained that the store was replacing "Merry Christmas" with "Happy Holidays" and then got the following outrageous email response from Wal-Mart's Customer Service:

"Wal-Mart is a worldwide organization and must remain conscious of this. The majority of the world still has different practices other than 'Christmas' which is an ancient tradition that has its roots in Siberian shamanism. The colors associated with 'Christmas' red and white are actually a representation of the amanita mascara mushroom. Santa is also borrowed from the Caucuses, mistletoe from the Celts, yule log from the Goths, the time from the Visigoth and the tree from the worship of Baal. It is a wide, wide world."

To their credit Wal-Mart issued an apology, withdrew "its insane statement" on the origins of Christmas, revised its Christmas-discriminating website and fired the employee who sent the email.

Two years ago, Manuel Zamorano, a California media consultant, grew weary of seeing Christmas disappear from our culture and founded the Committee to Save Merry Christmas. Last year he launched an attack on Federated Department Stores (parent company of Macy's, Bloomingdale's and others), declaring, "Your company actively solicits our patronage and purchasing of gifts for the Christmas celebration, and now refuses to acknowledge Christmas in your stores."

Macy's Herald Square store in New York City is the symbolic heart of U.S. retailing and is known as the "world's largest store." It was the setting for the 1947 holiday film, Miracle on 34th Street. However, the store substituted generic phrases such as "Happy Holidays" and "Season's Greetings" in place of the traditional "Merry Christmas," suggesting that the phrases they are using embrace "all of the various religious, secular and ethnic celebrations" in November and December.

A spokesman for Federated Department Stores stated, "These expressions of goodwill are more reflective of the multicultural society in which we live today."

Bill O'Reilly, FOX News personality, at the time, stated, "All over the country, Christmas is taking flak, (and) all of this anti-Christmas stuff is absurd. But the real reason it's happening has little to do with Christmas and everything to do with organized religion."

Reilly added, "Secular progressives realize that America as it is now will never approve of gay marriage, partial birth abortion, euthanasia, legalized drugs, income redistribution through taxation, and many other progressive visions because of religious opposition. But if the secularists can destroy religion in the public arena, the brave new progressive world is a possibility."

It appears that the devil has a cleverly designed plan to take over America, a country with the resources to evangelize the world. The removal of Christmas from the landscape is only a small part of the total plan, but the enemy is working his plan exceedingly well and the church is not putting up much of a fight.

Several years ago, World Magazine published an article entitled "How the West was lost" and stated, "A decline in courage may be the most striking feature that an outside observer notices in the West today. ...To defend oneself, one must also be ready to die; there is little such readiness in a society raised in the cult of material well-being. Nothing is left, then, but concessions, attempts to gain time, and betrayal."

Changing "Merry Christmas" to "Season's Greetings" may not seem too significant today, but what will be the next step in the onslaught of secularism? If we do not take a stand against the relentless march of this godless philosophy the day will come when preachers will have their sermons monitored and censored.

In November Ake Green, a Swedish pastor, faced imprisonment for preaching a sermon on what the Bible says about homosexual behavior. This happened in a "developed" Western country and the entire case was televised live in Sweden; Parliament stopped their session to watch the proceedings. The American Civil Liberties Union carefully observed this case, because it is doing everything in its power to use international law as a precedent in the courts of the U.S. Last week, Green was acquitted, but many believe the outcome could have been quite different.

Please take note: "Happy Holidays" is no substitute for "Merry Christmas."

The Unsanitized Version of Christmas

Our children were born more than 40 years ago, but they had the advantage of being born in sanitized hospitals with competent physicians clothed in Martinized smocks doing their work with disinfected hands washed with soap containing Chlorhexidine Gluconate.

Expectant fathers were not allowed anywhere near the labor rooms or delivery rooms for fear they would bring some kind of contamination into the area where the newborn child would enter the world. Christian comedian Ken Davis indicated that he was so desperate to get into the room where his wife was giving birth to their daughter that the hospital had to put out a restraining order on him. So, in an effort to keep soon-to-be fathers at some distance from the birthing place waiting rooms were designed as far away from the delivery room as possible.

After the children were born they were properly bathed and placed in a sterilized nursery. That too was off limits to both the mothers and the fathers for the most part. However, we got to go see our precious newborn children through a window from a parent's observatory. Essentially, in those days we could see, but not touch.

Times have changed, and the husband is no longer considered persona non grata in the delivery room. In fact, he now gets to coach his wife in the birthing process. But in developed nations children are born in fresh, sparkling, hygienically clean medical facilities that are maintained in the most favorable of conditions.

Because of our experiences we prefer to think that all births occur in the most idyllic of circumstances. And certainly, we'd like to think that there was nothing crude or barbaric about the birth of our Savior. We picture him in a warm stable that has been decontaminated and sanitized and scotch-guarded for his protection.

Even our most beloved Christmas carols picture his birth circumstances as ideal. Consider the words of perhaps the most well-known carol of all:

Silent night, Holy night, all is calm, all is bright

Round yon virgin mother and child.

Holy infant so tender and mild,

Sleep in heavenly peace, sleep in heavenly peace.

Do you think the Christ child got much sleep that night in the stench of a cold, filthy stable with sheep bleating and cows bellowing? I doubt it.

We want Christmas to be a warm sentiment with pleasant memories, a festive celebration with lavish decorations and a cozy, comfortable season marked by family conviviality.

All of that is well and good, but the first Christmas was all about a poor carpenter and a young woman who may have been disgraced by her pregnancy, both part of an oppressed race and living in an occupied country … and it's all about a birth in a barn, an unsanitized barn.

I actually think there is a hymn, which on the basis of the words of the chorus, could qualify as a Christmas carol, but it does not portray the kind of Christmas scene that we have painted for our own comfortable, casual brand of Christianity. Consider the words of "Ivory Palaces:"

His life had also its sorrows sore, for aloes had a part

And when I think of the cross He bore,

My eyes with teardrops start.

Out of the ivory palaces into a world of woe,

Only His great eternal love made my Savior go.

Christmas for Jesus was a condescension whereby He left the glories of heaven, and "took upon himself the form of a servant, and was made in the likeness of men ... and became obedient unto death, even the death of the cross."

He left the thrill of heaven for the threats of Herod. Van Horn calls Herod the "Ebenezer Scrooge without the conversion, the Grinch without a change of heart." We Christians like to talk about putting Christ back into Christmas, but let's not forget to put Herod back into Christmas.

Herod reminds us that Jesus came into a "world of woe" as the hymn suggests. II Corinthians 8:9 says it so well: "For ye know the grace of our Lord Jesus Christ, that though he was rich, yet for your sakes he became poor, that ye thorough his poverty might be rich."

The incarnation is all about a Savior who came into our broken world to redeem outcasts, refugees and nobodies like you and me. In your commemoration of the incarnation don't forget that the wood of the cradle almost touches the wood of the cross.

The Abomination of High Doctrine, Low Conduct

The inexorable slide toward a loss of faith typically begins with a willingness to devalue the Word of God. When some pedigreed religion professor uses his classroom or some animated question mark uses his pulpit to cast suspicion upon the Bible he or she typically does it with the most surreptitious approach.

Some may dare to dismiss the divine inspiration of the Bible with unabashed boldness, but most are subtler. They call the authority of Scripture into question with a "Hath God said?" approach. They advise, "The Bible is not the Word of God, but contains the Word of God; and the Bible is not the Word of God, but it is the words of God.

John P. Jewell, Jr., in his book, *The Long Way Home*, writes, "The rejection of the Bible as the Word of God has somehow come to be assumed as a requisite of intelligent, thinking people … all this takes place in the name of freedom."

John MacArthur, pastor of Grace Community Church in Panorama City, Calif., has stated, "The church in our generation is drifting from the fundamentals [of the faith] and has already begun to embrace post-modern ideas uncritically. Evangelicalism is losing its footing, and the church is becoming more and more like the world."

MacArthur continued, "Fewer and fewer Christians are willing to stand against the trends, and the effects have been disastrous. Subjectivity, irrationality, worldliness, uncertainty, compromise, and hypocrisy have already become commonplace among churches and organizations that once constituted the evangelical mainstream."

It was this downward spiral away from the infallibility of the Scripture that prompted Harold Lindsell to write his book *The Battle for the Bible* in 1976.

Subsequently, a conservative resurgence took place in the SBC and Southern Baptists valiantly contended for the right to be called "the people of the Book." I am personally grateful for the biblical conservatism that characterizes our Convention.

However, an uncompromising allegiance to "The Book" carries with it grave and solemn responsibilities. Forty years ago, I heard a sermon entitled "The Abomination of High Doctrine and Low Conduct." The preacher avowed that our behavior must match our beliefs; that our conduct should measure up to our convictions; that a profession without a performance equals a pathetic pretense.

Yet, when I read the Bible I am made painfully aware of my own wretchedness, and I am constantly resolving to let the transforming power of Christ change me so that my faith is not betrayed by my footsteps.

Gallup and Barna polls continue to show that evangelicals live just like the world. Born again Christians and evangelical Christians get divorced just as often, if not more often, than the general population. Studies show that physical and sexual abuse in theologically conservative homes is about the same as elsewhere.

Regarding racism, a Gallup poll discovered that when they asked the question, "Do you object if a black neighbor moves in next door?" the least prejudiced were Catholics and non-evangelicals. Evangelicals and Southern Baptists were most likely to object to having black neighbors.

Evangelicals are apparently gripped with the stranglehold of materialism. Only nine percent of evangelicals tithe and the average church member gives about 2.6 percent of his or her income to the church. If the average Christian tithed, we'd have another $143 billion for missions and ministry.

We have also lost our passion for the things of God and allowed the world to impose its preoccupation with temporal things upon our personal agenda so much that "the cares of the world and the deceitfulness of riches" have caused us to replace a fiery, dynamic Christian life for a dispassionate, mediocre substitute.

In spite of a weakened witness, it would appear that evangelicals still have a great opportunity to raise the standard concerning moral values in this society, but unfortunately, we have forfeited much of our influence and power by lacking the integrity to be taken seriously.

Ron Sider, in his new book, *The Scandal of the Evangelical Conscience*, writes, "The Lord doesn't take hypocrisy and disobedience lightly. He punishes, and there's an inevitable kind of decline that sets in if you are hypocritical and don't practice what you preach."

It is time for God's people, and Southern Baptists in particular, to put an end to the charade, stop playing church, and having renewed our commitment to the principles of the Bible, become doers of the Word.

Down Syndrome Babies
Targeted for Abortion

Over 40 years ago Jane Roe (whose real name was Norma McCovey), a pregnant single woman who was residing in Dallas County, Texas, brought a class action, challenging the constitutionality of the Texas criminal abortion laws, which proscribed procuring or attempting an abortion except on medical advice for the purpose of saving the mother's life.

Henry Wade was the Texas Attorney General who defended the anti-abortion law. The case was argued before the U. S. Supreme Court on Dec. 13, 1971 and Oct. 11, 1972.

On Jan. 22, 1973, U.S. Supreme Court Justice Harry Blackmun, delivering the opinion of the court, declared the abortion statutes void and indicated that abortion falls within the right to privacy protected by the Fourteenth Amendment to the U.S. Constitution. The decision gave women the right to abortion during their entire pregnancy and defined different levels of state interest for regulating abortion in the second and third trimesters.

It is now estimated that on an average more than one million women receive abortions in America annually. Approximately 60-million abortions have been performed since 1973.

Abortion is simply wrong and is a violation of the Sixth Commandment, "Thou shalt not kill." Furthermore, this nation was founded upon the belief that every human being is endowed by our Creator with certain "inalienable rights." Chief among them is the right to life itself.

This right should never be extended just to the strong, the independent, or the healthy. That value should apply to every American, including the elderly, the unprotected, the weak, the infirmed, and even the unwanted.

Researchers now say that by using a test called first-trimester combined screening, they can now detect Down Syndrome earlier in pregnancy than ever before.

The National Institute of Child Health and Human Development, which funded the $15-million, eight-year study of more than 38,000 women, found that the screening method – which combines a blood test with an ultrasound exam – can pinpoint fetuses with the common genetic disorder 11 weeks after conception.

The report said that the results of this study would provide those who might opt to terminate a pregnancy with sufficient information to make that decision when an abortion is safer and less traumatic.

Down Syndrome is the most common major chromosomal abnormality, occurring in 5,000 babies born each year in the United States. The syndrome results when a baby has three, rather than two, copies of the 21st chromosome, causing distinctive physical features, developmental problems and an increased risk of a variety of health problems that usually shorten the life span.

My sister, Miriam Hope, had Down Syndrome. She had a hole in the aorta of her heart and by the time such surgery was perfected her heart had enlarged too much for the surgery to be ventured. She had many of the physical characteristics of a Down Syndrome individual. She went to public schools, but received a "social" promotion year after year, because she simply could not comprehend many of the things taught in the school she attended.

She never had a boyfriend, never had a date, never drove a car, never had a job, never did many of the things most of us would call essential to a fulfilled life, but she understood spiritual things better than most preachers I know. Hope was proof that what God has hidden from the wise and the prudent, He has revealed unto babes (Matthew 11:25).

Few people I have known loved the Lord and His church more than my sister. She never missed going to church when it was physically possible for her to go. She passed out church bulletins at the door of the church and greeted people with the warmest smile you have ever seen.

She loved the Bible and read it through every year the last 20 years of her life. She also kept a diary each year and never missed a day of journaling. On Jan. 2, 1991 she wrote in her diary, "This morning took a walk with my father and mother. I washed and dried the dishes for my mother after lunch. This afternoon I went with my mother to deliver Sunday School quarterlies to the members of her class. Tonight, I went to prayer meeting. I also read three chapters from the Bible. I read my Bible through every year."

Hope also knew how to love her family. She died in our mother's arms in the summer of 1999 at age 49; and we all suffered a great loss. She was an incredible blessing to many people. It grieves me to think of how impoverished we would be if she had been aborted.

Judas Scheduled for Re-Imaging, Renovation & Rehab

Judas Iscariot, whose greed prompted him to betray Jesus for 30 pieces of silver, may be given an extreme makeover by Roman Catholic scholars. At least that is what *The London Times* recently reported.

Monsignor Walter Brandmuller, head of the Pontifical Committee for Historical Science, claims that Judas was not deliberately evil, but was just "fulfilling his part in God's plan." He insists that believers should look "kindly" at this disciple who has been reviled for 2000 years.

Al Mohler, former editor of *The Christian Index* and president of Southern Seminary in Louisville, Ky., addressed this subject recently on his radio program and commented, "Was Judas fulfilling a divine mission in betraying Christ? Jesus clearly knew that Judas would betray him (a fact mentioned as early as John 6:70). Furthermore, on the Day of Pentecost, Peter preached that the crucifixion of Jesus was 'according to the definite plan and foreknowledge of God'" (Acts 2:23).

Mohler added, "But does the affirmation of divine sovereignty mean that humans are not morally responsible? Not hardly. The omniscience and omnipotence of God are affirmed in these crucial texts, but the sovereignty of God is never cited to nullify full human responsibility."

In the Gospel accounts, Jesus reveals to the disciples at the Last Supper that one of them will betray him and adds, "Woe to that man by whom the Son of Man is betrayed!" In his high priestly prayer in John 17:12 Jesus says, "Those that thou gavest me I have kept, and none of them is lost, but the son of perdition ..." Scholars almost unanimously contend that this is a reference to Judas. The Greek word the Lord used here for "lost" is the word "apollumi" and is one of the strongest words that can be used to describe final and hopeless destruction.

The Bible clearly states that once a person dies in his/her sins there is no hope for a reprieve, a change in venue or a reassignment for one's eternal destiny. The account of the rich man and Lazarus in Luke 17 attests to the fact that once a person dies and goes to hell there is no exit from the place of eternal retribution. The dye is cast. Their doom is sealed. The verdict is carved indelibly in marble. The writer of Ecclesiastes alludes to this truth when he writes: "In the place where the tree falleth, there it shall be" (Ecclesiastes 11:3).

What does the Vatican hope to accomplish by this proposal to exonerate Judas? I fear that they will emerge from this muddled deliberation looking as if they have furthered the cause for ethical relativism or universal salvation.

First of all, let me declare that ethical relativism is the philosophical position that all points of view are equally valid and all truth is relative to the individual. In fact, I believe the vast majority of people in our western culture have come to believe that values are like fashions – a matter of personal taste and inclination, subject to rapid change and without final significance.

In fact, a recent Barna Group study revealed that six out of ten people 36 and older embraced moral relativism and 75% of the adults

18 to 35 did so. Therefore, it appears that relativism is gaining ground and the proposal to absolve Judas Iscariot by the Catholic Church will do nothing but hasten the move toward minimizing sin and maximizing existentialism.

Secondly, the effort to vindicate Judas would appear to promote the doctrine of universal salvation. Hypothetically, if Judas could be acquitted of his treachery, then no one should be left outside the fold of God. However, Judas, though filled with remorse over his dastardly deed, never repented of his sin of betraying Christ and is thus called the son of perdition, which means the son of everlasting punishment.

God is a god of love, but He is also a god of righteousness, and it is the holiness of His Person and the righteousness of His government that preclude Him from any mere benevolence that would make light of sin. In fact, sin is sufficiently sinful to require eternal retribution as the divine penalty for it. Furthermore, if God could save one soul from one sin by mere benevolence, He could save all souls from sin by benevolence and the death of Christ thus becomes the greatest possible divine blunder.

There is only one way to God and that is through Jesus Christ. Catholics need to know that, and Baptists must never forget it.

Needed: Fearless Prophets

Several years before his death I heard Robert Greene Lee, perhaps the last great pulpit orator in America, preach. He said, "One of these days I am going to cast off this earthy tabernacle and do something common to all men. I am going to die; and they are going to bury me in this terrestrial soil. And there is some chance that some little pusillanimous preacher will stand over my grave and say, 'There lies the body of R. G. Lee, a man who did not have an enemy in this world.'"

Lee stated, "If such a foolish, absurd, ludicrous, preposterous, nonsensical thing should happen, I hope the dear Lord of glory will give me enough of His omnipotence to kick the lid off that coffin and say, 'That's a lie.' I'd hate to think I preached for over 50 years and did not make one enemy."

In this day of religious pluralism and cultural diversity a Christian who stands for the truth of God's Word will make some enemies.

A secular worldview is slowly but surely replacing a Biblical worldview in America. Fifty years ago, most people never questioned Biblical ethics or morality. Now the philosophy of relativism has so blurred the concept of absolute truth that almost nothing is wrong; and it causes one to wonder if anything today is actually morally reprehensible.

Back then most people looked upon divorce as disgraceful, but now it is so commonplace and has so touched most of our lives in some way that it is scarcely a blip on the moral Richter scale.

Fifty years ago, most folks thought conceiving a child outside of marriage was a disaster, but now it is called an unplanned pregnancy and can be covered up with an abortion. My parents taught me that chastity was a good thing, but now Hollywood, having become secular society's champion, portrays chastity as bad and promiscuity as good.

Of course, Isaiah prophesied that such a day was coming. He wrote: "Woe unto them that call evil good, and good evil; that put darkness for light, and light for darkness; that put bitter for sweet, and sweet for bitter!" (Isaiah 5:20).

Furthermore, there was a time when an honest day's work was the responsibility of any respectable and dependable employee - that honesty was the best policy - but not today. Things have changed. Those who hold to the values that were acceptable fifty years ago are looked at today as archaic and out of touch with reality.

But when there is the demise of conviction and the emergence of compromise the result is chaotic. When people in the church don't have a Biblical worldview, the church becomes one huge intellectual and spiritual disaster area. It no longer knows how to out-think, out-live and out-die the unbeliever. Instead of being different, modern church members blend in nicely with the materialistic world.

Through years of subtle acquiescence and compromise church folks have come to the place where they yearn for and fret over the same things the secularists do. Such church members are more interested in their own personal kingdom than the Lord's kingdom. Their look is not upward or outward, but inward.

And preachers who buy into this secular worldview will ultimately abandon preaching on the once-honored Biblical virtues of sacrifice and surrender and will begin to twist and mold the Bible to fit the "felt needs" of the "itching ears" of their congregations.

To the modern church member, discerning God's will simply means learning about the things God has approved that they have already decided they want to do. Instead of being in an intimate relationship with the Lord, he thinks himself to be in a "limited partnership" with Jesus. This enables him to call himself a Christian, while being totally absorbed in the pursuit of "self."

When the church drifts into the ways of the world, it measures itself as the world measures itself - by size, wealth, power, and success of programs. But when the church is called back to its purpose, it sees itself in terms of Christlike character - the only means by which God can be glorified in his people. God sends prophets to beckon people to this high calling.

What we need today - at the risk of ridicule, perhaps even persecution - are prophets who are willing to risk all for the sake of the truth. Carmen Conner, a retired pastor in New Mexico said, "The danger to the church is not overt rebellion, but unconscious drifting. God sends prophets to awaken his people from their slumber and draw them back on course."

Carmen says that a prophet is someone with the long look, able to see into the nature of God's purpose and plans, uncompromising with truth, (and) willing to be unpopular.

Five Things that can Cripple a Church

The dear Lord Jesus loves the church and has given Himself for it, and He obviously wants the church to be healthy and vibrant. The devil hates the church and since its inception has been hurling all the weapons in his diabolical arsenal in an effort to cripple its witness and its effectiveness.

Let me mention five of the things that weaken the church and minimize its effectiveness.

First, there is the problem of a scandalous leadership. When immorality, bred by lust or greed, is found among the leadership of the church the results are devastating. That is precisely why pastors, church staff and lay leaders such as deacons must have lives marked by physical chastity, moral purity and spiritual integrity.

I have pastored a church that was marked by a staff member who was guilty of immorality of the worst sort and the results of his sin had a devastating impact, not only upon him, but also upon his family, friends, the church and even the community. In fact, the church may still bear the stigma of that heinous sin. Someone said that it might take the church a generation to overcome the humiliating and ignominious scars suffered from the grievous sins of one staff member.

Second, there is the problem of a discordant member. I am not speaking of the person who registers an occasional disagreement. I am not referring to the person who may infrequently raise a voice of dissent. I am speaking of the person who is born in the objective mood and negative case – the person who is never happy with what happens in the church and actually creates dissention.

In Proverbs 6:16-19 the Bible actually tells us that there are some things that God hates or considers an abomination and one thing God despises is the person who sows seeds of discord among the brethren. Such an individual can make life miserable for the pastor, sandbag decisions in a church business meeting, discourage other church members, repel the lost and summons an ominous cloud over the entire church.

Third, there is the problem of apathy. Vance Havner said, "We have anarchy in the world, apostasy in the professing church and apathy in the true church." An indifferent, indolent, lukewarm church nauseates God and renders the church helpless and ineffective.

One pastor went down to the train station every day to see the one westbound passenger train that came through their small town each afternoon at 4:30.

One day the ticket agent, who saw the pastor watch the train pull out of the station each day, asked, "Preacher, why are you always here to see the 4:30 train pull out of the station?"

The weary pastor said, "I just like to see something moving forward that I don't have to push."

Did you hear about the company that makes blank bumper stickers? They're for people who don't want to get involved. Too many churches have too many people who just don't want to get involved. Such apathy cripples the cause of Christ and paralyzes the effort to build healthy kingdom churches.

Fourth, there is the problem of inflexibility. Some churches do not grow because the members are so unwilling to change, so unyielding, so set in their ways. I have known Sunday School class members that were so married to their class that they would never agree to serve anywhere else or move to another class or help start another class.

Some classes have their own budget in order to purchase their own chairs, carpet their own classroom, and purchase their own television in case they want to watch a certain television preacher instead of having their own teacher teach the lesson. The class is like a country club and for the most part visitors and new members are not welcome unless they are "approved."

Gordon Venturella says, "Inflexibility leads to idolatry; and change is the only road out of self-centered control to servanthood." Yet many churches are inflexible – unwilling to change.

Fifth, there is the problem of purposelessness. One church put a sign on their church door in 1963 that stated, "Gone out of business. Didn't know what our business was."

Thomas Carlyle said, "A man without a purpose is like a ship without a rudder – a waif, a nothing, a no man. Have a purpose in life, and, having it, throw such strength of mind and muscle into your work as God has given you." The same is true of a church. Proverbs 29:18 emphasizes: "Where there is no vision, the people perish…"

Is your church avoiding the problems that cripple the family of God?

Spiritual Malpractice

Those of us who serve on the Southern Baptist Convention Funding Study Committee finished our recent meeting in Arlington, Texas ahead of schedule. I decided to try to get an earlier flight home via a stand-by status. When they called my name to inform me that I had been awarded a seat I was elated even though it was a middle seat between two other passengers.

When I sat down I warned the ladies on either side of me that I was a Baptist preacher and told them I hoped that wouldn't make them uncomfortable. I soon discovered that they were both believers and the young woman on my left, Jessica Atteberry Quinn, was a radiant Christian who grew up in First Baptist Church of Milton, Fla.

Jessica has her own public relations firm and she was returning from a meeting at Prestonwood Baptist Church, where she had the joy of listening to one of her clients, David Jeremiah, speak. She is promoting his new book, *Captured by Grace*.

Jeremiah is the pastor of a Southern Baptist Church, Shadow Mountain Community Church in El Cajon, Calif.; he is also an insightful preacher and a prolific writer.

Jessica told me that Jeremiah, a cancer survivor, presented a hypothetical case in one of his messages at Prestonwood, saying, "What if an oncologist examined a patient and said to him, 'Your blood pressure is perfect, and your cholesterol is at an acceptable level. Your skin is healthy, and your reflexes are good. Have a good day.'"

Jeremiah continued, "Then suppose the patient left and the nurse turned to the physician and said, 'but doctor, you didn't tell him that the tests show that he has cancer.'"

And the doctor replied, "Well, that is true, but I just didn't want to ruin his day."

The California pastor indicated that in a similar fashion many preachers today are painting life in the pastel hues of garden walks, spring flowers and lovely rainbows. They are not speaking of the grief, sorrow, heartache and separation caused by sin. Therefore, they are guilty of spiritual malpractice.

Secular humanism has attempted to humanize God, deify man and minimize sin; and these views have begun to insidiously infiltrate the church.

First of all, there is the attempt to humanize God. It has been said that in the beginning God made man in His image, and ever since the Fall man has tried to return the favor. Sinful man tries to re-make God into his image rather than being conformed to the image of Christ. This is the underlying problem of Romans chapter one. When they "knew God" they refused to "glorify him as God." Their downward spiral accelerated as they "changed the glory of the incorruptible God into an image made like to corruptible man" (Romans 1:23). This is the terrible sin of humanizing God.

Furthermore, in much of the preaching today God is humanized by stripping Him of his unappealing attributes. Many sermons today avoid those aspects of God's perfect character that bring guilt to imperfect people. In doing so, God is reduced to a passive, non-threatening deity.

Secondly, there is the matter of deifying man. Humanizing God naturally paves the way for the second sin of deifying man. After exchanging the glory of God for the image of man, the object of worship is no longer God, but man himself. Romans 1:25 states, "Who changed the truth of God into a lie and worshipped and served the creature more than the Creator."

Humanism has begun to dominate the cultural values of our society and has virtually turned the Christian world upside down – a reversal of Acts 17:6. This indicates the weakness of Christianity in our world, and that must be changed.

Finally, there is the matter of minimizing sin. When man has a lowered vision of God and a heightened vision of himself, sin does not appear exceedingly sinful. Therefore, men are prone to see their failures as nothing worse than poor judgment at best and a character flaw at worst.

Churches are not meant to be primarily social clubs or entertainment centers, but soul-saving stations where sin is portrayed as creating an impenetrable barrier between God and man. God alone removed the barrier caused by sin, and its removal was costly, requiring the sacrificial death of His Son, Jesus Christ, upon the cross. God takes sin seriously. Therefore, those who preach must not be guilty of spiritual malpractice.

It is Time to set Things Right

O n a recent mission trip to Moldova I rejoiced to see the Christians of the city of Balti openly share their faith and gather in large numbers to worship in freedom. It has not always been that way. Religious liberty is a fairly new concept for many of the countries in eastern Europe once held captive by the Iron Curtain of communism. How exceedingly glorious it was to see the Moldovans exercise their freedom to worship God and how wonderfully encouraging it was to see their receptivity to the Gospel.

I spoke to one faithful soldier of the cross in the town of Floresti in northern Moldova who in years past had been imprisoned for his faith in Christ. When reflecting upon his three arrests for preaching the Gospel, it was obvious that he still bore the emotional scars of an oppressive regime that attempted to deny him the freedom to serve God.

There are still people all over the world who are persecuted for their faith in Christ. One organization, The Voice of the Martyrs, states that more than 70 million Christians have been martyred for their faith since 33 AD. Their website estimates that this year approximately 160,000 believers will die at the hands of their oppressors and more than 200 million will be persecuted, arrested, tortured, beaten or jailed.

For example, in China there is a crackdown on unregistered house churches through attempts to disrupt their worship services and arrest their leaders. In parts of central Asia, where Christianity is considered an intrusive import from the West, believers are considered traitors to their country and families. Family members are beaten, and then thrown out of their homes and into the streets.

In the Middle East and parts of India and Africa, laws prohibit Christians from owning a Bible and evangelizing and forbid citizens from choosing Christianity over the religion into which they were born. Christians caught sharing God's Word are chased out of town, beaten or worse.

Compass, a news agency that provides information about Christians who are being persecuted for their faith, reports that a Nigerian pastor and 48 members of his congregation were among 200 killed in February 2004. Religious militants attacked the church in a rampage within the predominately Christian village. In addition, they went through the village killing Christians and burning down their houses.

Yet throughout the world severely punished Christians do not ask us to pray for their persecution to end. Instead, they ask us to pray that they will have the strength to endure. They ask us to send Bibles, so they may witness more effectively.

Tertullian, a church leader and prolific author during the early years of Christianity, declared, "The blood of the martyrs is the seed of the church." And indeed, it has often been said that the church has flourished more in times of adversity than in times of prosperity.

I have often wondered how we as believers would stand up under the kind of persecution Christians in other parts of the world have to endure. Alas, the average church member seems to be taking a nonchalant, blasé, lackadaisical approach to Christianity. Perhaps the message of Amos to the people of his day – "Woe to them that are at ease in Zion." – would be appropriate for our day as well.

While Christians all over the world are risking their very lives for the sake of the Gospel, so many professing believers in God-blessed America seem to prefer a religion of comfort and convenience. How can we be at ease in Zion when the church is dormant? How can we be at ease in Zion when the world is doomed?

In his hymn "Am I a Soldier of the Cross?" Isaac Watts asked:

"Must I be carried to the skies on flow'ry beds of ease,

"While others fought to win the prize, and sailed through bloody seas?"

Alexis De Tocqueville, the Frenchman who wrote much about life in America, stated, "The prospect really does frighten me that they may finally become so engrossed in a cowardly love of immediate pleasures that their interest in their own future and in that of their descendants may vanish, and they will prefer tamely to follow the course of their destiny rather than make a sudden energetic effort necessary to set things right."

Hopefully, persecution will not be necessary in order for us to make that "sudden energetic effort necessary to set things right." And, invariably nothing is set right until it is set right with God.

Abuse of "Freedom in Christ" is Dangerous

Liberty is a costly commodity. It never comes without a price. I was reminded of that in a very succinct way on Monday evening, July 3. Martha Jean and I went with some friends, Dr. and Mrs. Walter McBride, to hear the Atlanta Symphony present their annual patriotic concert at Mable House Barnes Amphitheatre in Mableton.

In addition to the stirring music, including "Fanfare for Freedom," "This Is My Country," "Battle Hymn of the Republic" and "Liberty for All," Ric Reitz, an actor who has appeared in a number of films, did a heart-rending narration on the cost of liberty. He quoted from a speech George Washington gave at Valley Forge during the American Revolution. I do not remember all that he said, but I was reminded that freedom is never free.

History records the hardships Washington's troops encountered during the winter of 1777–1778, and I have always been intrigued, even traumatized, by the stories I have read about the deprivation of the soldiers at Valley Forge.

When New York's Governor Morris visited the troops there he exclaimed, "An army of skeletons appeared before our eyes naked, starved, sick and discouraged."

The Marquis de Lafayette stated, "The unfortunate soldiers were in want of everything; they had neither coats nor hats, nor shirts, nor shoes. Their feet and their legs froze until they were black, and it was often necessary to amputate them."

Those who have fought and died from the time of the American Revolutionary battles in Lexington and Concord to the present-day battles in Iraq and Afghanistan during Operation Enduring Freedom have purchased at a great price the liberty we enjoy in America.

John F. Kennedy understood the cost of liberty. He said, "Let every nation know, whether it wishes us well or ill, that we shall pay any price, bear any burden, meet any hardship, support any friend, oppose any foe to assure the survival and success of liberty."

The liberty we enjoy as Christians has also come at a great price. Jesus, God's only begotten Son, had to die a cruel, ignominious death in order for us to know freedom from sin, freedom from guilt, freedom from Satan, freedom from condemnation and freedom to be what God wants us to be.

But we must remember that freedom is always inexorably linked to responsibility. Sir Edward Gibbon, historian and one of England's premier wordsmiths, penned, "In the end, more than they wanted freedom, they wanted security. They wanted a comfortable life, and they lost it all – security, comfort, and freedom. When … the freedom they wished for was freedom from responsibility, then Athens ceased to be free."

At the Southern Baptist Convention in Greensboro last month Southern Baptists passed a resolution against the use of alcohol in America. The resolution was inspired because of "some religious leaders who are now advocating the consumption of alcoholic beverages based on a misinterpretation of the doctrine of our 'freedom in Christ.'" The Bible warns against "using your liberty for a cloak of maliciousness" (I Peter 2:16). One translation says, "Live like free men, only do not make your freedom an excuse for doing wrong."

Whether you are talking about "freedom in Christ," "the priesthood of the believer" or "soul freedom," you are not to misconstrue the concept so as to turn liberty into license.

Some might say that "freedom in Christ" gives them the liberty to drink wine, go shopping on the Lord's Day or use profanity to emphasize a point. Quite frankly, such behavior under the guise of Christian liberty is nothing more than a mask to conceal sin.

With regard to the Christian life, liberty may be more accurately defined as the spirit of doing right spontaneously. Christian freedom comes when the heart of a saint is so unalterably linked with Christ that he/she is unified with Him in sympathy and interest and has the same radical purpose, the same holy views and aims.

Therefore, there is such harmony with God in their affections, desires and ends that their actions become an established, settled state. They are no more in bondage than Christ himself was. They are in such accord with God that their conscience no longer goads them, but guides them into the sweet will of God.

When the conscience sinks into the sweet will of God there is the most glorious kind of freedom, for God's will is "good, and acceptable, and perfect" (Romans 12:2c). Conversely, the person who uses liberty in Christ as a mask for doing wrong is living life in a masquerade ball of fools.

Trapped in a War Zone

To say the Middle East is a powder keg is an understatement. Since the dawn of creation, the part of the world known as the cradle of civilization has been the center of strife and conflict. The jealous rage that provoked Cain to slay his brother, Abel, simply previewed the fury and frenzy that characterizes that region today.

In the southernmost part of the Fertile Crescent, Israel has been pounding the Hezbollah stronghold with a barrage of artillery fire. Hezbollah, which in Arabic means "party of god," is a Lebanese Islamic military and civilian group. Israel's recent campaign in Lebanon was launched after Hezbollah captured two Israeli soldiers and killed two others.

Hezbollah is generally regarded as a terrorist organization much like the Taliban in Afghanistan. Hezbollah's military responded to the Israeli attack by launching hundreds of rockets aimed at northern Israel, hitting some of the cities including Haifa and Nazareth.

Israeli warplanes continued their retaliation with airstrikes against Lebanon in a deadly and destructive assault. Beirut's southern suburbs, believed to be a Hezbollah stronghold, have been the target of the most vicious attacks by the Israeli Air Force.

Having never served in the military or been trapped in a war zone, I cannot imagine what it would be like to be hunkered down in some bomb shelter. I cannot imagine what it would be like to feel the earth shake from exploding rockets. I cannot imagine what it would be like to hear the helpless cries and blood-curdling shrieks of those who have been shredded by shrapnel. I cannot imagine what it would be like to have jet fighter planes strafe the nearest street in a nation virtually cut off from the outside world.

As reported in *The Christian Index*, nine members of Eagles Landing First Baptist Church were trapped in Beirut during the initial days of the Israeli offensive. However, after eight days of withstanding the raging bombardment the Eagles Landing church members, who were helping in a children's camp, were evacuated by the United States military. What a sweet deliverance that must have been!

Honestly, while we may not be hearing bullets buzzing over our heads or rocket grenades whistling through the air, we, like the folks from Eagles Landing, are trapped in a war zone.

I am not referring to America as a war zone because of the ever-present threat of a terrorist attack here in our homeland. I am speaking of the ideological war raging in our country that is far more deadly than the one fought with bullets and bombs.

The secular humanists have been sending their salvos of destruction for years in America. They contend that moral values derive their source from human experience rather than the Word of God. Thus, ethics is autonomous and situational, needing no theological and ideological sanction. The secularists deny that morality needs to be deduced from religious belief, and so they oppose absolute, objective truth or Biblical morality.

Because secularists believe that standards of human behavior are derived from within human experience and that the plurality of human beings and their experience requires pluralistic standards, then it follows that, for secularists, everyone in society must be permissive and tolerant of every other person's standards and behavioral conduct.

Secular humanism is a religion, and this false religion is being taught to the sons and daughters of Georgia Baptists in many of our public schools. Furthermore, our society is so inundated with this indoctrination via the media that the moral fabric of our country is unraveling.

Satan has even launched this ideological war against the church with such a relentless attack that it appears that many church members have been trapped in the assault and the churches have not been able to withstand the insidious and withering onslaught.

Churches have perhaps unknowingly acquiesced to this humanistic ideology by adopting a consumerism mentality or by designing their pulpit ministry to address felt needs. Such a ministry is more man-centered than God-centered.

We must especially make sure that our worship is never man-centered or cater to the whims and desires of man but insist that our worship is forever designed to please and praise the "God from whom all blessings flow."

The most encouraging contemplation the mind can embrace is that ultimately "wrong will be on the scaffold and truth will be on the throne," and the church will be victorious for not even the gates of hell can prevail against it.

ESPN, since when did Poker Become a Sport?

James Butler "Wild Bill" Hickok was playing poker at Nuttal & Mann's Saloon No. 10 in Deadwood, Dakota Territory on August 2, 1876. It was then and there that Jack McCall shot "Wild Bill" in the back of the head with a double-action .45 caliber revolver.

Some think the cold-blooded murder was nothing more than the act of a paid assassin. Others contend that McCall was in a drunken stupor and seeking revenge over a recent dispute. Yet others believe that McCall was furious over what he perceived as a condescending offer from Hickok to let him have enough money for breakfast after he had lost all his money playing poker the previous day. Although the motive for the killing is still debated, I choose to embrace the latter speculation for my purposes in this editorial.

Poker (gambling) is a dangerous and deadly proposition and it is proliferating. The latest rage is Internet poker. More than eight years ago Randy Blumer introduced the first poker website that used real money.

His PokerPlanet.com ultimately failed, but Internet poker has regrettably been phenomenally successful. Online gambling is currently a multi-billion dollar business with more than 400 different card rooms operating today, offering every variety of poker game and every level of stakes.

Nearly 2 million people, two-thirds of whom are residents of the United States, log onto a poker gambling site every day. About $75 million is wagered in Internet poker rooms every hour. The University of Pennsylvania's Annenberg Public Policy Center predicts that more than 20% of college students (mostly male) play online poker at least once a month. There have been horror stories of students failing out of classes or losing their tuitions due to online poker.

In five years, if some of the major Internet gambling moguls have their way, consumers will be able to place bets on their cell phones and PDA's while waiting to be served in a restaurant.

Some of those who get hooked on online poker get "on a tilt." In poker "tilt" is the term used for a spell of insanity that often follows a run of bad luck.

Greg Hogan, age 20, was apparently "on a tilt" when he robbed a bank to pay off online gambling debts he incurred by borrowing money from his fraternity brothers. CNN.com reported that Hogan, the son of a Baptist pastor and president of his class at Lehigh University, robbed a Wachovia Bank in Allentown, Pa. and got away with $2,871.

Televised poker is beginning to dominate some of the cable channels and is contributing to the increase in video poker. I counted 78 different listings for poker on television in July and August. Many of these programs are on ESPN, whose stated purpose is to provide comprehensive sports coverage and complete sports information and news.

Pray tell me when did poker become a sport? And who could possibly be entertained by watching four people sitting around a table with expressionless faces hiding their cards from everyone's view?

Gambling is not just a minor vice, but also a major social evil and menace to society. From the blatant forms of casino gambling to state lotteries to wagers at work on who will win the World Series to those who bet on who will par the hole in golf, gambling is a national scourge.

Gambling violates God's legitimate laws for earning a living by undermining our work ethic. It promotes profiteering and greed. "Epithumeo" is one of the Greek verbs translated into "covetousness" in the New Testament. It is a compound word that comes from two Greek words, "epi," which means "upon" and "thumos," which means "passion." Covetousness is to set your passion upon money or things.

Gambling distorts our view of stewardship and also indicates a lack of trust in God's ability to provide. We must remember that God, who clothes the lilies of the field and who feeds the birds, will provide for our physical needs.

We as Christians are supposed to care for the needs of the poor, the widow, the orphan and the oppressed, but gambling mercilessly exploits these most vulnerable members of our society. John MacArthur stated, "Gambling is the result of post-modern pessimism, the hopelessness of practical atheism, that says, 'There is no God, no hope, no future, no reason, no rationality – just luck.'

"And so, the senselessness of gambling makes sense. It succeeds in a mood of despair and hopelessness, in a mood of moral relativism and atheism, but it doesn't belong with Biblical Christianity. It is a sin to be avoided and bless God – a sin to be forgiven."

The Muslim (Islamic)
March Across America

Islam is the second largest religion in the world with more than 1.3 billion adherents. In the United States, Islam is the fastest growing religion, a trend fueled mostly by immigration. There are almost 7 million Muslims in the United States.

If we choose to continue to open our borders to radical Muslim immigrants and accept multiculturalism as a societal philosophy, then we must be willing to face the consequences of losing our British-based Christian culture and our Judeo-Christian morality.

It is the declared intention of Muslims in America to turn the United States into a Muslim state. They really do not want to integrate; they want to dominate. It is predicted that Islam will also be the second largest religion in America by 2015. There are now more than 1,200 mosques in America; there are more Muslims in this country than Methodists.

While the West has been busy inventing new medicines to alleviate human suffering and increase life expectancy, and while the West has been attempting to decode human genes in an effort to find the cure for cancer and heart disease, and while the West has been launching space shuttles to enhance exploration, and while the West has been developing better economic models for a more prosperous world, and while secular humanism has been promoting its doctrine of tolerance, and while the ACLU has been gaining control over common sense, and while many Christian churches in America have been resting in the victories of the past, the Islamic religion has been aggressively propagandizing, converting, proselytizing, and winning the war for the minds and souls of our fellow Americans.

A veteran missionary to Middle Eastern people recently stated, "If you want to look at a dedicated, sincere, committed Muslim, look at Osama Bin Ladin."

A former Muslim stated, "I left Islam when I understood that Islam is a sick and evil religion. The Islamic message to the infidels of the West is: 'We will fight the infidel to death. Meanwhile, American laws will protect us. Leftists will support us. UNO will legitimize us. CAIR will incubate us. The ACLU will empower us. Western universities will educate us. Mosques will shelter us. OPEC will finance us. Hollywood will love us. And UN Secretary-General Koffi Annan will pass politically correct, sympathetic statements for Jihadists.'"

When President George W. Bush addressed Congress following the terrorist attacks on Sept. 11, 2001 he stated, "I also want to speak tonight directly to Muslims throughout the world. We respect your faith. It's practiced freely by many millions of Americans, and by millions more in countries that America counts as friends. Its teachings are good and peaceful, and those who commit evil in the name of Allah blaspheme the name of Allah. The terrorists are traitors to their own faith, trying, in effect to hijack Islam itself."

However, Bush's comments do not ring true with many Americans, because many contend a closer analysis of the Muslim religion will reveal that their renunciation of violence is only superficial.

The Ayatollah Khomeini, former dictator of Iran, once said, "All those who study jihad will understand why Islam wants to conquer the world. Those who know nothing about Islam pretend that Islam counsels against war. [They] are witless."

Anis Shorrosh, in his book Islam Revealed, comments, "Religious liberty is unknown where Islam is the creed of the majority. Of course, Muslims are quick to take full advantage of the freedom of religion, which is practiced throughout the western world. This is demonstrated in the Muslim centers established in the last fifteen years."

The King Abdulaziz Chair for Islamic Studies, the King Fahd Chair for Islamic Shariah Studies, the Sultan bin Abdulaziz Al-Saud Program in Arab and Islamic Studies, the H. E. Sheikh Ahmed Zaki Yamani Islamic Legal Studies Fund, the King Fahd Chair of Oncology and Pediatrics, the Bakr M. Binladin Visiting Scholar Fund – you may think these studies are taking place in the Middle East, but these are branches of American universities. Saudi Arabia is funding most of them and using them as propaganda machines to promote the Islamic religion.

God promised Abraham a son, with whom He would establish an everlasting covenant. The Muslims believe that son of promise was Ishmael, but the Bible says, "He (Ishmael) will be a wild man; his hand will be against every man, and every man's hand against him" (Genesis 16:12). Jews and Christians believe, according to the scriptures, that the promise was given to Isaac who became the father of the Israelites, father of Moses who received the Torah, father of King David who ruled in righteousness over God's people and who also received the promise that from his descendants would come the king who would rule the world for ever and ever.

Christians and Muslims do not simply have two different fathers (Isaac and Ishmael) and two different books (the Bible and the Koran), but they have two completely different spirits: one brings freedom, the other brings bondage. One leads to life and one leads to death.

In the Bible we see that God wants us to make the choice (freedom). "I have set before you life and death, blessing and curse; therefore, choose life, that you and your descendants may live" (Deuteronomy 30:19). But according to the Koran, Allah chooses the way for us (bondage). "This day I have perfected your religion for you and completed my favour unto you, and have chosen for you as your religion Islam" (from the Koran, Sure 5:3).

Christianity has spread because Christ died to His own desire and in the end gave His life for us. Islam, on the other hand, has spread because Muhammad lived for his own desires and killed everyone who tried to stand in his way.

Muhammad said, "I will instill terror into the hearts of the unbelievers, smite ye above their necks and smite all their finger-tips off them: (Surah 8:12).

Jesus said, "A new commandment I give to you, that you love one another; as I have loved you, that you also love one another. By this all will know that you are my disciples, if you have love for one another" (John 13:34-35).

The Ayatollah Khomeini, former dictator of Iran, once said, "All those who study jihad will understand why Islam wants to conquer the world. Those who know nothing about Islam pretend that Islam counsels against war. [They] are witless."

Try Honey

October is Clergy Appreciation Month. It is a time to honor pastors and their families for their faithful service and sacrificial dedication.

The Bible declares, "How beautiful upon the mountains are the feet of him that bringeth good tidings, that publisheth peace; that bringeth good tidings of good things, that publisheth salvation, that saith unto Zion, Thy God reigneth!" (Isa. 52:7)

H. B. London, Jr., vice president of pastoral ministries at Focus on the Family, said, "In our tumultuous culture, pastors need encouragement more than ever to keep up the good fight."

Hopefully, your church is planning to do something significant to express appreciation to your pastor(s) for his (their) labor in the service of the Lord.

My grandfather was my first pastor, and I am sure he had times of trial and testing, seasons of sorrow and stress, days of discouragement and disappointment. He served as the pastor of churches during the Great Depression and got paid in chickens, produce, and canned goods. However, I don't think I would be in error to say that he was one of the most respected men in the community.

After my grandfather passed away, my father became the chairman of the committee who sought out supply preachers during the period of time the church was without a pastor. We often invited those supply preachers in our home for "Sunday dinner." I was taught to love and respect those "men of God" who graced our home with their presence.

I grew up thinking that the pastor was worthy of double honor because of his high calling; and I was taught that God said, "Touch not mine anointed, and do my prophets no harm."

My father often defended pastors who were unduly criticized and often quoted Isaiah 54:17: "No weapon that is formed against thee shall prosper; and every tongue that shall rise against thee in judgment thou shalt condemn. This is the heritage of the servants of the Lord, and their righteousness is of me, saith the Lord."

Yes, there are some pastors who are not worth their "salt" and others who have defiled the office and yet others who have abused their role in the church, but a good and faithful pastor is worth his weight in gold. The apostle Paul spoke of the pastor as a "gift" to the church and in Revelation the apostle John referred to the pastor as an "angel."

Yet, there is probably not a more demanding profession than that of the pastor of a local church. A pastor is never off duty and virtually everyone lays claim to his time. His work is under-estimated and under-appreciated.

Furthermore, pastors are some of the most criticized and denigrated people on the planet. A pastor would most likely never attempt to tell an attorney, pharmacist, mechanic, or software programmer how to conduct his business, but few people are hesitant to tell the pastor how to perform his tasks.

Scorned and ridiculed by the world and castigated and harangued by people within the church, it is no wonder that pastors are leaving their calling at record numbers and are wandering from church to church like gypsies.

According to a survey reported by PastorCare Network, 50 percent of those who go into full-time ministry drop out in 5 years; 80 percent of those interviewed believe pastoral ministry has affected their families negatively; 70 percent say they have a lower self-image now than when they started.

Incidentally, the same survey reported that a church that fired a pastor has a 70 percent chance that it will do the same to the following pastor.

If your pastor is not all that he should be, remember the words of Benjamin Franklin, who said, "A spoonful of honey will catch more flies than a gallon of vinegar."

Here are some suggestions that will bless your pastor: (1) Let your pastor know that you love him and that you are praying for him. (2) Take good care of your pastor's wife and family. (3) Give your best to the church, not your leftovers. (4) Pay him a fair salary with sufficient benefits, and (5) recognize him during Pastor Appreciation Month in October with a special love offering or a paid vacation.

No Homogenization of Bad Eggs . . .

I feel that it is the responsibility of *The Christian Index* to chronicle the work of Georgia Baptists, encourage the work of evangelism, missions, and ministry among Georgia Baptists, and provide some accountability for our institutions and agencies as we endeavor to stay on mission. We must not stray from our bedrock convictions and from our mission of reaching people for Christ, planting new congregations, and building healthy kingdom churches.

Southern Baptists have experienced significant decline in membership and attendance in the last twelve years, but it is important for us to be aware of what happens to churches and denominations that drift into liberalism. Their decline becomes precipitous.

In his address to the Southern Baptist Convention in 1988 the venerable old warrior, W.A. Criswell, proclaimed, "It is very apparent why [there is a] decline in all the old mainline denominations of America. The curse of liberalism has sapped their strength and their message and their witness to the Lord Jesus Christ. That's why."

Charlotte Allen, a Catholic journalist, wrote an article that appeared in the *Los Angeles Times* entitled "Liberal Christianity is Paying for Its Sins." She contends that although most mainline Protestant churches and many

American Catholics for the past 40 years have embraced liberal Christianity as the future of the Christian church, it has resulted rather in providing the death knell to their denominations.

Allen reports, "… all but a few die-hards now admit [that] all the mainline churches and movements within churches that have blurred doctrine and softened moral precepts are demographically declining, and in the case of the Episcopalian Church, disintegrating."

Allen writes: "It is not entirely coincidental that at about the same time that Episcopalians, at their general convention in Columbus, Ohio, were thumbing their noses at a directive from the worldwide Anglican Communion that they 'repent' of confirming the openly gay bishop, V. Gene Robinson of New Hampshire. Three years ago, the Presbyterian Church USA, at their general assembly in Birmingham, Ala., was turning itself into the laughingstock of the blogosphere by tacitly approving alternative designations for the supposedly sexist Christian Trinity of Father, Son, and Holy Spirit. Among the suggested names were 'Mother, Child and Womb'" and 'Rock, Redeemer and Friend.'"

Moved by the spirit of the Presbyterian revisionists Beliefnet blogger Rod Dreher held a "Name That Trinity" contest. Entries included "Rock, Scissors, and Paper" and "Larry, Curly, and Moe."

To me such disrespect for the blessed Trinity is blasphemy.

Allen also states, "Following the Episcopalian lead, the Presbyterians also voted to give local congregations the freedom to ordain openly cohabitating gay and lesbian ministers and endorsed the legalization of medical marijuana.

"As if to one-up the Presbyterians in jettisoning age-old elements of Christian belief, the Episcopalians at Columbus overwhelmingly refused even to consider a resolution affirming that Jesus Christ is Lord. When a

Christian church cannot bring itself to endorse a bedrock Christian theological statement repeatedly found in the New Testament, it is not a serious Christian church. It's a 'Church of What's Happening Now,' conferring a feel-good imprimatur on whatever the liberal elements of secular society deem permissible or politically correct."

Dave Shiflett, who has recently written a book entitled *Exodus: Why Americans are Fleeing Liberal Churches for Conservative Christianity*, contends that "God-lite" just doesn't cut it. Indeed, thousands of churches that preach a watered-down gospel are hemorrhaging and their constituents are finding homes in houses of worship that preach the exclusivity of the gospel and a more demanding ethic.

According to the Glenmary Research Center, mainline Protestant churches are rushing headlong into oblivion. According to John H. Adams, the Presbyterian Church USA, which had a membership of 4,254,597 in 1983, but that number had been reduced to 1,482,767 by 2017.

The Institute on Religion and Democracy reports that after 30 years of decline and over a million members lost, the Episcopal Church is desperately in need of reform and renewal. The reasons given for the decline are interesting: (1) seminaries that have abandoned Biblical Anglican theology, (2) public policy that may reflect leftist positions, (3) unrelenting pro-homosexual advocacy and undermining of the family by church leaders, (4) a House of Bishops that is divided and no longer offers moral leadership, and (5) church officials who embrace a radical feminist theology.

The United Church of Christ, the first major U.S. denomination formally to endorse same-sex "marriage," has lost 1.3 million members (almost 60 percent of its membership) in the past 40 years.

The United Methodist Church has lost four and a half million members since 1965, and both membership and attendance has decreased by a third in the past 10 years. A report from Concerned Women for America stated that although the denomination operates the largest seminary system in America, none of their schools are devoted to traditionalist Wesleyan doctrine, and essentially all of the seminaries and church agencies openly support "gay" rights.

The American Baptist Churches USA have also experienced a membership decline and suffered budget cuts in recent years. John Pierce, writing for Associated Baptist Press and quoting ABC General Secretary Roy Medley, reported, "Despite dealing with controversy, American Baptists are energized by growing relationships with other groups such as the Progressive National Baptist Convention, the Cooperative Baptist Fellowship, and the Church of the Brethren."

Two months ago in another ABP article, Pierce reported that the American Baptist Historical Society, which claims the largest collection of Baptist resources in the world, is moving to the Atlanta campus of Mercer University, also the national headquarters for the Cooperative Baptist Fellowship.

In April of this year former U.S. President Jimmy Carter and Bill Underwood, president of Mercer University, hosted leaders of other Baptist conventions and organizations including, among others, the Cooperative Baptist Fellowship and the American Baptist Churches, USA. Those present agreed to hold a convocation in 2007 "to celebrate these historic Baptist commitments and to explore other opportunities to work together as Christian partners."

Vance Havner, a great revivalist a generation ago, said, "A lot of folks are like the herd of swine into whom Jesus cast that legion of devils in Mark, chapter 5. I can imagine those swine conversing with one another as they were running down that hill toward that sea in which they were drowned.

"And one said to the other, 'Where are we going?'"

"And the other said, 'O, it doesn't make any difference as long as we stick together.'"

Southern Baptists must guard against alliances that would cause us to compromise and dilute our principles. Adrian Rogers once commented, "No homogenization of bad eggs will make a good omelet."

Allen also wrote, "When your religion says 'whatever' on doctrinal matters, regards Jesus as just another wise teacher, refuses on principle to evangelize, and lets you do pretty much what you want, it's a short step to deciding that one of the things you don't want to do is get up on Sunday morning and go to church."

Then the Catholic journalist concluded by writing, "Evangelical and Pentecostal churches, which preach Biblical morality, have no trouble saying that Jesus is Lord and they generally eschew women's ordination. These churches are growing robustly, both in the United States and around the world."

While our denomination is growing [slightly] larger, we must forever guard against lukewarmness, lethargy, legalism, and liberalism.

Why Christian Higher Education?

If you are a high school student, if you are the parent(s) of a high school student, if you are related to a high school student, if you teach a high school student, or if you know a high school student, I hope you will read this editorial.

First of all, an education beyond high school is recommended for most high school students, but beware of the negative influences of secular higher education. For example, some schools have a hedonistic atmosphere and are antithetic to a Christian worldview.

For example, *The Princeton Review* lists The Top Ten Party Schools each year, and for 2006 the number one "party school" is the University of Texas at Austin. The Austin institution of higher education ranked number 2 in hard liquor, number 3 in beer drinking, and number 13 in pot smoking to qualify for the dubious number one ranking.

Unfortunately, such schools are often not only antagonistic toward the Christian worldview outside the classroom, but inside the classroom as well. There are three worldviews competing for the minds of students today: Christian theism, naturalism, and postmodernism.

Naturalism is the view that there is no god and that observable events in nature are explained only by natural causes or by the physical sciences.

Postmodernism, on the other hand, rejects all traditional authorities, believes that there is no such thing as objective, absolute truth, but that truth is subjective, always changing. The postmodernist believes in religious pluralism, that all religions offer an equally valid path to God, and that faith is based on feelings, imagination, mysticism, and group consensus.

Christian theism is the view that God exists and has revealed Himself decisively in Jesus Christ. This view is in the distinct minority on the secular college or university campus. There are consequences that must be faced when Christian theism is regarded as incidental rather than fundamental.

A recent article by Howard Kurtz in *The Washington Post* entitled "Study Finds College Faculties A Most Liberal Lot," revealed that most faculty at non-Christian colleges disdain Christianity with 72% indicating they are liberal, 84% favoring abortion, and 67% accepting homosexuality. This is problematic because students often reflect the values of the college faculty they encounter in the course of their education.

Steve Henderson, who writes for Christian Consulting for Colleges and Ministries, comments, "Statistics show significant declines in religious attitudes, values, and behavior during college years and that 28.4 percent of those who called themselves born-again and attended secular colleges did not call themselves born-again four years later."

Henderson continues, "Students who dropped away from the born-again faith were not likely to end up in a conservative church where born-again commitment is considered essential, but instead dropped out entirely from affiliation with a religious group or moved to a liberal or moderate denomination where being born-again is not stressed."

Henderson states, "The secular college or university is saying at best that God is irrelevant to the real business of living."

Clearly, secular college/university environments are diametrically opposed to Christian growth (although there are some great Christians on the faculty, some great Baptist Campus Ministries faithfully ministering, and good Christians attending). Only a very few students actually increase their faith attending secular institutions. The odds are clearly against it.

Of course, some think that Christian schools should be theologically neutral. I am not an educator, but while it may be worthwhile for an institution of higher education to present all sides of an issue, it should unquestionably equip the student to "be ready always to give an answer to every man that asketh you a reason of the hope that is in you" (I Peter 3:15). We should not be afraid to tenaciously offer the apologetics for our faith in our Baptist college classrooms.

First of all, I believe the primary reason for considering a Christian college is to provide an education within the framework of a Christian worldview. As Christians we believe we live in a world that is "charged with the grandeur of God." This belief impacts every facet of our lives and tempers how we look at all the disciplines of study, including the arts, humanities, and sciences.

Secondly, the Christian campus should be a haven from a hostile, secular world where one's faith is strengthened and opportunities for worship, Christian fellowship, ministries, and missions abound.

Thirdly, the Christian college or university should be a place where the mind is renewed. Properly cultivated, the Christian mind is not limited to mere academic dimensions. Paul told us we are transformed by the renewing of our minds. Proverbs tells us that as a man thinks, so is he. To have a Christian mind is to have "the mind of Christ," and to think His thoughts so that the process of being transformed into His image is a daily reality.

Fourthly, Christian education has the responsibility of equipping students to stand for historical, Biblical values and thus change the culture. If we choose to resist the degeneracy of culture, we cannot afford to neglect the wisdom of people who have prepared themselves and banded together to teach new generations to transform the culture (Romans 12:1-2) The largest concentration of such teachers is to be found on Christian college campuses. Righteousness exalts a nation (Proverbs 14:34), and Christian colleges exalt righteousness in ways impossible in other educational settings.

Finally, in this trying time when scandals are commonplace, companies are returning to Christian college campuses to hire workers with integrity. While a person's alma mater can provide no guarantee of high moral values, choosing a Christian education reflects an inclination to pursue guidance that will help a person be an admirable contributor to company success.

Georgia Baptists have three wonderful institutions of higher learning – Brewton-Parker College and Shorter University and Truett-McConnell University – that are distinctively committed to the Christian worldview. I believe these great institutions deserve our prayers, our gratitude, our financial support, and our very best high school students.

Have a Very "Holy" Christmas!

Christmas has become so secularized that it is little more than a cosmic birthday party in most circles. To avoid being swallowed up by the superficial tinsel and trappings of the holiday, most of us tack on our own religious version of Christmas and appease our consciences by at least giving lip service to the real significance of the season.

Those who change "Merry Christmas" into "Happy Holidays" offend us, and we certainly don't want our children or grandchildren to get out of school for Christmas and have it called "Winter Solstice." Furthermore, we don't even like the idea of Kwanzaa or Hanukkah getting equal attention with "our" Christmas season.

But even our most noble attempts to capture the true meaning of Christmas seem to be diluted by the commercialization of a society so skillful in communicating its worldly message of merriment and merchandizing. All of us are probably guilty of compromising the true meaning of Christmas.

Our best Christmas pageants could never really capture the significance of the incarnation, the wonder of the shepherds, and the worship of the wise men. After all, Christmas is the incarnation of holiness, and the celebration of a doctrine central to Trinitarian Christianity.

The Incarnation is the foundation stone upon which the framework of all Christian doctrine is laid. In fact, without the Incarnation, none of the rest of orthodox Christian thinking makes any sense whatsoever. The doctrine is this: God became incarnate, that is, put on human flesh. Until the moment of conception, God had been completely other than this world, but in that moment took on humanity, still as much God as if he were not man and yet as much man as if he were not God – the God-man.

This is such a radical doctrine that some of the earliest theologians referred to it as "the scandal of the Incarnation." The term does not designate the Incarnation as a heresy, but describes the difficulty that some people had in accepting the Church's teaching that God became man. The Incarnation scandalizes people because they resist the idea that God would limit Himself in that way or stoop to our level at all.

How could a Being as holy, powerful, and filled with glory as God become sullied with human flesh? It would seem a diminution of God's holiness. And yet that is what Jesus' birth represents to orthodox Christians, and it is this Incarnation of holiness that is celebrated at Christmas.

We probably seldom reflect on the Incarnation of holiness, because as Matthew Henry said, "No attribute of God is more dreadful to sinners than His holiness." It is the holiness of God that sets the standard for our conduct.

We tend to play the comparison game and judge ourselves favorably because we regard ourselves to be more righteous than our neighbor, but our neighbor was never meant to be the standard for our conduct. Morally, our standard of living is determined by the quality of holiness in the character of God. We must set the clock of our conduct by the character of God and His Son, who is the express image of the invisible God.

The holiness of God also means that he hates sin. He loves everything in conformity to His laws and loathes everything contrary to His laws.

While we minimize, rationalize, and even glamorize sin, God despises it. It follows, therefore, that He must necessarily punish it.

If God hates sin, then it also surely incurs His wrath. We must not forget that "the way of the transgressor is hard" (Proverbs 13:15). For one sin, God banished our first parents from the Garden of Eden. For one sin, God instructed Joshua to have Achan stoned. For one sin, Elisha's servant was smitten with leprosy. For one sin, Ananias and Sapphira were cut off from the land of the living.

But this eternal God whose holiness stands in direct contrast to our sinfulness and who has been offended by our iniquity, rebellion, and disobedience has provided a way for us to enter once again into His favor. His holiness demands a perfect sacrifice for our sins and through the Incarnation the provision of such a sacrifice was made possible. For Jesus, throughout his life, was known to be "holy, harmless, undefiled, and separate from sinners" (Hebrews 7:26) thus qualifying Him as the only one who could atone for our sins.

A. W. Tozer has declared, "We must hide our unholiness in the wounds of Christ as Moses hid himself in the cleft of the rock while the glory of God passed by."

Oswald Chambers said, "Holiness, not happiness is the chief end of man."

Therefore, have a "holy" Christmas!

Whatever Happened to the Holy Spirit?

Joe Graham, GBC specialist in Collegiate Ministries, invited me to speak to our Georgia Baptist campus ministers at their December retreat. During their meeting I was privileged to hear Jim Slack, a representative from the International Mission Board, who was speaking about the growth of Islam in Europe and America. He asked rhetorically, "How are they managing to grow so rapidly when we have the Holy Spirit and they have nothing?"

However, since that Baptist Collegiate Ministers' meeting I have wondered, "Do we really have the Holy Spirit?" Don't get me wrong. I know that the Lord has given us the Holy Spirit. I believe that He indwells every believer. I believe that He is the divine enabler, the One who empowers and energizes us.

Yet, I fear that there has been so much misinterpretation and misunderstanding about the doctrine of the Holy Spirit that we have become reticent to preach on the subject or avail ourselves of the efficacious work of the Spirit.

It is also possible we have become so dependent upon our own ability, education, ingenuity, cleverness, and Madison Avenue promotional techniques that we have forgotten about the ministry of the Holy Spirit.

A.W. Tozer, the great Christian and Missionary Alliance pastor and author, stated, "In most Christian churches the Spirit is entirely overlooked. Whether He is present or absent makes no real difference to anyone … so completely do we ignore him that it is only courtesy that we can be called Trinitarian. The idea of the Spirit held by the average church member is so vague as to be nearly nonexistent."

We must remember that in this foreign mission field of pagan, post-modern America that no matter how many gimmicks and rousements we employ to implement our ministry, no one will ever be converted apart from the power of God and the Holy Spirit and no significant work can be accomplished without His enabling grace.

Peter Hammond, the founder and director of Frontline Fellowship, asks a similar question to the one posed in this editorial. He asks, "Whatever happened to the prayer meeting?" Hammond proclaims, "What was once a major emphasis of church activities has either been relegated to the sidelines and ignored by most members, or it has been dispensed with altogether.

"Furthermore, many prayer meetings today involve little prayer. Even in meetings set aside for prayer, other activities typically crowd in and leave little time for adoration, confession, intercession, and thanksgiving to the Lord."

It is only through prayer and the power of the Holy Spirit that we can effectively confront the secular society in which we live or have any hope of seeing a revival of Christianity in our day.

The people of Isaiah's day came to believe that God had lost His power, that somehow He was no longer omnipotent. The great statesman prophet responded to their doubts and fears by saying, "Behold, the Lord's hand is not shortened, that it cannot save; neither his ear heavy, that it cannot hear" (Isaiah 59:1). Isaiah was assuring the people that the ability of God was not limited in any way and that God was aware of every flutter of thought in their minds.

In verse two of Isaiah 59 the prophet declares that God is not to blame for our lack of deliverance, our bankruptcy of power, or our spiritual poverty. He insists that we, because of our iniquities, have created the wall of separation between God and ourselves.

The deadness and dearth in so many churches are not God's fault. He has all power and authority and longs to endue us with the power of His spirit and send revival. The problem is with His people who have lost their passion for Christ and become lukewarm and lackadaisical.

Vance Havner, one of Southern Baptists' more renowned authors and revivalists, once told about the little boys who were playing baseball. They just had one ball, but one little boy hit the ball over the centerfielder's head and they lost it. They looked out in the grass for the ball, but their efforts were in vain. Finally, one kid said, "Let's forget the ball and get on with the game."

The question is obvious: How are you going to play baseball without a ball? Furthermore, how are you going to live the Christian life and how are you going to have a dynamic, heaven-blessed, God-pleasing ministry in your church without the power of the Holy Spirit?

I hope and pray that no one will ever look at your life or your church and ask the question: "Whatever happened to the Holy Spirit?"

Beware of False Advertising

I don't want to be standing near Brian in a thunderstorm. He was raised a Catholic, and says he became a born-again Christian when he was 13. Now he professes to be an atheist and has entered a contest with God that makes the prophets of Baal in Elijah's day look like featherweights.

Brian, who refuses to divulge his last name for safety reasons, was on ABC News' Nightline to explain his anti-God campaign. The 30-year-old atheist has developed a website for The Rational Response Squad, whereby he challenges people to make videos of themselves denying, denouncing, or blaspheming the Holy Spirit.

Those who are conversant with the Bible know that Mark 3:29 reads, "But he that shall blaspheme against the Holy Ghost hath never forgiveness, but is in danger of eternal damnation."

"Blasphemy against the Holy Spirit" is generally regarded as the "unpardonable sin."

Brian boldly stated, "Initially we wanted to find a way to allow atheists to come out of the closet, speak up, and show other people that there are people that think like this. We wanted to do it in such a way where we stripped the power from religious institutions that instill fear in people.

We did that by blaspheming the Holy Spirit, by showing that we are not scared of this unforgivable sin."

ABC reports that one of the posts on Brian's website is from a young man named Chandler, who wrote: "I've come to the conclusion that alongside the fact that there is no Santa Clause and there is no Easter Bunny, there is also no God. So, without further ado, my name is Chandler and I deny the existence of the Holy Spirit."

Another post stated, "My name is Joel. I deny the Holy Spirit, as well as God, Jesus, Buddha, Zeus, Mohammad, Joseph Smith, Sponge Bob, the pope, Santa Clause, Mother Mary, the Easter bunny, the tooth fairy, Optimus Prime, all the saints, and Spiderman."

Brian and his Rational Response Squad are targeting teenagers by taking their blasphemy challenge to websites for students, like Tiger Beat. Brian says, "[Teens] are not so indoctrinated and set in their ways that they cannot overcome this religious superstition that has been put in their brain unfairly."

Brian's website has links to other websites, one of which sells bumper stickers and buttons inscribed with messages such as "Born Again Pagan," "I Pledge Allegiance to the Earth," "Nothing Fails Like Prayer," and "I Asked God, She's Pro Choice."

Interestingly, the Bible never provides us with any formal arguments to prove the existence of God. In fact, the Bible assumes that everybody knows deep down that there is a God. That is why the first book of the Bible begins with the words, "In the beginning God created the heaven and the earth."

The world has been designed and created with incredible beauty and intricate detail. The symmetry, the colors, the variety, the complexity, the climate, the exquisite facets of all of creation suggests a Designer, because every effect requires a cause, and nothing comes from nothing.

Furthermore, Psalm 14:1 clearly says, "The fool hath said in his heart, there is no God." But before I launch into a tirade on atheists, let me give an idea as to why some folks are atheists. I think we (Christians) are responsible for many people turning away from God and denying the faith and embracing the cloudbank of atheism.

I would have to question Brian's "experience with Christ" at age 13 because "a faith that fizzles before the finish has a flaw from the first." However, would his quest for God have taken a different path if he had seen vibrant Christians who were empowered by the Spirit of God, if he had seen a church aflame with a passion for the souls of men, if he had seen less hypocrisy and more authenticity among the saints, if he had seen the church bravely marching in the train of our triumphant Lord?

Daniel 11:32 asserts, "The people who know their God shall be strong and do exploits." The implication is that those who know God will adorn the gospel of God and be advertisements of His precepts and His power.

In our churches we sing "What a mighty God we serve," but most folks see no indication that God is manifesting Himself in our lives.

We are lacking in spiritual strength and dynamism. We talk about a God of might and miracles, but the world is longing to see evidences of the Almighty in us and through us.

I deplore what Brian and his Rational Response Squad are doing, but those of us who comprise the church of the living God must make sure we are not guilty of false advertising. If we sing and preach about a mighty God, we need to make sure that people can see Him at work in our lives.

Nine Reasons why I Love the Church

In the course of human history few institutions have been more misunderstood and maligned than the Christian church. Indeed, it would be foolish to insist that the church is perfect, because it is made up of frail and fallible people like you and me. Unfortunately, the criticism being leveled against the church today is not only coming from those outside the church, but from those within.

However, those who have a gloom-and-doom attitude toward the church are certainly overstating the case. Surely, the picture is not as bad as some would have us believe.

George Bernard Shaw, the Irish dramatist, playwright, and literary critic who at best was a mystic and at worst an atheist, once stated what would happen if the church went out of business for a while. He proclaimed that it would have "a very salutary effect. It would soon evoke an irresistible desire for the re-establishment of the church." No matter what people say, the world just can't live without the church.

Here are nine reasons why I love the church:

First, I love the Christ of the church. The church belongs to the Lord Jesus Christ. He bought it with His own blood. The Bible says, "Christ also loved the church, and gave himself for it" (Ephesians 5:25). I believe that we should loathe what Jesus loathed and love what Jesus loved.

Second, I love the creation of the church. The church originated in Christ and was forged by a handful of believers who had been on their knees in prayer and empowered by the Holy Spirit to change the world. They emerged from an upper room with an indomitable faith and an unconquerable zeal to face a world that had previously intimidated them into a paralyzing fear. Inspired by the miracle of Pentecost they launched out on a grand adventure that resulted in churches being planted throughout the whole world.

Third, I love the convictions of the church. The convictions of the church are drawn from the Bible. The Word of God is an infallible handbook that is "profitable for doctrine, for reproof, for correction, for instruction in righteousness" (II Timothy 2:16). When a church fails to embrace the Bible as altogether true its doctrines and values are subject to weaken or disintegrate. However, praise the Lord for those churches that don't try to change the Bible or find fault with it, but just believe it.

Fourth, I love the congregation of the church. There are always some surly, cantankerous, obstreperous people in the church, but the best people I know are also in the church. I have received great acts of love from caring church members. I have made intimate and lifelong friends in the church. I thrill to find warm, convivial fellowship among God's wonderful people wherever I go.

Fifth, I love the commission of the church. Of course, the commission of the church is articulated in Matthew 28:18-20, and it charges the church with the responsibility of evangelizing the world. We are to preach the gospel of Jesus Christ to every person. Only when man's heart is changed will the world be changed. No institution, entity, or organization has a higher or nobler commission.

Sixth, I love the cooperation of the church. The world is known for its anarchy and competition, but the church is known for its camaraderie and cooperation. When God's people get together incredible things are accomplished for the good of mankind and the cause of the Kingdom.

Seventh, I love the charity of the church. Think of all the needs that have been supplied, all the hurts that have been alleviated, all the homes that have been blessed, and all the lives that have been changed because the church is motivated by love. So long as the church insists on love being the quality which crowns her ministry worthwhile things will be attempted and achieved.

Eighth, I love the celebrations of the church. I have seen the revelry that comes with winning a championship football game and the festivities that follow the final out in a Major League Baseball World Series, but there is nothing that compares with a worship service when the Spirit of God is moving, souls are being saved, heaven comes down, and glory fills the souls of the saints. Now that is a celebration!

Ninth, I love the consummation of the church. The church will outlive and outlast every other organization on earth. Jesus promised that the gates of hell would not prevail against the church. The church is the bride of Christ and one of these days He is going to receive the church unto Himself. It is going to be a "glorious church, not having spot, or wrinkle, or any such thing: but that it should be holy and without blemish" (Ephesians 5:27).

Perhaps you can add a tenth reason for loving the church. At any rate, make sure you hold the church in high esteem.

The Cross and the Empty Tomb

Paul spoke of "the offense of the cross" in Gal. 5:11. And, of course, Jesus himself has been referred to as "a stumbling stone and a rock of offense" (Rom. 9:33).

Therefore, it is not surprising that the ACLU threatened Los Angeles County with a lawsuit unless they removed a small cross from the official seal of the county. The tiny cross was placed on the seal over fifty years ago to memorialize the early Christian impact on Los Angeles by Spanish missionaries.

Although the seal primarily featured a prominent picture of Pomona, the Roman goddess of the harvest, the tiny cross has been removed and the Roman goddess remains on the seal.

In Charlotte, N.C., Caldwell Memorial Presbyterian Church voted unanimously last year to lease the congregation's gymnasium and educational building to an Islamic school in order to bolster their weakening financial status. At the insistence of the Islamic school and with the acquiescence of Caldwell's leaders, two large crosses were removed and stained-glass windows displaying Christian symbols were covered up.

You may also be familiar with the fight to remove the 29-foot Mt. Soledad cross from the landscape of La Jolla, Calif. The fate of the cross was uncertain for 18 years until a recent California Supreme Court decision announced that it would not hear an appeal challenging the right of the cross to remain on property where it has stood for more than 50 years.

Now, American atheists have gone to a federal court to stop certain state highway patrol and department of transportation officials from erecting Christian crosses on state property that honor state troopers killed in the line of duty.

Furthermore, in February the Supreme Court refused to hear a New York City policy that bans public school displays of nativity scenes (and presumably crosses), but allows Jewish menorahs and the Islamic star and crescent to be on display.

Now, in addition to attempting to remove the cross from public view, Simcha Jacobovici and Charles Pellegrino have written a book, *The Jesus Tomb*, declaring that the bones of Jesus, Joseph, and Mary have been found in a burial chamber near Jerusalem. The book has been made into a documentary film.

This ludicrous claim is nothing more than the attempt of entertainment exploiters who hope to line their pockets with "filthy lucre" by hitching a ride on the reputation of Jesus.

Professor Amos Kloner, one of Israel's prominent archeologists and the scholar who supervised the discovery of the bones in an ossuary 27 years ago, in a recent interview with *The Jerusalem Post* declared emphatically that the current theory "is impossible. It's nonsense."

Kloner added, "There is no likelihood that Jesus and his relatives had a family tomb. They were a [poor] Galilee family with no ties in Jerusalem. The Talpoit tomb belonged to a middle-class family from the 1st century C.E."

The question of the ages is: What happened to the body of Jesus? Some think the Jews stole it, but they were the ones who insisted that the

Roman guards be posted to ensure that his body remained in the tomb and His teachings died with Him.

Others suspect that the Romans stole the body of Jesus, but they had no motivation for doing such a thing. Others think the disciples stole the body of Jesus, but they were cowardly. They would have needed to overpower the Roman soldiers to steal the body of Christ.

To me the three most convincing proofs that Jesus rose from the dead and evacuated that tomb are: (1) The Bible declares it. "And the angel answered and said ... He is not here, for he is risen, as he said, Come, see the place where the Lord lay" (Matt. 28:5-6).

(2) The changed lives of the disciples after they had seen the risen Christ is another mark of the story's truthfulness. They were no longer cowardly, but courageous. They were no longer timid, but tenacious. They were no longer doubting, but shouting. They were persecuted for proclaiming the resurrection and ultimately gave their lives for this message: "Jesus Christ rose from the dead and He is alive."

(3) Let the scoffers scoff. Let the doubters doubt. Let the critics criticize. Let the atheists howl. Let the ACLU (Anything Christian Looks Unlawful) sling their lawsuits against the cause of Christ. I can only say that I believe the message of Easter and the reality of the resurrection, because He is alive in my heart.

"Hooray for Hollywood?"

Johnny Mercer wrote the lyrics for "Hooray for Hollywood" in 1938 when Hollywood was much different than today. He declares, "Come on and try your luck. You could be Donald Duck. Hooray for Hollywood."

Actually, Hollywood hit the skids soon after that and has gone downhill like a toboggan sled on an icy slope ever since.

The very next year Hollywood released Gone with the Wind and had Rhett Butler (Clark Gable) using a four-letter word, which was a "no-no" back in the 1930's when society was more genteel compared to the present-day fare of an avalanche of profanities and expletives.

Year after year, Hollywood pumps out the same formulaic dross, appealing to the very basest elements in the human character. It is a rare and wonderful Hollywood film that elevates the soul and inspires us with a sense of human potential.

Edouard Metrailler, editor of *The Harvard Salient* in 1997, wrote, "Attending movies is nowadays an exercise in numbing oneself to gratuitous violence, drug abuse, and sleaze. We are finally experiencing the dangerous consequences of this corrupting education. We must acknowledge that society cannot long endure if its children are so infected by Hollywood's perverted attitudes." *The Harvard Salient* was founded in 1981 by students at Harvard University to provide a journalistic alternative to the predominately liberal campus press.

Interestingly enough, a higher percentage of Americans went to see movies each week during the Great Depression, which swept the United States in the 1930's, than during the times of economic expansion and great prosperity the United States has seen since.

In 1930 (the earliest year from which accurate and credible data exists), weekly cinema attendance was 80 million people, approximately 65% of the resident U.S. population. However, in the year 2000, only 27.3 million people attended the cinema weekly – a mere 9.7% of the U.S. population. A brief look at the raw numbers will clearly indicate that cinema attendance has taken a steep decline in seventy years.

Michael Medved, in his book *Hollywood Vs. America,* suggests that the entertainment industry is forfeiting both profits and paying customers in a crazy campaign to foist its own loony lifestyles and muddled world views on the American people.

Hollywood is the primary purveyor of popular culture. In fact, American life is becoming victim to the onslaught of Hollywood culture; its selfish, greedy vapidity; and its far-left agenda. Furthermore, we must resist the debasing of our political life by keeping the boundaries between politics and popular culture clear and distinct.

Politics, though often marred by corruption, should be an arena for virtue. By welcoming popular culture into the political sphere, the prospects for virtue become very bleak indeed.

That bleak prospect is exacerbated by a motley aggregation of Hollywood glitterati – bullhorn radicals like Sean Penn, Susan Sarandon, Martin Sheen, Tim Robbins, Alec Baldwin, Barbara Streisand, and yes, Jane Fonda, whose combined college credit units would probably not get you one decent college degree, although Sean Penn did study auto mechanics at Santa Monica College. What legitimate reasoning qualifies them to have a platform to express their opinion on politics, the Iraq war, or anything else?

Charlie Sheen is best known in Hollywood for his sexploits (Maxim, a heterosexual magazine, reported last year that Sheen claims to have had sex with 5,000 women). The Tinseltown gigolo is reportedly in talks to narrate an Internet documentary that suggests that elements of the United States government were behind the Sept. 11 attacks on the World Trade Center.

The 79th Academy Awards, hosted by the openly gay Ellen DeGeneres, was more a brazen act of wartime propaganda by the shameless secular-progressives than an awards show.

Rosie O'Donnell, the raunchy standup comedienne and talk show host, but hardly a Hollywood starlet, has frequently appeared to be sympathetic toward terrorists groups threatening America and has even said that we ought "not to be alarmed by terrorists." She frequently insults the collective intelligence of the American people and recently demonstrated her contempt for followers of Christ by comparing radical Islam to radical Christianity on ABC's The View.

David Limbaugh, best-selling author and attorney, recently commented, "Until Hollywood hotshots demonstrate some modicum of the diversity of thought they sanctimoniously demand of others, they will not and do not deserve to be taken seriously."

Medved states, "America's long-running romance with Hollywood is over. Tens of millions of Americans now see the entertainment industry as an all-powerful enemy, an alien force that assaults our most cherished values and corrupts our children. The dream factory has become the poison factory."

Maybe we could say "Hooray for Hollywood" in 1938, but certainly not today.

Politically Correct Chameleons or Passionately Committed Christians?

I am absolutely exasperated, infuriated, and indignant over the whole concept of political correctness. Political correctness is just another term for social, national, and religious demolition.

Because of political correctness our country has stopped getting stronger and more influential and has become weaker and less influential. We have lost all respect for authority in the home, school, church, and nation. Instead of authority ruling its constituents, the constituents rule authority. There is an insidious rebellion taking place whereby power is methodically being wrested from the traditional rulers and placed in the hands of "the occasional will of the people."

In political correctness all language, philosophy, and beliefs are reduced to the lowest common denominator so that no one is offended. Tolerance is exalted and convictions are diluted.

For example, since there are those who now believe that climate change has moved from scientific theory to dogma, there are now proposals that "global warming deniers" be treated the same as "holocaust deniers" and suffer professional ostracism, belittlement, ridicule, and even jail.

Some politically correct advocates think "history" is a pejorative term and prefer "herstory," because it takes the male element out of the word. Though there are more than 800,000 Google citations for "herstory," they are all based on a mistaken assumption. When Herodotus wrote the first history, the word meant simply an "inquiry."

To press home the point, the staff at a coffee shop refused to serve a customer who had ordered a "black coffee," believing it to be "racist." He wasn't served until he changed his order to "coffee without milk."

Furthermore, the headmistress of an elementary school had to divide a grade into two equal classes. Although the students were divided purely by alphabet, parents objected because they feared that the children in class 1b might be perceived as academically inferior to the children in class 1a.

Since 9/11 some of the PC activists believe that we should use the term "misguided criminals" for terrorists, because the word "terrorist" can be a barrier rather than an aid to understanding.

And, of course, the PC fanatics think we should pray, "Our Mother and Father Who are in heaven" and insist that if we must sing during the winter solstice, a term which they prefer over Christmas, that we should sing "God Rest Ye Merry Persons" for "God Rest Ye Merry Gentlemen."

The Common Era (C.E.) is much to be preferred over A.D. (Latin for: in the year of our Lord) for proponents of political correctness.

Tony Perkins, who heads the Family Research Council in Washington, recently reported that Great Britain is drowning in a wave of political correctness. He states, "As the country copes with an influx of Muslims, the church and government find it extremely difficult to maintain their British identity. As an example, the Church of England is considering removing the cross of St. George from its flag because of its association with the medieval crusades. The debate has enraged citizens who are concerned that the country may soon become unrecognizable in its pursuit of cultural pluralism."

Perkins also exposed a growing problem in the public-school curriculum of England. He explained, "For fear of 'offending' Muslim students, teachers have become increasingly hesitant to teach history lessons on the Holocaust because of the students' predominantly anti-Semitic feelings. A government study found that educators are also afraid to tackle the 11th century crusades, in which Christians fought Islam for control of the Holy Land, or the Arab-Israeli conflict. Since the curriculum often conflicts with what some children are taught at the local mosques, some teachers are dropping the lessons altogether."

The developing trend in Great Britain, America, and across the world is to use history as a means, not for teaching the truth, but for promoting a value-free form of tolerance. It is utter madness and will ultimately dismantle our Judeo-Christian-structured American society and the traditions we hold dear.

As we stand at the front of the third American century, most citizens of our country know all too little about the first two. As a nation we don't visit historical sites, don't learn our nation's stories, don't recognize the people and places that shaped this nation, and, unfortunately, much of our history has now been rewritten to reflect the cultural diversity and religious pluralism that prevails today. Consequently, we are gradually losing our national sovereignty, our role as a world power, and most importantly our distinctiveness as a Christian nation.

Unfortunately, the cancer of political correctness has metastasized in American life and has infected our schools, our entertainment, our media, and even many of our churches. Those who name the name of Christ must make a choice! Do we want to be politically correct chameleons or passionately committed Christians with the will to learn the truth, speak the truth, and live the truth regardless of the consequences?

Old Fashioned? Guilty as Charged!

I love to read the sermons of preachers of days gone by. Maybe it is because some of those stalwart characters were my contemporaries – almost.

There was Mordecai Ham (1876-1959), referred to as the Iron Man of God. He was raised in Kentucky and Arkansas and a great soul winner. Catholics bullied him, thugs threatened to kidnap his son, and on one occasion they knocked him down in the street with a car and dragged him for several blocks on the bumper. A man wielding a .45 pistol once accosted him, but he resisted all the threats on his life and was the man who was preaching when Billy Graham got saved.

Baxter McClendon – "Cyclone Mac" – (1879-1935) was an itinerant Methodist preacher who impacted the western part of North Carolina where I grew up as a boy. His circuit riding days were a few years before my time, but as a lad I could sit for hours and listen to the stories about Cyclone Mac's revival campaigns.

Rodney "Gipsy" Smith (1860-1947) was born in England, but often came to America to preach. Although he often preached to thousands of people, on his third trip to America he was invited to hold special "drawing room" meetings for some of the elite in one of the largest mansions on Fifth Avenue in New York City.

It was not a public meeting, but personal letters were sent to various aristocratic ladies of New York, inviting them to be present. When he faced Mrs. John D. Rockefeller and her peers, he simply preached on "Repentance." He said, "I only remembered that they were sinners needing a Savior."

Sam Porter Jones (1847-1906), described as the South's most famous preacher in the late nineteenth century, was born in Oak Bowery, Ala. However, he moved with his family to Cartersville, where he grew up and lived for most of his life.

Jones overcame early battles with alcohol, was called to preach the gospel, and began to hone his oratorical skills. A revival in Nashville, Tenn., in 1885 put Jones in the national limelight. Tom Ryman, whose riverboats carried much of Nashville's river trade and also featured barrooms, gambling casinos, and dancing girls, was converted in that meeting.

Because of Ryman's newfound religious zeal, he cleaned up his boats and constructed a building where Jones and other preachers could hold revivals. Ryman's Union Gospel Tabernacle later became the home of the Grand Old Opry.

William "Billy" Ashley Sunday (1862-1935) was the most colorful of the evangelists in those days. Sunday, born in Iowa, was a professional baseball player who became a fiery preacher.

Sunday said, "I'm against sin. I'll kick it as long as I've got a foot, and I'll fight it as long as I've got a fist. I'll butt it as long as I've got a head. I'll bite it as long as I've got a tooth. And when I'm old and fistless and footless and toothless, I'll gum it till I go home to Glory and it goes home to perdition."

Sunday also had a passion for revival. He asked the question, "When is revival needed?"

He also provided the answer to his own question; and his response is as relevant today as it was 80 years ago. He contended that revival is needed "when the members are careless and unconcerned, when the church has degenerated into a third-rate amusement joint, with religion left out."

Sunday continued, "Revival is needed when carelessness and unconcern keep the people asleep, because it is the duty of the church to awaken and work and labor for the men and women of the city as it is the duty of the fire department to rush out when the call sounds. What would you think of the fire department if it slept while the town burned?

"Revival is needed when Christians have lost the spirit of prayer, when the church wants revival and feels the need of it."

Space will not permit a full disclosure of Sunday's appeal for revival, but nothing short of revival will restore our nation's reason and sanity today. I long for revival. I pray for revival. I am trusting God for revival. Maybe a heart-cry for revival is old fashioned in this postmodern culture, but Sunday said something else that made great sense to me.

Sunday said, "I am an old-fashioned preacher of the old-time religion, that has warmed this cold world's heart for two thousand years."

I vote for a heartwarming!

Filling the Pulpit or Filling the Pew?

There is much symbolism in the church of the Lord Jesus Christ. The two ordinances of the Baptist church, baptism and the Lord's Supper, are beautifully symbolic. The cross that is displayed in so many churches is emblematic of the atoning death of our blessed Redeemer. The church spire originated in the 12th century as a symbol of heavenly aspiration.

For years the pulpit has been placed in the center of the platform of Baptist churches to symbolize the centrality and priority of preaching the gospel.

Years ago, during a pastor's conference sponsored by the Billy Graham Evangelistic Association, a well-known pastor proclaimed, "If the church is alive, it's because the pulpit is alive – and if the church is dead, it's because the pulpit is dead!"

Today many churches are flirting with death, because there is a greater focus on filling the pew than filling the pulpit.

Several things may contribute to this postmodern focus. First, there are those who suggest that preaching is an antiquated, outdated, outmoded method of communicating the gospel and that we should replace the sermon with dialogue, films, panel discussions, dramatic presentations, and concerts. While a church may use these methods of communicating truth they should be supplemental, and even incidental, to the preaching of the gospel.

Secondly, there is a prevailing mood today that is antithetical to the dogma of preaching – the rejection of absolute truth. In this "postmodern" age everything is relative or subjective and everybody has his or her own convictions. Furthermore, many consider their convictions to be just as good as the preacher's. These people are of the opinion that it would be presumptuous for a preacher to lay down the law with an uncompromising conviction.

Another argument foisted by society against the "the foolishness of preaching" is that we live in a visual society and people are accustomed to looking at images, not listening to arguments. This is an indication that people have become intellectually lazy. They would rather be entertained than think.

It would be disastrous for the church to replace the sermon with some multi-media presentation. However, our preaching must not be dull, ponderous, and monotonous. This doesn't mean that we should be anti-visual. The Bible is not anti-visual, but in God's economy the Word predominates. The visual is an accessory to the Word, not the other way around.

Another factor that may militate against the focus on preaching is the church growth movement. It all started with good, old-fashioned American pragmatism: find a method or strategy that works well and use it to build up the church and fill the pews.

Unfortunately, after years of training seminarians to fill the pulpit many young pastors arrive on the field for their initial pastorates only to meet a host of people who want to make their church as appealing as the mega-churches. Immediately, their focus shifts to filling the pew, and their heroes become "successful" pastors who are known for what they are doing rather for their convictional life and message.

In a recent conversation on this subject with IMB Senior Vice President for Spiritual Nurture and Church Relations Tom Elliff, he asked, "Are pastors going to conferences today to hear what others are doing or to savor the impact of a life of faith and to discover what and how men are preaching?"

The church growth gurus have suggested that numerical increase is a sign of health.

"In order to fill the pews, the church growth advocates have developed marketing strategies to attract the attention of the world, created programs packaged to appeal to consumer's demands, designed strategies to accommodate "felt needs," and crafted messages commensurate with the doctrine of tolerance."

Phil Kenneson and James Street, in their book, *Selling Out the Church,* suggest that we risk great harm when we pander to the tastes and desires of the world around us. The authors proclaim that clever marketing strategies create churches that reflect the culture rather than shape it. Then Kenneson and Street lay out arguments for why a marketing orientation inherently changes not just the style, but the message and mission of the church.

It is possible to artificially fill the pews without the Word and Spirit. I Cor. 3:15 indicates such ministries will someday "burn" because their builders preferred the wisdom of the world rather than the foolishness of Christ.

Someone has said, "The important things have not changed." While outward forms and fashions have changed, God is still holy, mankind is still depraved, and Jesus is still the way, the truth, and the Life. The Bible still stands as God's inspired word and is still profitable for doctrine, for reproof, for correction, and instruction in righteousness. Preaching is still the primary way to tell others of these truths.

John R. W. Stott, a noted evangelical Anglican, writes, "It is God's speech that makes our speech necessary. We must speak what He has spoken. Hence the paramount obligation to preach."

Jesus was anointed to preach, but many stopped following Jesus after his sermons (see John 6:66, John 8:30, and John 8:59). Although there were times when He failed miserably to "fill the pews," He received the approval of His Father in heaven.

So, what do you think pleases God the most? Is it filling the pulpit or filling the pew?

The Trilogy of the Alamo

One of the joys of attending the Southern Baptist Convention is the opportunity it affords of renewing old acquaintances and establishing new friendships. While in San Antonio for last week's annual meeting of the Convention, I had the opportunity to meet Dr. Daniel Sanchez. Sanchez, a professor of missions at Southwestern Seminary in Fort Worth, is a native of San Antonio.

One day the missions professor and I were discussing the Alamo, situated only a few blocks from the Henry B. Gonzales Convention Center where we were meeting. He said, "You know, The Alamo was once a church, then a battlefield; now, it is a museum."

His comments inspired me, and I thought, "This is the perfect outline for a sermon – or an editorial."

The Alamo – a Church

The Alamo was originally a Catholic church, named Mission San Antonio de Valero. The mission was authorized in 1716 by the viceroy of New Spain and was established two years later by Fray Antonio de Olivares, who brought Indian converts and records with him from the San Francisco Solano Mission near San Juan Bautista on the Rio Grande.

The present site was selected in 1724 and the cornerstone was laid on May 8, 1744. The church served as a home to missionaries and their Indian converts until 1793 when the mission was abandoned.

The Alamo – a Battlefield

In the early 1800s, the Spanish military stationed a cavalry unit at the former mission, but the Alamo is best known for the strategic battle between Texan loyalists and the army of Mexico's General Antonio Lopez de Santa Anna. On February 23, 1836, Santa Anna's army arrived in San Antonio to quell any hope for Texas independence. The Texan and Tejano volunteers prepared to defend the Alamo and held out for 13 days against a massive Mexican army.

Colonel William B. Travis, the commander of the Alamo, drew a line on the ground and asked any man willing to stay and fight to step over the line. Every person, with the exception of one man, stepped over the line indicating his willingness to fight for Texas liberty. Jim Bowie, the well-known knife fighter, and David Crockett, famed Tennessee frontiersman, were among those who devoted themselves to the fight for Texas independence.

The defenders of the Alamo were finally overwhelmed by the relentless siege launched by Santa Anna and his hordes. Indeed, the Alamo is remembered for the heroic struggle of those brave men who fought until the death against impossible odds.

The Alamo – the Museum

Today the Mision San Antonio de Valero is a museum and shrine dedicated to the memory of the men who fell in defense of Texas liberty. Since 1905 The Texas State Legislature has entrusted the Daughters of the Republic of Texas with the preservation of the Alamo as a historic site.

I am afraid that there are many churches that have a grand and glorious beginning, but in the course of years become a battleground. Quite often the warfare lacks any significantly eternal purpose and unfortunately amounts to no more than infighting and power struggles that disrupt the fellowship of the "Saints."

Strife and contention, spawned by the devil and hatched in hell, begin to characterize the spirit of the church. However, those who are engaged in the daily dog-eat-dog competition of the business world, those who have to battle the hostility and fierceness of the secular society, and those who must contend with the din and strife of ungodly men all during the week, don't want to go to church and face conflict and warfare there.

So, what happens? At first, the problem may be almost imperceptible. But the difficulty turns into dissention; and the dissention turns into disenchantment; and the disenchantment turns into disillusionment; and the disillusionment turns into decline; and ultimately the decline turns into death. At last, the church becomes nothing more than a stodgy museum.

Churches are meant to represent the resurrection life of Jesus Christ. They must be marked by vitality, passion, enthusiasm, brotherly love, and vision. Salvation means that we have left the region of death and emerged into the light and life of God's grace. Thus, we must leave those old grave-clothes that are tainted with corruption and reeking with death.

History is important, some traditions are to be honored, and some battles must be fought, but when a church insists upon holding on to the relics of the past rather than seizing the present moment for the glory of God it is courting death and destined to become a museum.

Remember the Alamo!

Is Jesus the only way to Heaven?

I believe the greatest doctrinal issue confronting the church today is the exclusivity of the gospel, or the belief that salvation is possible only through a personal relationship to Jesus Christ. It is incredible to think that the most fundamental doctrine of the Christian faith could be called into question or debated among people who call themselves Christians, but that is precisely what is taking place in our world today.

From a Christian viewpoint, the very idea that there are many ways to heaven is unreasonable, unscriptural, and offensive. If there are many ways – or even two ways – to God, Jesus Christ was a deceiver. For Jesus avowed more than once that he is the only way to heaven. He declared, "I said therefore unto you, that ye shall die in your sins; for if you believe not that I am he, ye shall die in your sins" (John 8:24).

However, apparently there are those who do not believe that Jesus is the only way to heaven as emphatically declared in John 14:6. For example, a reporter of *The Edmonton Journal* in Edmonton, Alberta, Canada interviewed Tony Campolo, professor emeritus of sociology at Eastern University in St. Davids, Pa., an ordained Baptist minister, on Jan. 17. The professor was asked, "Do you believe non-Christians can go to heaven?"

Campolo responded, "That's a good question to ask because the way we stand is we contend that trusting in Jesus is the way to heaven. However, we do not know who Jesus will bring into the kingdom and who He will not. We are very careful about pronouncing judgment on anybody. We leave judgment in the hands of God and we are saying Jesus is the way. We preach Jesus, but we have no way of knowing to whom the grace of God is extended."

Another example of a tap dancing, fence straddling, non-answering minister in line with Tony Campolo is Joel Osteen, pastor of one of the largest churches in America, Lakewood Church in Houston. He was interviewed on Larry King Live and asked if atheists go to heaven. He replied, "I am going to let God be the judge of who goes to heaven and hell."

When Osteen was asked where Jews or Muslims go without trusting Jesus, he replied, "I'm very careful about saying who would and wouldn't go to heaven. I don't know."

Although the Houston pastor issued a clarification of his response to King's questions on his website, the fact remains that he refused to unashamedly respond with a definitive answer, choosing to waffle in his reply so that no one would be offended.

There was a time when nearly all people in our western culture shared the same general worldview. America had a spiritual environment in which religion flourished as it did in no other western country. In time the postmodern left threw out absolute truth and replaced it with "tolerance," a vague word of indeterminate meaning, which they applied selectively at the expense of the Christian worldview.

When I was growing up the word "tolerance" meant "bearing or putting up with someone or something not especially liked." However, now the word has been redefined to suggest that "all values, all beliefs, all lifestyles, all truth claims are equal." Denying this makes a person "intolerant" and thus worthy of contempt.

The left has used its institutional leverage, the influence of the media, and the glamour of Hollywood to drive the Christian voice out of the public square and nullify the assumptions of the Christian worldview. Thus, doctrine is out, and tolerance is in. We are told that for the sake of unity, doctrine should not be tested or contested. We are not to draw any definitive lines or declare any absolutes. Doctrinal issues that were once painted black and white are now seen as gray.

Paul forewarned us that this time would come as he wrote: "For the time will come when they (the people of the church) will not endure (tolerate) sound doctrine; but after their own lusts they shall heap to themselves teachers, having itching ears; and they shall turn away their ears from the truth, and shall be turned unto fables" (II Tim. 4:3-4).

Paul had no tolerance for those who did not preach the gospel. In Galatians 1:8 he said, "But though we, or an angel from heaven preach any other gospel unto you than that which we have preached unto you, let him be accursed."

This is no time for "lite," topical, entertaining preaching that whips doctrine into a creamy filling suitable for topping canapés that are palatable and rich, but ultimately not really sustaining food. Charles H. Spurgeon, pastor of the great Metropolitan Tabernacle in London, wrote an article in the late 1800s titled "Feeding Sheep or Amusing Goats?" What Spurgeon saw blossoming in his day is in full bloom today.

Ray Stedman, long-time pastor of Peninsula Bible Fellowship, wrote, "The greatest contribution the Church can make today to a troubled and frightened generation is to return to a consistent and relevant preaching of the Word of God! All Christians would agree that what is most needed in the present age is a loosing of the power of God among us, but what is often forgotten is that the proclamation of His word has always been God's chosen channel of power."

"He sent his word and healed them," the psalmist declares. And it is not so much preaching from the Bible that is needed, as it is preaching the Bible itself – in a word, expository preaching.

And dear church member, it is time for some expositional listening. When you go to church don't look for some syrupy homily that will bolster your self-esteem, some engaging anecdotes and vivid vignettes that will help you find fulfillment, or some entertaining monologue that will give you a cheery heart.

Desire the "strong meat" of the Word of God. When members cultivate the habit of expositional listening they guard themselves against "itching ears" and they protect the gospel from corruption.

God-called preachers, who have an uncompromising allegiance to the Bible, and discerning listeners, who insist upon sound doctrine, love the truth of God's Word, and insist upon the exclusivity of the gospel, fully understand that Jesus is not just a good way to heaven or the best way to heaven, but the only way to heaven. "The way of the cross leads home … and there is no other way, but this."

Don't put your Christianity in a box

Several of our thirteen grandchildren enjoy playing the game of Monopoly. Once we have completed the game and all participants have sufficiently demonstrated their greed and avarice I insist on being the one to put all of the components of the game back in the box.

I know precisely where everything goes – each denomination of currency, the houses and hotels, the cards of Chance and the Community Chest, the dice, the deeds to the property, and the tokens. I want each component to go in its specific compartment. I don't want $10 bills to get mixed in with the $100 bills and I would be horrified to find the Baltic and Mediterranean property mixed in with Park Place and Boardwalk.

That is also the way I like my closet. There is an item of clothing for every place and a place for every item of clothing. Some may say I am obsessive compulsive, but that is nonsense. However, in my opinion there is a divinely-ordained place for white shirts, a predestined plan for blue shirts, a providentially-designed place for striped shirts, etc.

I wouldn't be gripped with a panic attack or be hurled into a fit of apoplexy if I found a pair of blue slacks mixed in with a pair of grey slacks, but it would seriously infringe on my normal state of serenity.

While some of us may wisely compartmentalize facets of our lives, it is undeniably true that there are those of us who profess Christ who regrettably either carelessly or unintentionally relegate Christianity to some small corner or segment of our lives.

What happens when we compartmentalize or trivialize Christianity? What happens when we consign our faith to Sundays, but refuse to let it permeate our lives the rest of the week? What happens when we reduce our religion to some antiquated tradition or a form of godliness, but deny the power thereof?

A compartmentalized faith becomes like an addendum to a book, a postscript to a letter, or a codicil to a will. It is like a side street rather than a major highway, a strip mall rather than a downtown shopping district, a minor skirmish rather than the main battle, a pinch hitter rather than the starting line-up, the appetizer rather than the main course, a computer program rather than the operating system.

When professing Christians fail to integrate their faith into the whole of their lives and do not boldly live out their beliefs in the neighborhood, the school campus, the factory, and the marketplace, the church loses its influence and becomes nothing more than an irrelevant sideshow rather than the primary focus of life.

Consequently, the world recognizes Christianity as just one minority among many. We are tolerated and sometimes defended, just like any other minority, but not really taken very seriously. Sadly, modern Christianity has for the most part accommodated to the culture rather than successfully called the culture to accommodate to Christ.

Jesus gave us two metaphors – salt and light – that teach us that Christianity is designed not to just be a minor part of the society, but the defining part. Salt permeates! It flavors! It arrests corruption! Similarly,

Christianity should influence everything it touches and arrest the decay of a society that is tending toward corruption.

Similarly, light has a permeating influence. It drives out darkness completely. In a very dark room, a small candle will give an individual enough light to see. The good thing about light is that it affects everything within its domain. A light does not touch part of the room. It drives out darkness totally from its sphere of influence.

Light and darkness are totally incompatible. Where one exists, the other is driven away. Wherever Christ is, evil must flee away. Wherever truth is, deceit and dishonesty must excuse themselves. Wherever Christians are, society should be better.

Martin Luther, the 16th century Augustinian monk, said that the Christian was worthless until he could vibrantly live a profane life – which in Latin means "outside the temple." Luther not only brought clarity to the gospel message, but he also catapulted believers beyond the stained-glass walls of the church, exhorting them to be salt and light in places where they might be skewered and lampooned.

George McLeod commented, "I am trying to recover the claim that Jesus Christ was not crucified in a cathedral between two candles, but on a cross between two thieves; and that on the town garbage dump where cynics talk smut, thieves curse, and soldiers gamble. That is where the church must be and that is what churchmanship must be about."

True spirituality is incredibly practical, robust, and workable no matter where you dwell or what you do. If your Christianity isn't viable and stout in the most difficult of cultures, then it isn't made of the same stuff that characterized the believers of the early church.

To help you take your Christianity out of the Christian ghetto where the secularists would love to have it remain, here is a simple prescription:

Stop compartmentalizing Christianity and love God with all of your heart, all of your mind, and all of your soul - all the time and in every place.

No one is allowed to take a break from following Christ. Either we follow His precepts or we do not. If we refuse to do what He has commanded us to do and fail to live out our faith wherever we are, we are no better off than the most ardent agnostic. We are even worse: lukewarm.

You can put all the pieces back in the Monopoly box in the compartments specifically designed for them, but don't put your Christianity in a box. Get the salt out of the shaker! Get the light out from under the bushel! Shine! Permeate! Saturate! Integrate!

Needed: A Wholesome Respect
for Authority

I was taught to respect authority when I was growing up. I memorized the Ten Commandments in public school and learned to honor my father and mother as the fifth commandment specifies. My parents taught me that my teachers in school and church were to be respected and admired. I was also instructed to highly esteem the pastor of our church, who was God's man and worthy of honor.

I learned at an early age that the leaders of our community, our state, and nation were to be held in high regard. Holding my hand over my heart when pledging allegiance to the flag or when listening to or singing the National Anthem was also ingrained into my mind and heart. However, today it seems that those who should be honored are the primary objects of scorn and ridicule.

I'm not exactly sure when we lost respect for authority, but it seems that the 1960s was a decade filled with ferment and rebellion that fostered a whole new disrespect for authority. I remember well the riots and demonstrations that took place on many college and university campuses in 1967-68. There was a crusade to "tear down the establishment."

This "crusade" carried over into the 1968 Democratic National Convention in Chicago. Abbie Hoffman, a self-proclaimed communo-anarchist, was arrested and tried for conspiracy and inciting to riot as a result of his role in protests that led to violent confrontations with police during that fateful Democratic National Convention. Hoffman, along with other individuals, became known, collectively, as the Chicago Seven. In his autobiography Hoffman wrote: "Kids need to be educated to disrespect authority. Otherwise, democracy is a farce."

I would never recommend Hoffman's book, but somehow his message, which was conceived by the devil and hatched in hell, has found a lodging place in the minds of many.

I was in a restaurant last week and in the booth behind me a mother was eating lunch with her two small children. There was constant bantering between the poor beleaguered mother and the two very vociferous and rambunctious children.

The children were apparently born in the objective mood and the negative case. They were not happy with the restaurant their mother had chosen, the color of Crayons they had received from the server, the food, or the surroundings. At one point the mother said to her son, "Landon, eat your chicken fingers."

He responded by shouting loud enough for the chef in the kitchen to hear, "I hate this food and I don't have to do what you say!"

If I had ever said that to my mother or father in public or private the wrath of Khan would have seemed like a walk in the park compared to the retribution I would have received from my parents. But then, my parents taught me to have a reverence for God, a respect for authority, and a reason for living.

To me it is of little wonder that many children fail to respect the authority of their parents, because there is a lack of respect for authority on just about every level of our society. When adults fail to respect those in authority over them, why should we expect any less from children? Unfortunately, in our day we not only see authority disrespected, but demeaned.

In fact, it appears that respecting authority is out of vogue today. When we fail to have a high regard for those who are in places of leadership we are flirting with anarchy.

The funny boys on the television talk shows take potshots at our president and those who are leaders in government to get a laugh. I didn't like it when Mr. Clinton was president and I haven't liked it during Mr. Bush's administration. Speaking derisively of the political leader of our country opens the door for authority to be disdained on all levels.

Americans have the right to dissent, but the protestations of some have reached a level of disrespect and dishonor that is shameful, even reprehensible.

In the grand scheme of things, I suppose that disrespect for authority is nothing new. In fact, in the first pages of the Bible we find that Satan entered the Garden of Eden and tempted Eve by challenging what God had said. The first sin was not a matter of whether the action was right or wrong; it was a matter of whether or not authority should be respected.

Satan led Adam and Eve to believe that God was an inadequate authority trying to hide power from them and lying to them about the outcome of their choices. He convinced them to reach around God, due to His "inadequacy," and reach for godhood on their own. Obviously, this same tendency follows us today. We have an enormous problem with authority and have been searching for a way to get authority for ourselves since Eden.

Any time we disrespect the authority that is over us, it is a blatant attempt to reach around the authority God has established. People who fail to honor the authorities God has placed over them may ultimately get the leadership they deserve.

The Church of the Comfortable

Vance Havner, a preacher's preacher of the last generation, used to say, "It is the responsibility of the preacher to comfort the afflicted and afflict the comfortable."

God instructed the prophet Isaiah, saying, "Comfort ye, comfort ye my people." In every congregation of people there are hurried, hurting, haggard, helpless people who need to be comforted. It is a noble thing to provide solace and consolation to those in such distress.

However, most church folks have broadened their comfort requirements to the extreme – to include things that actually border on the ridiculous. For example, the temperature in the Sunday School classrooms and worship center must be exactly 72 degrees Fahrenheit. Some church members would consider anything more or less than that ideally controlled climate intolerable.

Other church members must be greeted with a cup of coffee upon their arrival at church each Sunday morning. There must be the right kind of cream and a preferred kind of sweetener to satisfy the tastes of each coffee connoisseur. Any deviation from that expected welcome would be considered unsatisfactory.

Furthermore, the volume of sound in the worship center must remain within a certain parameter of decibels or the comfort level would be compromised.

The time of the worship services must also be factored into the comfort equation. If the services were ever too long, some people would presumably become wearied, uneasy, and just plain miserable.

In fact, most of us are extremely interested in our personal comfort; and we spend a lot of time and energy making sure that the church is a comfortable place for people to come – a place that doesn't scare or turn people off. But in making it a comfortable place to visit, perhaps we have made it too comfortable of a place to stay. Church folks don't want to leave the "sanctuary" – the safe, comfortable place of worship – to witness or serve.

One of the primary dangers in being comfortable in our Christianity is that over time comfort tends to begin to feel like something that God – or the world – owes us. What we once called 'luxury' we now call 'need'.

Therefore, let me use the next few paragraphs to afflict the comfortable. Why would I want to do something like that? Jesus did precisely that when He was here on this earth. He was not always a comforting person. In fact, he said some very disturbing things to the Pharisees and religious leaders of his day.

Today there is a strong justification to afflict those who are "at ease in Zion" because a comfortable kind of Christianity will not be able to withstand the ferocious storms and the diabolical attacks that threaten to sink the ship of faith.

First, storms will come that will threaten to undo the foundations of our security. Secondly, Satan is launching some of his heaviest artillery against the church. In his hymn "A Mighty Fortress Is Our God" Martin Luther wrote, "... and though this world with devils filled should threaten to undo us." Such disturbing storms and demonic attacks tend to make a comfortable Christianity nothing more than an illusion.

When I read the New Testament, I don't see any evidence that the early Christians had a cushy, comfortable life. There was no comfort zone among the early believers where they could seek refuge from hostility and persecution. They had to rely on God for their every need.

Today, the Christian has to battle the tendency to fall into a casual, easy-going approach to his faith. In fact, the believer who is very comfortable in this life can also become sluggish, complacent, and dependent upon the securities of life instead of the Lord.

For the extent of his ministry here on earth, Jesus Christ called those around him to live a life much different from the average person. Many aspects of this new life charged followers to step outside of their "comfort zones" and seek the paradoxical relationship between being his friend and surrendering as a slave.

I fear that somewhere along the way, we have lost the uncomfort-able part of the paradox and refuse to surrender.

F. B. Meyer once said, "The one thing that pierces the heart of God with unutterable grief is not the world's iniquity, but the church's indifference."

There is nothing like being at home on a cool autumn night with a good book and a cup of hot chocolate, but can we be content to "relax" when our grandchildren may have to inherit from us a nation that does not know God?

Are you afflicted yet?

A Placebo Cannot Cure an Ailing Patient

The sincere Christian who is sensitive to the climate and character of our present American culture would have to be gravely concerned about the present condition of our society. Subjective, situational ethics have replaced biblical morality. Tolerance and indulgence have replaced absolute, objective truth. Independence and self-reliance have replaced faith and a dependence upon the sufficiency of God.

Antinomianism has replaced God's standard of integrity and righteousness. Unbridled freedom has replaced God's narrow parameters of decency and honesty. A secular worldview has replaced the biblical worldview. In short, the revered principles upon which this nation was founded have been cast into oblivion's depository.

Our noble history has been rewritten. Our Christian heritage has been discarded. Our values have been replaced. Our educational system has been rendered ineffective. Our cities have become dens of iniquity. Our media cannot be trusted. Our health care system has been abused. Our airwaves are filled with profanity. Our cable networks are filled with salacious programming. Our creed is greed; our god is gold. An honest appraisal of our future is frightening.

In essence, our culture is in chaos. Ideally, the church's mission is to save the society. Christians are to be the saving salt that prevents the world from tending toward corruption.

But is the church in a position to be that saving salt? Are we really that light that shines brightly enough to dispel the darkness that is beginning to permeate the world? Can a lukewarm church exert the power necessary to rescue the world from its moral and spiritual decline?

Jesus said, "... but if the salt have lost his savour, wherewith shall it be salted? It is thenceforth good for nothing, but to be cast out, and to be trodden under foot of men."

An impotent, anemic church cannot reclaim a decadent society any more than a placebo can cure an ailing patient. A powerless church cannot rescue a faltering nation any more than an illiterate pedagogue can teach a student to read.

I know it sounds crazy, but there are many churches that should forget trying to change the world until they get their act together. If your church is marked by dissention, discord, immorality, immaturity, and impotency, what do you have to offer a self-absorbed society that sees nothing in your fellowship that commends Christ to them?

In Luke 4:23 we find the phrase, "Physician, heal thyself." Jesus feared the people of his hometown of Nazareth might use that phrase in relation to him, because of the belief that a prophet is not honored in his own county. The phrase alludes to the readiness and ability of physicians to heal sickness in others while sometimes being unable or unwilling to heal themselves.

Before we can propose to change the world, we must make sure that we are distinctively different from the world. The world must see in us something that adorns the gospel of God (Titus 2:10), something that makes Christianity attractive and appealing.

There was something attractive about Jesus to His followers. It was His purpose, because He steadfastly set His face to go to Jerusalem where He was determined to make atonement for our sins. It was His passion, because His heart beat with an unqualified compassion for the souls of men. It was His purity, because His life was the epitome of integrity and righteousness. It was His power, because He worked the works of God among men.

The church must emulate His purpose, His passion, His purity, and His power. When we are able to effectively follow His example, the world will begin to ask us to give the reason for the hope that is within us. That is what Peter says will happen when we are living for Christ as we should (see I Peter 3:15).

The problem is that the world has not noticed anything so remarkable and compelling about our lives that they are inspired to ask us to explain the reason for our hope.

All of this simply suggests that we need revival. Once the church is truly revived all heaven will break loose; and the church will be able to change the world.

We often speak of the revival at Pentecost when 3,000 people got saved. I am of the strong opinion that the revival occurred before Peter preached his renowned sermon recorded in Acts 2. It took place in the upper room as those 120 disciples "tarried" as Christ had compelled them to do. I have an idea that they confessed their sins, reconciled strained or broken relationships, got in one accord, and prayed until the Holy Spirit filled them.

In fact, the Spirit shows up at least 60 times in the first 20 chapters of Acts, acting to possess, empower, and compel people. Enlivened by the Spirit those early disciples went forth to share God's story in their own language and to undermine the ecclesiological and political powers of the day.

We need to learn from the first century church and realize that we cannot change the world until God has changed our lives and given us the subduing, elevating, overcoming, and conquering power of the Holy Spirit. God will never be able to use a lukewarm, anemic, powerless church to change our society.

However, an individual or a church that is wholly committed to Christ and empowered by His Spirit was in the first century and is today an amazingly formidable force in the hands of almighty God!

Trying to fit Church into Super Bowl Sunday

When I was a pastor I worked hard to adjust the time of our Sunday evening worship service to suit everyone's plans to watch the Super Bowl. We met earlier to accommodate those who wanted to go home in time for the game. We occasionally set up a viewing area in the fellowship hall for those who wanted to stay after the service to watch the game. On at least one occasion we had a viewing of the game in our gym and crammed our service into the half-time segment of the game.

None of the above methods worked well, because many people were more interested in the Super Bowl than having church. We finally decided to have our regularly scheduled worship service and force people to decide between God and the gridiron. In days of yore no such choice was necessary, because there was no Super Bowl.

When I was growing up as a boy in western North Carolina my parents saw to it that we meticulously observed the Lord's Day. My grandfather was my first pastor and going to church twice on Sunday was more natural than breathing.

I started getting ready for Sunday School and church at least by Saturday. We lived on a dirt road and by Saturday my shoes needed a good shine for the Lord's Day services and so a part of the preparation was shining my shoes and selecting the clothes I would wear, which always had to pass my mother's approval.

We had church offering envelopes that included a report card for the "Eight Point Record System." There were little boxes where each member was to indicate such things as: (1) being present, (2) being on time, (3) bringing a Bible, (4) reading the lesson, (5) staying for worship, (6) giving an offering, (7) making a contact, etc. To be honest I cannot remember the eighth point of the record system to save my life, and there are only a few people around old enough to remember; and those who are old enough can't remember much of anything.

Going to church was the most significant event in the week for our family; and it seemed to be important to the whole town where I grew up. Very few people had television sets and there were a limited number of programs for viewers to watch. The only movie house in town was closed on Sundays and there were no ball games to attend or watch – at least not within 400 miles.

We also had "blue laws," which originally applied to laws supposedly enacted by the Puritans in seventeenth-century Connecticut. These laws regulated moral behavior and restricted certain activities on Sunday to accommodate the Christian observance of the Lord's Day.

Consequently, retail shops were closed on Sunday and as a general rule no businesses were open on the first day of the week with the possible exception of some few drug stores that would only sell medicine and perhaps a service station that dispensed gasoline to traveling motorists.

David Wilkerson, pastor of Times Square Church in New York City, has stated, "Even the rankest sinner didn't think of buying anything on Sunday."

In those days public schools were careful not to plan any programs or sporting events that would conflict with church schedules – even Wednesday night church activities.

The Lord's Day was revered by most Christians and regarded as holy. Using the day for pleasure or self-gratification was abhorrent to people of piety. Almost everyone ceased from their labors and made it a day of worship and rest.

However, a lot has changed in the last half century. Wilkerson declared, "[Sunday] has become the biggest retail shopping day of the week. More money is spent on Sunday than on any other day. If you drive by any suburban mall on a Sunday afternoon, you'll see the parking lot absolutely packed. Blue laws are now a thing of the past.

"Sunday has also become a time for pleasure and recreation. People fill the day with football, sports, shopping, and picnics. And if it doesn't interrupt their leisure activities, they may squeeze in an hour for church, just to ease their consciences."

Yes, I know it sounds legalistic and unreasonable, maybe even Pharisaical to measure one's spirituality by evaluating them on the basis of what they do and don't do on the Lord's Day, but there was a time when the observance of the fourth commandment was far more important that it is today.

And I realize that the book of Hebrews tells us that Christians have entered into that reality of which the Sabbath command, now superseded, was only a precursor – that God is interested in our entering His own rest, the eternal Sabbath, and his own rest is not a day of the week. This eternal, spiritual rest is the rest God offers believers, and it is a rest that is eternal, not by setting aside one day a week, but by faith, by believing in the One whom God has sent.

Many believers have embraced the concept of the Christian Sabbath, but use the freedom it provides as a license to do just about anything they want to do. In addition, the secular world has dismissed the idea of any kind of Sabbath rest. Consequently, there is nothing distinctive about Sunday for most people. It is a day for recreation, shopping, traveling, and working.

But it is refreshing that the late Truett Cathy, king of the Chick-fil-A empire, never open his restaurants on Sunday. Statistics show that 20 percent of all fast-food revenue comes on Sunday, and while Cathy believes everyone should "Eat Mor Chikin," he does not serve the public on the Lord's Day.

Cathy, was a member of First Baptist Church in Jonesboro, taught a boy's Bible study on Sunday mornings for 51 years and later served as an assistant teacher. He is convicted that Sunday is a day for worship, meditation, and rest. With nearly 1,340 restaurants in 37 states and sales topping $2.275 billion in 2006, Cathy is known not so much for what he has done as a businessman, but for what he hasn't done: Open up shop on Sunday.

There is something about Cathy's conviction to honor the Lord's Day that is attractive to me. It speaks of commitment, reverence for God, integrity, good values, and character. The Lord's Day should at least give us time to focus upon the God who has created us, who sustains us and who has redeemed us through the blood of His dear Son. How we observe it should serve as a witness to others. What are you doing to "hallow" the Christian Sabbath?

Dare to be the 'Bad Guys' of the Future

I believe that America is still the hope of the world. We have the capability, the resources, and enough gospel light to change the world.

However, something is happening to the soul of our nation. I have tried to discern exactly what is taking place in this country, but like a dike that has sprung multiple leaks, it is difficult to know where to start the reparations.

First, some would point to the public-school system in our country and contend that much of our undoing has come from the humanistic philosophy that characterizes many of our educational institutions.

Al Mohler, president of Southern Seminary in Louisville, Ky., stated, "Some now argue that Christian parents cannot send their children to public schools without committing the sin of handing their children over to a pagan and ungodly system.

"Fueled by a secularist agenda and influenced by an elite of radical educational bureaucrats and theorists, government schools now serve as engines for secularizing and radicalizing children."

While there are many public schools that are commendable and acceptable to Christian families, there is great concern for what is happening at the national level where policies are made and the future is shaped.

Many public schools have embraced the philosophy of Outcome Based Education (OBE), a system of education that is less concerned about the curriculum and more concerned about the student. With this approach to education, a list of desired outcomes in the form of student behaviors, skills, attitudes, and abilities is created.

One of the goals of OBE includes minimizing the distinctions between various sexual relationships. OBE suggests that sex within marriage between those of the opposite sex is not morally different from sex outside of marriage between those of the same sex. The goal of such programs is self-actualization and making people comfortable with their sexual preferences.

If transformational outcome-based reformers have their way, students would not get credit for classes taken until their attitudes, feelings, and behaviors matched the desired goals of the proponents of this system of education.

The public-school system may be the launching pad for this new doctrine of tolerance. And in our society, there is increasing evidence that everything is tolerated but evangelical Christianity. Josh McDowell recently stated that the general public is becoming so anti-Christian that within 36 to 60 months, the good guys (evangelical Christians) will become the bad guys in the United States.

Second, some would point to the government as the primary advocate of this new kind of tolerance. In Micah 3:1-2 the Old Testament prophet declares, "And I said, Hear, I pray you, O heads of Jacob, and ye princes of the house of Israel: Is it not for you to know judgment? Who hate the good, and love the evil ...."

Micah is referring to the governmental leaders of the house of Israel and seems to suggest that they abhor that which is good and embrace that which is evil. Micah's words seem applicable for today because, it is absolutely true that today's view of tolerance blurs the distinction between right and wrong.

Marcia Barlow, writing for the Arizona Conservative, avows, "Stating that a particular idea or behavior is unacceptable and should not be encouraged has been labeled as 'hate speech' and is now a justifiable reason for an individual to be pelted with derogatory names (Racist! Religious bigot! Homophobe!), threatened with potential lawsuits, or at the very least to be chastised as being 'intolerant.' The new doctrine of tolerance has become the foundation of a social movement that permeates the media and has found root in both our judicial and legislative systems.

"Under the guise of 'separation of church and state,' the new tolerance is bent upon neutering or eliminating traditional religion. No person or institution is allowed to identify right and wrong or say 'Thou shalt not …' The new tolerance states that there are no moral absolutes – thus no Supreme Being."

While in Canada a month ago I met a young pastor, Jonathan Chisholm, who said, "When the United States was attacked on September 11 your president called your people together and had prayer for the nation. The president of Canada also called our people together, but there was no prayer, because he didn't want to offend the unbelievers and those with no religion."

Who knows but that we may be only one presidential election away from experiencing the same kind of response to a national tragedy?

In Proverbs 29:1-2 we find these sobering words: "He that being often reproved hardeneth his neck, shall suddenly be destroyed, and that without remedy. When the righteous are in authority, the people rejoice; but when the wicked beareth rule, the people mourn."

Third, many churches in America have bought into this doctrine of tolerance, which is subtly and insidiously stripping our culture of every vestige of absolute truth.

I do not believe Southern Baptists have fallen into this trap and are thus often scorned by the media for being narrow and sectarian. It sounds so warm, inviting, and loving to be accepting of all religions and all systems of thought. But those who buy into the idea of religious pluralism and replace truth with tolerance are being misled by their own gullibility.

A. W. Tozer said, "Gullibility is not synonymous with spirituality. Faith keeps its heart open to whatever is of God and rejects everything that is not of God." We must always be ready to reject what is false and embrace what is true.

Yet, at the same time, be prepared to endure the slings and arrows of those who are tolerant of everything but manifestly intolerant of Bible-believing, Christ-loving, soul-winning Christians. Those of you who fit that description of unashamed Christians may be the "bad guys" of the future.

Why I am not Running for
President of the SBC

In the May 25, 2006 edition of The Christian Index I wrote an editorial entitled "Bring it on – your nomination, that is." In that editorial I wrote, "I understand that constant vigilance must be maintained to preserve the victory of the Conservative Resurgence, but I think we have come to the time when we need to see multiple nominations for each convention office both on the national and state level."

So far, this year, we have reported that six people are going to be nominated as president of our Convention, although one promising candidate, Dr. Al Mohler, had to withdraw his name from consideration due to health issues. Who could have ever expected that the field of candidates would be so crowded?

It remains to be seen what other candidates may throw their hats in the ring, but I wanted to let Southern Baptists know that I am not a candidate this year and I have ten reasons why I will not allow my name to be placed in nomination.

In other words, mark it down and put a star by it. If I am nominated I will not run; and if I am elected I will not serve. So, here is what I think to be a reasonable justification for me not being SBC president:

First, there has been no groundswell of interest in my candidacy. No one has called to urge me to run. I have had not one single email to suggest that I should allow my name to be placed in nomination. And there has certainly been no cadre of convention leaders compelling me to enter the race.

Second, no one has offered to nominate me – no one. Not even my wife or brother. My son-in-law is also my pastor and will be going to the convention, but he has not even hinted that he would be willing to nominate me. Of course, I could do like Anis Shorrosh did years ago and nominate myself, but I wouldn't know what to say in the nomination speech.

Third, If I were to be nominated and elected I would be expected to go to a lot of meetings, because the SBC Constitution says, "The president shall be a member of the several boards and of the Executive Committee." Also, I once heard Adrian Rogers say, "The only difference in a drunk and an alcoholic is an alcoholic has to go to all those meetings." I actually think I have an Attention Deficit Disorder and attending all those meetings would be difficult for me to endure.

Fourth, the ballots only have ten chads to be punched out for the various votes during the course of the convention and I am afraid the number of candidates this year will exceed the number of chads. I am sure I don't want to create a chad controversy in the Southern Baptist Convention.

Fifth, I am afraid something would come up that I didn't understand, like that Garner amendment last year. As I recall, we voted on that twice – once by raising our hands and then by ballot. I was so confused about that motion that I voted both ways in order to make sure I didn't make a mistake. I would hate to preside over the business session when something like that came up.

Sixth, I have heard that the Convention president has to do a lot of traveling. In the first place who would want to travel outside Georgia? In the second place, to get across the nation it would be necessary to fly and the notion of flying out of Hartsville-Jackson International Airport more than once a month gives me panic attacks, the heebie geebies, apoplexy, nervous prostration, and peptic ulcers.

Seventh, most SBC presidents get invited to the White House during the course of their presidency. I am not sure there will be anyone in the White House I will want to see in the next two years.

Eighth, in April I witnessed an oyster-eating contest on television. There were people with cast iron stomachs in the French Quarter of New Orleans attempting to win the lion's share of a $1,750 prize by eating dozens of raw oysters. The goal was to break the world's record by eating more than 552 oysters. I was glad to be a spectator rather than a participant in that event. By the same token I think I will enjoy being an observer rather than a participant in this year's SBC presidential race.

Ninth, the only person that I am absolutely sure would vote for me is my mother and so far they are not picking up ballots in heaven where she is enjoying the blessings of being saved without the hassles of earthly trials.

Tenth, I am not qualified to be the SBC president. I am certainly not qualified like the two candidates I know best, those two fashionable, formidable, and faithful Georgia Baptist candidates who are ready, able, and willing to serve.

If these ten reasons have not convinced you that I am not a viable candidate I could come up with ten more for the next issue of The Christian Index, but hopefully this will suffice.

Some Pastors Become
Universalists at Funerals

As a pastor for many years I discovered there were certain things that were extremely difficult to do. It was difficult when I had to tell young women (or men) in the churches I served that I could not perform their wedding if they insisted on marrying an unbeliever (I Cor. 6:14).

I also found it particularly difficult to carry the news of a sudden or accidental death to the spouse or family of the deceased loved one. It was likewise painful to see promising church members wreck their lives through wrong choices. It was difficult to see bright high school students go off to college and have their faith shattered by the insidious teachings of liberal and humanistic professors.

However, one of the most difficult things I ever had to do as a pastor was conduct funeral services for those who had never professed faith in Christ or who never lived out their once-professed faith. And I had to do it on many occasions – probably many more times than I even realized.

It happens like this: a grieving widow calls and says with a broken heart and with tears in her voice, "Pastor, my husband had a heart attack last night and we took him to the hospital, but he was dead on arrival.

I can't believe it has happened, but we need your help. I know he was not a church member, but we would like for you to preach his funeral."

What does a pastor say to an understandably emotional woman who has not even yet come to grips with the dimensions of her loss? You do the only reasonable and respectable thing you can do and respond in the affirmative.

A visit is typically made to the home of the deceased to console the bereaved and get some information in order to write the funeral message. In the process of gathering information it is obvious that the woman's departed husband never professed faith in Christ.

In certain cases, a pastor may be called upon to conduct the funeral for an individual who may have joined a church years earlier, but never gave any indication of being born again or that Christ was vitally important to him.

In either case some pastors are torn between integrity and compassion and in an effort to add comfort to the family they become Universalists – giving the family some hope that their loved one may have been granted eternal life by a gracious and benevolent God. Universalism is the belief that there will be a universal reconciliation between humanity and the divine and that God is too good to send anyone to hell.

We have all heard eulogies ushering celebrities, politicians, athletes, and entertainers into heaven who in some cases were as far from that celestial city as a downtown tomcat is from *Home Life* magazine.

Judy Garland attained international stardom, but died in 1969 in London, England at 47 years of age. The coroner stated at the inquest that she died from "an incautious self-overdosage" of barbiturates.

She had been married five times, lived a life of promiscuity, "read the psychoanalytic pioneers – Freud, Jung, and Adler as if they were holy scripture," and was certainly not known for her Christian faith.

However, at her funeral the Rev. Peter A. Delaney, of Marylebone Church in London, gave her a Christian eulogy in a 20-minute Episcopal service. Mourners sang "The Battle Hymn of the Republic" and I Corinthians 13 was read.

Deborah Jean Palfrey, known as the D.C. madam, committed suicide by hanging herself last month. She was facing prison time for money laundering and racketeering charges in connection to what prosecutors described as a high-end prostitution ring whose clients included members of Washington's political and social elite.

In a suicide note left to her sister Palfrey stated, "Know I am at peace, with complete certainty, I believe Dad is standing watch – prepared to guide me into the light."

On her blog Gina de Vries wrote a eulogy for Palfrey, stating, "I always do what Nana (Franscesa, my great-grandmother) taught me to do when grieving – light candles, say prayers, cook a meal for friends, buy some flowers if I can find them fresh, set up an altar. Wish the person well on their way home.

"Deborah, I hope you get there with ease and peace. I'm sorry your way out of this world was so rocky, that you were not treated with the grace and graciousness that every human being deserves. I'm praying that Franscesa – or someone very like her – is there to greet you with a meal, some flowers, and some sweetness on the other side."

I am not judging Judy Garland or Deborah Jean Palfrey and hope somehow they were redeemed by the blood of the Lamb, but Garland's Christian funeral and Palfrey's eulogy seem to be lacking reality.

In actual fact, a funeral service is not for the deceased. It is primarily for the family and friends; and while a Christian minister may be called upon to conduct the service, he must not be guilty of suggesting that the unredeemed will inherit eternal life. To do so is to be disingenuous at best and dishonest at worst.

If a pastor is true to the Word of God, he cannot change or minimize the Bible's warning that the consequence of unbelief is condemnation (John 3:18).

To suggest or hint that someone who has never been saved is somehow headed for heaven does nothing but confuse the mourners and give the false impression that one can go to heaven without trusting in Christ who is the only way to God (John 14:6).

John M. Spence, professional toastmaster and non-religious funeral officiant, promotes his availability to conduct memorial services by saying, "According to recent surveys the vast majority of ordinary people these days do not profess to have any religious faith, yet only a tiny portion of all funerals are arranged on a non-religious basis."

While Spence and others may want to have their say at the funeral of the non-believer, the carefully-crafted remarks of a Christian minister can convey the gospel message of hope and certainty to those who need it most.

Adjusting the Bible to our Philosophy Doesn't Work

There are some hard sayings in the Bible. Most of us who are conservative actually believe more than we obey. For example, it's really hard to turn the left cheek to the ogre who has just smacked you on the right cheek (Matt. 5:39).

Furthermore, I don't know of anyone who has had their right eye extracted in order to avert a lustful look; and I know of no one who has had their right hand amputated in order to curb any attempt to activate their avarice (Matt. 5:28-30).

In John 6 when Jesus had fed the 5,000 with five loaves and two fish He began to declare himself and delineate the terms of discipleship. Some of the disciples remarked, "This is a hard saying; who can hear it?" (John 6:60)

In John 6:66 the Bible says, "From that time many of his disciples went back, and walked no more with him."

Many of the truths of the Bible are hard to take. The Bible presents a perfect ethical standard and sets forth the objective of holiness. It could be no other way, for God is holy and a holy God must have a perfect standard of ethics and holiness.

Interestingly, for centuries individuals have attempted to adjust the Bible to accommodate their own level of morality or justify their own theology or philosophy of life.

When I was at Southeastern Seminary in the 1960s it was extremely liberal, except for a few good and godly professors. One Wednesday at chapel we had a professor who so dissected and discredited the Bible that one student threw his Bible in the aisle of the chapel except for one page that he salvaged and ran out of the building screaming, "This is all I have left." He was emphasizing the only part of the Bible that remained after the professor had demythologized and rationalized the rest of it into oblivion.

Thomas Jefferson attempted to summarize his views of Christianity by taking scissors and snipping out every miracle and inconsistency he perceived to be in the New Testament Gospels of Matthew, Mark, Luke, and John. Then, relying on a cut-and-paste technique, he reassembled the excerpts into what he believed was a more coherent narrative comprised of 46 pages, resulting in what has been called the Thomas Jefferson Bible.

A couple of years ago the Western Bible Foundation in the Netherlands published a new Bible translation that caused great controversy, because they cut out difficult references related to economic justice, possessions, and money. Their goal was to "make the gospel more palatable."

The chairman of the foundation, Mr. De Rijke, stated, "Jesus was very inspiring for our inner health, but we don't need to take his naïve remarks about money seriously. He didn't study economics, obviously."

According to De Rijke no serious Christian takes these texts literally. "What if all Christians stopped being anxious, for example, and started expecting everything from God? Or gave their possessions to the poor, for that matter? Our economy would be lost. The truth is quite the contrary: a strong economy and a healthy work ethic is a gift from God."

The foundation wanted to "boldly go where no one else has gone before: by cutting out the confusing texts."

Meanwhile, in the United States, the Colorado state legislature recently passed SB-200, a bill that places the preaching and teaching of the Bible in jeopardy and criminalizes beliefs that oppose the homosexual rights agenda.

The Liberty Counsel reported, "As homosexual activists push for more rights, the result will be their attempt to criminalize beliefs that oppose their lifestyle – especially Christian beliefs. The Liberty Counsel specified that this bill "outlaws communication that discriminates based on sexual orientation – in essence outlawing the Bible in that state."

Outlawing God doesn't lessen His power and voting the Bible unconstitutional or unacceptable doesn't lessen its truth.

Another recent attack on the Bible has come from Bradley LaShawn Fowler, a gay man, who claims his constitutional rights have been infringed upon by Zondervan Publishing Co., and Thomas Nelson Publishing, both of which, he claims, deliberately caused homosexuals to suffer by misinterpretation of the Bible.

Fowler, age 39, is seeking $60 million from Zondervan and another $10 million from Thomas Nelson. The man from Michigan claims the intent of the Bible revisions that refer to homosexuals as sinners reflect an individual opinion or a group's conclusion. He claims that the changes made to 1 Corinthians 6:9 "referring to homosexuality as a sin have made him an outcast from his family and contributed to physical discomfort and periods of demoralization, chaos, and bewilderment and has caused him and other homosexuals to endure verbal abuse, discrimination, episodes of hate, and physical violence … including murder."

I suppose some of us would like to eliminate some of the indicting, convicting verses of the Bible at times, but Matthew 5:18 specifically tells us that "one jot or one tittle shall in no wise pass from the law, till all be fulfilled."

A.W. Tozer said, "The Word of God well understood and religiously obeyed is the shortest route to spiritual perfection. And we must not select a few favorite passages to the exclusion of others. Nothing less than a whole Bible can make a whole Christian."

I guess I wonder how Bradley LaShawn Fowler's story could be different. I wonder if anyone ever extended grace to him. For indeed, the Lord who condemns sins and who will one day judge sin now offers abounding grace for healing and freedom from the bondage of sin.

No homosexual may like 1 Corinthians 6:9, but they may love 1 John 1:8-9. No one will have success in eliminating one syllable of the Word of God, but those who come to God will find salvation, satisfaction, and security by living in its precepts.

Trustees are Accountable
to Billy and Betty Baptist

Every year the national Southern Baptist Convention and its state conventions elect trustees to oversee the work and operations of their various institutions and agencies.

In the course of a long ministry I have had the privilege of serving as a trustee for a variety of those entities. In the beginning I accepted this role as an honor and was proud to be given the recognition that accompanied the role of trustee.

Generally, being a trustee has certain amenities that are easy to appreciate. While a trustee of the Baptist Sunday School Board I enjoyed the times when we traveled to Glorieta and Ridgecrest for our board meetings.

It is not at all difficult for a trustee to become ingratiated by an agency leader, enamored by the position itself and captivated by the proprieties offered to those who hold that strategic role.

However, being a trustee of a Baptist entity is far more than an honor to be coveted. It is a serious and solemn responsibility to be upheld.

The Board of Trustees – the governing body of an entity – operates its entity in trust for the Convention and has a fiduciary duty to protect its assets through efficient operation.

Trustees are also generally responsible for establishing the entity's mission, bylaws, and strategic policies. Trustees select the administrative leader of the institution and ensure that the entity remains true to its stated mission. Failure to do this would be a serious dereliction of duty and constitute a breach of trust.

Former SBC president and current SBC Strategist of Global Evangelical Relations Bobby Welch believes, "Trustees are elected by the SBC and thereby given the right and responsibility to govern the entities to which they are elected. The trustees owe and own ultimate accountability to the SBC which holds possession of the particular entity."

Frank Page, immediate past president of the Convention, adds, "The role of trustees in SBC life is one of extreme importance. While entities and agencies rely on staff for day-to-day operations, it is the role of the trustees to ensure that the Lord's money is properly utilized in the accomplishment of the Great Commission. Thus, theirs is the responsibility of stewardship and therefore is a holy responsibility. When these fiduciary as well as spiritual responsibilities are fulfilled properly God's people can be confident that their trust in trustees is well placed."

The trustees of the North American Mission Board demonstrated a remarkable understanding of this concept in October of 2006 when they approved Executive Level Policies and expressly stated, "Our first responsibility as trustees is to the Southern Baptist Convention, not to NAMB team members."

We live in a critical day when our institutions and agencies must function at maximum effectiveness. Good and responsible trustees can be instrumental in keeping their entity on mission successfully.

First, if trustees are primarily accountable to their Southern Baptist constituency – Billy and Betty Baptist – they will do everything they can to see that every penny their agency spends is well-placed and used to accomplish the greatest good for the Kingdom. This will build credibility and transparency and give people the assurance that their Cooperative Program dollars are being used effectively.

In the secular world, trustees protect the best interests of their shareholders. They want the company to grow and prosper, but at the end of the day they are responsible for providing a good return on the investment of those who own stock in the company. In the denominational world those shareholders are the tithers who purchase an interest (shares) in the ministries of the Convention through deposits in the offering plate.

Second, responsible trustees will make wise, Christ-honoring decisions when choosing entity leaders and should be wary of nepotism and avoid things that would suggest a conflict of interest. Any leader of a Baptist agency should be a sold-out Christian with a clear biblical worldview, have a passion for Christ, be a personal soul-winner, and completely committed to the purpose of the entity to which he has been called.

Furthermore, trustees should make sure that the entity leader is building a team of workers that are marked by an explicit agreement, a visible unity, extraordinary prayer, high motivation, and a high level of collaboration with constituents and/or partners to work efficiently and effectively to fulfill the Great Commission. If our agencies are not committed to these things it is unlikely that their employees will rise above the example of their leaders – those whose salary they pay.

Third, trustees and employees should be able to converse freely. This will undoubtedly allow staff to relate stories of how God is at work in and through the staff. On occasion an employee may need to confide in a trustee to register a concern. This should always be allowed without the employee being fearful of retribution or marginalization.

Fourth, trustees who are committed to their entrusted assignment will serve as a liaison between their entity and the pew. The people in the pew need to know the good things that are happening through our institutions and agencies. Trustees have an up close and personal view of what God is doing in the entity and should be able to relate "God stories" to thrill the hearts of fellow Baptists within his/her sphere of influence.

I had the privilege of serving on the administration committee of the Georgia Baptist Convention and always rejoiced when someone from the New Church Development Ministries would request money for a new church start or when someone from Language Missions Ministries would tell about what God was doing in terms of reaching a new ethnic group in Georgia. I often wished that all Georgia Baptists could sit where I sat and hear the glowing reports of what God was doing through our state convention. I was similarly impressed when I was on the SBC Executive Committee's Cooperative Program Budget Committee.

When the president of the International Mission Board, North American Mission Board, or one of our seminaries came to share their vision and make their budget requests, I could only wish that we had enough money to meet every need. I longed for every Southern Baptist to hear the reports of what God was doing among his people around the world.

Fifth, trustees must demonstrate an exemplary degree of spiritual and financial support for the entity they represent. Every agency and institution need prayer support and financial support. Trustees should be pacesetters by leading their churches to give generously to the Cooperative Program and to SBC missions offerings.

The point of this editorial is that the trustees of our agencies – both in Georgia and in Southern Baptist life – have an awesome responsibility. Their first responsibility is to Billy and Betty Baptist. We are depending upon them to do their job. We joyfully express our gratitude to all those who are.

God is Still Able in
a Postmodern Culture

While some churches are growing spiritually and numerically others are struggling. Have you stopped to consider why your church may not be prospering? Senior church members sometimes wistfully recall the days when the church was flourishing, God was moving, and the baptismal waters were being stirred on a regular basis.

Things have changed. In the 19th century and through the first half of the 20th century public education in the United States had a distinctly evangelical protestant flavor. In the mid-20th century several developments helped to create a greater sensitivity to the need to remove religious advocacy from public education.

I have been a witness to this transformation. When I was in school we had chapel with preachers from the community preaching sermons. We celebrated Christmas with Christmas carols and the reading of the Christmas story from Luke's Gospel. I memorized scriptures like Psalm 100 and Psalm 23 in a public-school classroom.

In the '50s such practices posed no apparent problem for the vast majority of people because they reflected society's attitudes, but for an increasing minority prayer and Bible reading became an affront. That minority has continued to grow in number and confidence and has raised its voice to the point that they have a powerful influence. In fact, they have affected a shift in our culture and values.

D. A. Carson, in his book *The Gagging of God*, writes, "Although it is notoriously difficult to chart simple causes and effects at the societal level, few would be so bold as to deny that one of the factors that has powerfully contributed to the changes convulsing Western culture is the decline in Judeo-Christian assumptions, allied with (but emphatically differentiable from) the shift from modernity to postmodernity."

All of this has brought about a decline in three things I would venture to mention in this editorial.

First, there has been a decline in dogmatism. *USA Today* recently described religion in America as "a salad bar where people heap on beliefs they like and often leave the veggies – like strict doctrines – behind."

Pew Forum on Religion and Public Life recently surveyed 35,000 Americans whereby they discovered that although 92 percent of our population believe in God, there is a "stunning" lack of alignment between practices and their professed faiths.

D. Michael Lindsay, a Rice University sociologist, explains, "The survey shows religion in America is, indeed 3,000 miles wide and only three inches deep. There is a growing pluralistic impulse toward tolerance and that is having theological consequences."

Dogma is defined as "a doctrine or a corpus of doctrines relating to matters such as morality and faith, set forth in an authoritative manner by a church." Have we gotten to the place that we are afraid to embrace and proclaim strong doctrine for fear someone will be offended?

Rather than dogmatically denounce sin have we mollified it and tempered it as nothing more than a mistake in judgment? Have we skirted the biblical doctrine of judgment and theoretically air-conditioned hell so as not to provoke the ire of a culture lying in the warm, fuzzy lairs of tolerance?

Jesus preached to thousands in John 6, but when He began to dogmatically delineate the terms of discipleship there were some of His followers who said, "This is a hard saying; who can hear it?"

Jesus knew his strong message caused the disciples to murmur, so He asked, "Does this offend you?"

The sixth chapter of John shows us that you can have a crowd by giving them what they want, and that dogmatic doctrine will produce a winnowing. In the final analysis what would you rather have – a vacillating multitude or a dedicated minority? If this question stumps you read Judges 7.

In a day of declining dogmatism, we must sound forth the trumpet that will never sound retreat.

Second, there is a decline of exclusivism. Exclusivism, the view that one religion has the absolute and exclusive truth, has gotten a bad rap in America today. Religious pluralism is the "in" thing today, because it is politically correct and advocates the validity of all religions. According to religious pluralists: Judaism, Christianity, Islam, Sikhism, Hinduism, Buddhism, et. al., are equally worthy, even equally true religions.

Oprah Winfrey expressed the thoughts of many in our age of spiritual pluralism, saying, "One of the biggest mistakes humans make is to believe there is only one way. Actually, there are many diverse paths leading to what you call God."

While this view seems kind and generously open to all faiths, the belief is as foolish as saying that every sequence of notes on a page of music results in "Amazing Grace" or any grouping of mathematical numbers equals 1,000 or all roads in Georgia lead to Ludowici.

Because the gospel and the souls of men are at stake, we must always fiercely contend that Jesus was wounded and crushed for our sins and died for us by bearing our sins on the cross as our substitute. In other words, we must remain steadfast in our conviction about the exclusivity of the gospel and that there is no possible means of salvation apart from Jesus Christ.

Third, there is a decline of institutionalism. Americans are deeply suspicious of institutional religion. Some see religion as about money, rules, and power. That is not a positive connotation for anyone.

Angus Ritchie in his article, "Do We Need Institutional Religion?" comments, "It appears that spirituality is in vogue today, but institutional religion is rather less fashionable. It is quite common to contrast the dynamic spiritual message of Jesus with the stagnant institutional church." The gospel of God's grace seems distant from the worship wars, the business meetings, and the power struggles in most churches.

However, we must not diminish the religious institutions, because it is through the churches (institutions) that the gospel is proclaimed, believers are nurtured, Christ's ministry on earth is accomplished, missionary endeavors are launched, and God's purposes are fulfilled. The slings and arrows of the church's critics may be hurled against it, but it is the one thing on earth that Jesus promised the gates of hell would not prevail against.

Because of a secular society's influence and the decline of dogmatism, exclusivism, and institutionalism many churches are struggling, but God is not through with the church and He is still able – able to give added momentum to a growing church, able to reverse the trend of a declining church, and even able to resurrect a dead church.

Knowing the Difference
Between Cost and Value

Sometimes I find myself living in the past and longing for the price
tags of 1959, the year I graduated from high school. That was when
first class postage stamps sold for four cents and a gallon of gas cost a
quarter.

In fact, a year or two later I remember driving back to my home in
North Carolina from Mercer University one weekend and finding Rutherford
County engaged in an all-out gas war. I purchased gasoline for 16 cents a
gallon. In other words, I drove over almost 600 miles that weekend in my
straight-shift, six-cylinder, Plymouth Mayflower for less than $4.

In 1959 milk sold for $1.10 a gallon, a loaf of bread cost 20 cents,
and a Ford Skyliner sold for less than $2,500. The average cost of a new
house was $12,400. My wife tells me that on those rare occasions when I
go shopping with her I never buy anything because I am still looking for
those 1959 prices. As usual, she is probably right.

Today's prices are mindboggling to me. I was browsing on the Internet
to see where I could get the best price for a certain brand of footwear and
came across a website for Moreschi shoes. I noticed they have their Esquire
Shoe made from crocodile skin priced at $1,800.

I gasped for breath and nearly hyperventilated. I did find the shoe I was looking for on Shoebuy.com. – a pair of Johnston and Murphy Classic Dress Shoes at $99.95 and considered that highway robbery. I remember buying a great pair of penny loafers at Belk Department store in my hometown in 1959 for $6.95.

So far, we are talking about nickel and dime stuff. Have you heard the price tag for President Obama's Inauguration? The New York Daily News estimated the cost of the Washington extravaganza at $160 million dollars.

Talk about extravagance – the New York Yankees recently forked out $423 million for baseball superstars CC Sabathia, Mark Teixeria, and A.J. Burnett.

In case you are not impressed with any of the preceding price tags, let me clue you in on the price of tickets to Sunday's Super Bowl in Raymond James Stadium in Tampa, Fla. Two seats in the upper corner of the stadium are selling on StubHub for nearly $4,000. Seats closer to the playing field are in the five-figure range. Seats in the luxury suites have been listed for as high a $369,330 per seat.

The National Broadcasting Company recently announced that a thirty-second television ad during the Super Bowl is priced as approximately $3 million. An estimated 20 minutes of advertising (it probably will be much more than that) will produce $120 million in revenue for NBC. That amount of advertising appears to be a total waste of money in the midst of a recession.

Today we seem to know the cost of everything and the value of nothing. We can become so enamored with "things" that we lose sight of eternity. Jesus warned us against laying up treasures on earth. We need to be laying up treasures in heaven.

Each day brings us closer to death. If your treasures are on earth that means each day brings you closer to losing your treasures.

John Wesley toured a vast estate with a proud plantation owner. They rode their horses for hours and saw only a fraction of the man's property. At the end of the day they sat down to dinner. The plantation owner eagerly asked, "Well Mr. Wesley, what do you think?"

Wesley replied, "I think you are going to have a hard time leaving all this."

The real question here is this: Is my heart seeking after self and the things of this world or a real, vibrant relationship with God? In a lot of ways we can put on masks so people perceive us as spiritual or godly, when in reality, deep in our hearts, there is a civil war going on between the flesh and the spirit and we end up desiring the things of this world more than the things of God.

Jesus had a way of addressing the heart of an issue by asking pertinent questions, like "Where is your treasure?" He says in Matthew 6:21 "For where your treasure is, there your heart will be also." Our treasure typically betrays the inner desires of our heart. And there are a lot of things vying for our heart, because the heart is the control center of your life.

I am reminded of the old Scotsman who was frugal to a fault. Instead of buying his wife a present for their wedding anniversary he gave her an x-ray of his chest. He said, "I didn't get you a present, but I did want to show you that my heart is in the right place."

In this time of economic recession when many have lost their jobs and others have suffered financially don't forget the needs of your church and place your treasures in Kingdom causes (the church offering plate) to really prove that your heart is in the right place.

Incidentally, the Lord's work cannot be funded on 1959 prices, but on the cost of things today.

A Hard Look at Church Business Meetings

One church sign revealed, "Today's sermon: What is hell like?" Underneath the sermon title were the words "Church business meeting tonight."

Some church business meetings have been alarmingly similar to the place of torment.

In Dr. W.A. Criswell's famous sermon, "The Old Time Religion," he tells about a church conference or church business meeting he had in the church he served as pastor when he was a student at Southern Seminary.

Criswell reported, "We had a man in our church who was born in the objective mood, negative case. No matter what we were considering he was 'agin it.'

"At one church business meeting we were discussing the prospect of building a fence around the church cemetery, and this obstreperous, cantankerous, argumentative church member rose to state his position on the matter at hand.

"He vociferously exclaimed, 'I am agin it! I am agin it! Why should we build a fence around the cemetery? Do you know anyone in the cemetery who can get out; and do you know anyone outside of the cemetery who wants to get in? Why build a fence around the cemetery?'"

Your church probably doesn't have anyone born in the objective mood and negative case, but I have encountered a few people like that in the course of my ministry.

I have presided over heated discussions regarding who should be in charge of the thermostat in the church worship center, the color of the carpet in the church, and whether or not to buy an electric typewriter or just keep the old manual Underwood typewriter for the church secretary.

The minutes of one church business meeting recorded the following: The committee charged with reducing the electrical costs in the church building reported that they had been standing outside the bathrooms after services and reminding people to turn out the lights as they leave.

Mr. Tom Brown objected that this might create the wrong impression with visitors but was quickly shouted down by Deacon Holstein who opined that anyone who couldn't follow a few simple posted rules weren't the kind of people we wanted around this church anyway. After another thirty minutes of discussion, the matter was tabled until next month.

It is true that wherever there are two Baptists together you could have up to three opinions on any given subject.

A blogger from Winnipeg, Manitoba, Canada has obviously been around a church business meeting or two. He observed, "Local churches all over the world are shattered so often that it is almost an expected result. Pastors are fired, members storm off, staff members take a group from one church to start another just down the road. Business meetings become filled with yelling, fighting, and screaming, believers taking sides against fellow believers. Then there are power plays, deception, and alliances that would make reality TV look sane."

I have a few rules I would like to suggest that churches employ for their business meetings.

First, non-tithers should not be allowed to speak or vote at church business meetings. If that rule seems unfair then the time allotted for members to speak should be in direct proportion to how much they give. For example, a person who gives 2 percent of their income to the church should be given the opportunity to speak for 20 seconds, the person who gives 4 percent should be allotted 40 seconds, the person who gives 10 percent for 1 minute and 40 seconds and the person who gives 20 percent should be allowed to speak for 3 minutes and 20 seconds, etc.

Second, no one should be allowed to speak or vote at the church business meeting who is more knowledgeable and conversant with the church constitution/by-laws and Robert's Rules of Order than the Bible. I have known deacons who could quote Article III, Section 4, paragraph 6 of the church constitution, but couldn't find the Gospel of John in the Bible.

Third, the only members who can speak or vote at church business meetings should have at least a 75 percent attendance record. In other words, if the church has Sunday morning, Sunday evening, and Wednesday evening worship services or Bible studies each week or 12 such meetings a month, a member should be in attendance for nine of those meetings in order to participate in a business meeting.

Having this rule will prohibit conniving members from importing scads of inactive members for crucial votes – like for the termination of a pastor.

Fourth, a man who is silenced and controlled by his wife should not try to make up for his lack of authority at home by attempting to assert himself and control the church business meeting. Unfortunately, some men are as bold as a lion at a church conference and as meek as a lamb at home.

Fifth, some church business meetings should be held in a wrestling arena or hockey rink, because there is nothing spiritual about them and they hardly qualify to be held in a "house of prayer." Half nelsons and flying pucks are more likely to be seen in some church business meetings than grace and unity.

In case you think the preceding suggestions are manifestly unspiritual I want you to know that I have written them facetiously or tongue-in-cheek – well, maybe somewhat facetiously. Others of you may be cheering the suggestions because if they were employed your church business meetings would be significantly improved.

Here is the question: What kind of impression would an unsaved person get about your church if his only exposure to it were a business meeting? Furthermore, if the resurrected Christ were to visibly walk into your church business meeting would He feel at home in His Church?

May the Lord be exalted in your church's next business meeting and in the Southern Baptist Convention's business meeting in Louisville this month. Why? The media will show up as usual and the world will be watching and quite often the only impression the world gets of us is the impression they get of our business meeting.

Spectators in the Circus Maximus

I f you lived in Rome 1,900 years ago you might have had season tickets to the Circus Maximus. Circus Maximus is Latin for "greatest circus." The Circo Massimo, as it would be called in Italian, was built in 326 BC and could hold 250,000 spectators. It was a mass entertainment venue located in a valley formed by the Palatine and Aventine Hills.

Originally, the aristocracy of the Roman world used the Circus Maximus for non-public games and entertainment. Chariot races were of particular interest to the elite citizenry of Italy.

The charioteers raced around a dividing wall called a spina. Crowds of Romans loved watching these races and often charioteers were killed when their cart tipped over. Somehow the potential for catastrophic collisions fueled the interest of the spectators.

Perhaps it was this appetite for fast races and sensational crashes that set the stage for the Circus Maximus becoming the site of treacherous contests involving the slaughter of Christians.

No Roman was more ruthless than Nero when it came to the persecution of Christians. He did not just kill Christians; he wanted to make them suffer first. Nero enjoyed dipping the Christians in wax before impaling them on poles around his palace and lighting them on fire, yelling sarcastically, "Now, you truly are the light of the world!"

Nero used the Circus Maximus for some of his most gruesome murders. In that massive stadium he would have Christians wrapped in animal skins and thrown to lions or dogs that would then tear them apart in front of thousands of entertained spectators. At other times he would crucify them and after the crowd would get bored, set the Christians on fire.

The above description of spectators sitting in a mammoth arena and observing Christianity being dismantled one believer at a time is not vastly different from what is happening in our culture today.

Why? There is a striking similarity, because many of our Christian structures and principles are being dismantled before our very eyes and many people are sitting idly by in the comfort of their own private "Circus Maximus" and watching it happen.

For example, the House of Representatives recently passed the "hate crimes" bill and it is presently (as of this writing) pending in the Senate. World Net Daily reported that the bill "would give special protections to homosexuals, essentially designating them as a 'protected class.' However, it could leave Christian ministers open to prosecution should their teachings be linked to any subsequent offense, by anyone, against a homosexual person.

"A renowned expert on the life and work of sex scientist Alfred Kinsey, widely considered the 'father of the sexual revolution,' says the 'hate crimes' bill pending in Congress would be just another step in the conversion of the United States into a nation without sexual limits, where polygamy, incest, and worse are common practice.

"Judith Reisman says it would be a nation in which those who hold religious views that do not approve of homosexual behavior and the myriad other sexual lifestyles would be censored and arrested."

These atrocious decisions are made in full view of modern day church members who sit as spectators in some ecclesiastical "Circus Maximus" and watch as sexual perversion is given a protected status and Christianity is trivialized and marginalized by a 2009 culture hostile to the gospel of Jesus Christ.

Then last week there was a Jihad Al Qaeda Group meeting at a Hilton Hotel in Chicago. The group that hosted "The Fall of Capitalism and the Rise of Islam," Hizb-ut Tahrir America, was allowed to gather in America despite its activities that have been banned from other countries for having reported ties to terrorism.

Frank Gaffney, former deputy assistant secretary of defense and current president of the Center of Security Policy, stated, "The mission of [Hizb-ut Tahrir America] is to establish a Khalifate, a theocratic form of government, that will rule the world, subjecting all of us, Muslim and non-Muslim alike, to what authoritative Islam calls Sharia Law, which is a pretty repressive, brutal program."

Hizb-ut Tahrir is one of the oldest, largest indoctrinating organizations for the ideology known as jihadism (holy war). It often says that its indoctrination "prepares the infantry" for subversive Al Qaeda operations.

Having an Al Qaeda recruitment meeting in our nation is the logical equivalent of having Jeffery Dahmer over for dinner and giving him free rein to prepare the meal.

All the while we continue to sit in our box seats in the Circus Maximus and watch the forces of evil flex muscles being developed to undermine our faith and target Christianity for extinction.

President Obama went to Georgetown University to make a speech, but insisted that the monogram "IHS" – symbolizing the name of Jesus

– be covered. The White House had asked the University to cover up all Christian symbols and signs because they could potentially be an impediment to his purposes.

Then when the president went to Turkey in April he stated that we Americans, "do not consider ourselves a Christian nation, or a Muslim nation, but rather a nation of citizens who are bound by a set of values."

Then in May Mr. Obama decided to downplay the National Day of Prayer with a paper proclamation instead of an event at the White House.

Shirley Dobson, chairwoman of the National Day of Prayer, stated, "We are disappointed in the lack of participation by the Obama administration. At this time in our country's history, we would hope our president would recognize more fully the importance of prayer."

Each time the president minimizes or dismisses Christianity as a tertiary matter we simply adjust our seats in the Circus Maximus and idly observe the events with mild outrage or bored disinterest, but doing little to affect any change.

According to Voice of the Martyrs, "More Christians have been killed for their faith in the 20th century than have been martyred in the total history of Christianity."

Perhaps there are no Christians in America being slaughtered for their faith, but there are those being persecuted. For example, Christians who stood for Proposition 8, banning gay marriage in California, have been ridiculed, warned, and threatened. One writer stated, "Burn their [expletive] churches and then tax the charred timbers."

Rick Scarborough of Vision America, in summarizing the backlash from the Prop 8 vote, remarked, "Shame on anyone who would dare to say that the persecution of Christians has not begun in America! And if we refuse to speak out about it now, while we still have the right to speak, we will see the day when we cannot speak out without experiencing real persecution. Mark my word."

We have done little to thwart the subversive attacks on Christianity. In fact, we have seemingly been content to observe the dismantling of our faith from the grandstand, the sidelines, the Circus Maximus, even occasionally drifting into some kind of idyllic daydream that gives us the false assurance that it will never come close to us.

Muslims Should be Able
to Pray in Public Schools

Muslims who are truly faithful to their religion are supposed to pray five times a day. To the Muslim prayer is considered the most important act of worship. The Muslim guideline for prayer states that it is a great sin to neglect praying.

"The Basics of the Muslim's Prayer" states, "If a believer is shopping at the mall or waiting at the airport and there is no way to get home or to a mosque, he is still obligated to perform the prayer within its due time instead of purposely leaving out or delaying the prayer. This indicates the importance of the obligatory prayer. Doing the obligatory prayer on time takes priority over other non-obligatory matters."

Sometime ago I was in Dulles International Airport in Washington, D.C. and saw a Muslim unroll a small rug, kneel down – I presume toward Mecca – and pray. He seemed to be oblivious to everyone else in the airport and was undaunted by surrounding circumstances. He was devoted to his time to prayer.

Let the Muslims pray – in the airport, on the street corner, in the mall, or even in the public schools. I do not believe the United States Constitution prohibits such prayers. But let Christians pray also. Let us pray wherever we would like to pray, including in the public schools of our land.

The First Amendment was never intended to bar voluntary expressions of religion. The relevant part of the amendment says, "Congress shall make no law respecting an establishment of religion, or prohibiting the free exercise thereof."

Unfortunately, the Supreme Court and others have inanely focused only on the first clause, which prohibits the establishment of religion, at the expense of the second clause, which protects the right of Americans to worship as they please including the offering of voluntary prayers in public schools.

Recent Supreme Court decisions have gone well beyond giving privilege to secularism; they suggest an actual hostility toward religion. The secularism of our schools has done great harm to our educational system.

The prejudice, however, seems to be not just against religions generally, but Christianity specifically. For example, Von Steuben High School in Chicago has set aside a place for Muslim students to observe one of their five daily prayers.

When recess comes at an elementary school on the outskirts of San Diego, some students rush out for a quick game of hopscotch while others gather in a room for Muslim worship. Like a growing number of school districts around the country, San Diego is changing its ways to meet the needs of its Islamic students.

In Nyssa, Ore., students are taught how to say Muslim prayers, the Five Pillars of Islamic Faith, and key scriptures from the Koran. Teachers ask students to dress like Muslims, play-act Islamic skits, and build Muslim props. All this is mandated by the state of Oregon according to School Superintendent Don Grotting.

At George Mason University in Fairfax, Va., Muslim students are given a "prayer" room when no such room is available to Christians or Jews.

At Irmo High School in Columbia, S.C., students are required to create a pamphlet which would teach people about Islam, discuss the Five Pillars of Islam, listen to a guest speaker who told them all religions are based on Islam, and that the U.S. is a "Judeo-Christian-Muslim" nation according to the beliefs of the Founding Fathers. Muslim students are allowed to use the school library for prayer each day.

Fine, let the Muslims have prayer in the public schools and the institutions of higher learning in America. To me it is the equivalent of the prophets of Baal going through their ritualistic prayers on Mount Carmel in Elijah's day.

The Bible says, "[They] called on the name of Baal from morning even until noon, saying, 'O Baal, hear us.' But there was no voice, nor any that answered. And they leaped upon the altar which was made" (I Kings 18:26). They even tried to get Baal's attention by cutting themselves with knives and lancets. However, their God did not respond to their plaintive appeals because he was non-existent.

Let the Muslims, the Buddhists, the Hindus, the Mormons, and the Jehovah's Witnesses pray, but don't prohibit the Christians from praying. Don't allocate prayer space for other religions and fail to accord Christians the same rights. To register a prejudice against Christians praying anywhere in America is to deny our heritage and fight against God Almighty.

Frank Lay, principal of Pace High School in Pace, Fla., asked Robert Freeman, the school's athletic director, to offer a prayer before the meal at a luncheon to honor the school's boosters and other adults. However, a federal judge may rule that they violated a court order forbidding an employee from "promoting, advancing, aiding, facilitating, endorsing, or causing religious prayers or devotions during school-sponsored events."

Baptist Press reported on Aug. 17 that the prayer could land the principal and the AD in jail. BP stated, "U.S. District Judge Case Rodgers initiated criminal contempt proceedings and has referred the men to the United States attorney's office for prosecution. The case is scheduled for trial in U.S. District Court in Pensacola on September 17."

I don't want to admit that I am given to conspiracy theories, but there seems to be a cleverly devised plan to undermine Christianity in America. Why? The devil detests the prayers of God's children.

It is time for another Mount Carmel contest. The prophets of Baal have shown up for the battle. They are praying their prayers to their own specially contrived deity, but we could lose by default. I mean, it is foolish to cry "foul" and plead for "equal access" if no one really wants to pray.

If ever it was true, it is "knee time" in America today. We must pray for our churches, our denomination, and our nation. Our prayers could very well result in God demonstrating His power to the extent that the multitudes would cry out as did the Israelites in Elijah's day, "The Lord, He is the God; the Lord, He is the God."

Reinventing Christianity

We have heard much about the Emergent Church for almost two decades. Some have looked with favor upon this movement - or "conversation," as its proponents prefer to call it. Others view the Emergent Church with skepticism, if not outright disdain.

What is the Emergent, or Emerging, Church? The late evangelist Sam Cathey asked, "What is it emerging from and what is it emerging into?" Those are reasonable and appropriate questions.

Its own advocates describe the Emergent Church as "a growing generative friendship among missional Christian leaders seeking to love our world in the Spirit of Jesus Christ." The proponents of the "conversation" also admit that they began meeting because many were disillusioned and disenfranchised by the conventional ecclesiastical institutions of the late 20th century."

However, it is also apparent that this movement crosses a number of theological boundaries and supports the deconstruction or the reinvention of Christian worship and evangelism as well as the nature of the church.

Some have even warned that the Emergent Church is nothing more than a repackaging of the New Age philosophy or a movement toward religious pluralism.

Pam Sheppard, a staffer with Answers in Genesis, defines the Emergent Church by writing: "Emerging churches are an informal network of worldwide Christian communities who believe God's way for today's generation is to focus more on relationships and emerging ideas than hard-and-fast truths and traditional statements of faith."

Brian McLaren, founding pastor of Cedar Ridge Community Church in Spencerville, Md., is regarded by many as one of the chief spokespersons for the Emergent Church movement in America. In 2005 *Time* magazine recognized McLaren as one of the top 25 Most Influential Evangelicals in America.

In his book, *The Last Word and the Word After That*, McLaren recounts several conversations with his daughter Jess, who at the time was a second-semester freshman in College Park, Md.

Jess came home one weekend and asked her father, who at the time was on a leave of absence from his church for his questionable theology, to answer a question.

Jess asked, "If Christianity is true, then all the people I love except for a few will burn in hell forever. But if Christianity is not true, then life doesn't seem to have much meaning or hope. I wish I could find a better option. How do you deal with this?"

McLaren, who admitted he had generally avoided the subject of hell in his preaching over the years, responded by telling her about "inclusivism" which was an alternative to the "exclusivist" view she was unhappy with.

McLaren stated, "While exclusivism limited eternal life in heaven to bona fide, confessing Christians, inclusivism kept the door open that others could be saved through Christ even if they never identified as Christians."

McLaren's answer didn't satisfy his daughter, so she came back with another question: "How can I deal with the fact that even one person could be tortured for an infinity of time for a finite number of sins?"

McLaren said, "Then I told her about 'conditionalism,' the idea that hell is temporary and leads to extinction rather than eternal torment."

Still not satisfied with her dad's answer Jess came back the next morning with a question about the validity of universalism.

Although McLaren considered universalism one small step from atheism, he writes, "I didn't know what to say, so I made a joke about not answering theological questions before 9 a.m. on Sunday morning, and she let me off the hook."

It would appear, therefore, that there might be no right or wrong answers in the Emergent Church movement - that there are no clear doctrinal positions and there is a significant commitment to tolerance.

In a Baptist Press article on March 23, 2005, Southern Seminary president Al Mohler said that McLaren "embraces relativism at the cost of clarity in matters of truth and intends to redefine Christianity for this new age, largely in terms of an eccentric mixture of elements he would take from virtually every theological position and variant."

Mohler added, "As a postmodernist, he (McLaren) considers himself free from any concern for propositional truthfulness, and simply wants the Christian community to embrace a pluriform understanding of truth as a way out of doctrinal conflict and impasse."

Mohler, speaking on a panel about the Emergent Church, said, "If you get the truth question wrong you are going to be aberrant in every dimension of the life of your church and in your personal understanding of Christianity; and if we forego that, if we surrender that, if we come off the heights of that commitment then I don't care what you call it - emerging or emergent, it is going to be a new form of liberalism in the church."

John MacArthur believes the Emergent Church is heretical. He contends, "You won't learn much about the holiness of God or the importance of obedience. That's because if a church's primary focus is to encourage unbelievers to attend, it will invariably soften the truth to make it more palatable. It will skirt the hard teaching of Scripture on matters of repentance and the cost of discipleship, choosing instead to focus on God's grace and how easy it is to become a believer."

I don't know what you think about the words of McLaren, Mohler, or MacArthur, but I am unconditionally convinced that the Gospel is absolutely true and amazingly relevant in every culture and to every man in every age and in every society. It is the truth that transcends all humanity.

And there is no need to "reinvent" it by compromising its wholeness in order for it to be relevant.

Christless Preaching

The title of Michael Horton's book, *Christless Christianity: The Alternative Gospel of the American Church,* is a jarring oxymoron. How can there be even a semblance of Christianity without Christ? It is impossible. It would be like having an alphabet without letters or having a sumptuous meal without food.

The great London preacher Charles Haddon Spurgeon said, "A sermon without Christ is like a brook without water; a cloud without rain; a well which mocks the traveler; a tree twice dead, plucked up by the root; a sky without a sun; a night without a star. It was a realm of death – a place of mourning for angels and laughter for devils. O Christian, we must have Christ."

I had a former church member call recently and inform me that she had visited a Georgia Baptist church and that the name of Jesus was not mentioned in the entire sermon. Hopefully, that Sunday was an anomaly, a rare exception, a unique day unlike any other day in the church's history. Do Baptist churches – Christian churches – dare conduct a service where Christ is not at the very heart of the service, the theme of every song and sermon?

In other churches Christ may be preached, but is He lifted up as Savior and Lord, as the only way to God? Or is he mentioned as some kind of good luck charm, as the key to prosperity or the steppingstone to success?

In his book Horton writes, "The focus still seems to be on us and our activity rather than on God and His work in Jesus Christ. In all of these approaches, there is the tendency to make God a supporting character in our own live movie rather than to be rewritten as new characters in God's drama of redemption.

"Assimilating the disruptive, surprising, and disorienting power of the gospel to the felt needs, moral crises, and socio-political headlines of our passing age, we end up saying very little that the world could not hear from Dr. Phil, Dr. Laura, or Oprah."

In commenting on Horton's book Richard Doster declares, "It's motivated by a concern that there's this creeping fog of what sociologist Christian Smith called 'moralistic-therapeutic-deism.' This has turned God into a tool we can use rather than the object of our faith and worship. I'm concerned that the Gospel is being taken for granted, that Christ is a sort of life coach, but not the Savior.... There is a shallowing of the Christian faith."

In contrast to that you have the example of Spurgeon. Someone said to him, "All of your sermons sound exactly the same. Why is that?"

Spurgeon responded, "Because I just take a text anywhere in the Bible, and then make a beeline straight to the cross."

The Gospel is essentially the death, burial, and resurrection of Christ. Paul declared, "For I am not ashamed of the Gospel of Christ, for it is the power of God to salvation for everyone who believes, for the Jew first and also for the Greek" (Rom. 1:16).

Michael Spencer, who is a Southern Seminary graduate, Baptist pastor, and author of Internet Monk (www.internetmonk.com), writes on the subject of Christless preaching and pens, "I've just heard yet another sermon that never mentions Jesus anywhere or in any way."

Then Spencer adds, "No, no, it is not an oddity or anywhere close to the first time. I'll estimate that in the last five years I've heard at least fifty sermons that totally omitted any mention of Jesus, and many more where there was no real reason for Jesus to be included – sermons that could have been preached by Jews, Mormons, even Muslims in some cases, without any real changes. Some of those sermons were preached by ordained, and often, educated, Baptist ministers."

Horton asks, "What would things look like if Satan actually took over a city?" He suggests that most would imagine mayhem on a massive scale: "widespread violence, deviant sexualities, pornography in every vending machine, churches closed down, and worshipers dragged off to City Hall."

Over a half century ago, Donald Grey Barnhouse, pastor of Philadelphia's Tenth Presbyterian Church, gave his CBS radio audience a different picture of what it would look like if Satan took control of a town in America.

Barnhouse said, "All of the bars and pool halls would be closed, pornography banished, pristine streets and sidewalks would be occupied by tidy pedestrians who smiled at each other. There would be no swearing. The kids would answer 'Yes, sir,' 'No, ma'am,' and the churches would be full on Sunday … where Christ is not preached."

Horton adds, "Satan lost the war on Good Friday and Easter, but has shifted his strategy to a guerilla struggle to keep the world from hearing the Gospel that dismantles his kingdom of darkness."

In preaching we must do exactly what Peter enjoined us to do in I Peter 2:9 when he wrote, "Declaring the excellencies of Him (Christ) who has called us out of darkness and into his marvelous light."

Paul declared, "I am determined not to know anything else save Jesus Christ and Him crucified."

I have heard a lot of Georgia Baptist pastors preach and I think they are among the finest, but in order to be faithful to our calling we must forever lift up the Lord Jesus.

Attacks on National Day of Prayer may be a Good Thing

The publishing date for this issue of The Christian Index, May 6th, is also the National Day of Prayer in the United States. Throughout the nation's history there have been several national days of prayer, but the idea of an annual National Day of Prayer was introduced by evangelist Billy Graham in 1952.

Graham was hosting a rally in Washington, D.C., in which he called for a National Day of Prayer and envisioned a "great spiritual awakening" for the capital with "thousands coming to Jesus Christ."

Graham's idea was introduced in the House the next day, then later to the Senate as a measure against the "corrosive forces of communism which seek simultaneously to destroy our democratic way of life and the faith in an Almighty God on which it is based."

On April 17, 1952 President Harry S. Truman signed the bill proclaiming each following president must declare a National Day of Prayer at an appropriate date of his choice.

In 1988, at the urging of Campus Crusade for Christ and the National Day of Prayer Committee, Congress enacted legislation requiring the president to issue an annual proclamation declaring the first Thursday in May as the National Prayer Day. President Ronald Reagan signed the bill into law.

However, last month U.S. District Judge Barbara B. Crabb (who was appointed to her position by Jimmy Carter in 1979) of Madison, Wis., ruled that the National Day of Prayer is unconstitutional. The federal judge stated that the law designating the day and requiring a presidential proclamation for the day violates the First Amendment prohibition against laws respecting an establishment of religion.

Crabb's ruling has received mixed reviews. Some have criticized the judge's pronouncement. Milwaukee Archbishop Jerome Listecki suggested that eliminating the day of prayer would constitute "a missed opportunity to acknowledge our nation's identity, which was founded on our dependence on God.

Then you have author Tommi Avicolli Mecca, who writes, "A day of prayer is a stupid idea! It's time to turn the tables on the religious right.

"Atheists, agnostics, and other nonbelievers (about 22 percent of Americans, according to the latest study) should seize the moment and declare the day as our own, a 'National Day Without Prayer.' On the first Thursday of next month (May), we should wear T-shirts and buttons declaring ourselves free from religion."

The differences of opinion simply illustrate the cultural war we are facing. William Dembski might well view this debate as healthy. Dembski is a research professor in philosophy at Southwestern Seminary, a prolific author, and a champion of intelligent design.

In his book "The End of Christianity," Dembski recalls what he encountered in his pursuit of a postdoctoral fellowship at the Massachusetts Institute of Technology (MIT). He mused, "I was struck by how readily my colleagues regarded Christianity as passé. They did not think that

Christianity was dangerous and had to be stamped out. They thought that Christianity lacked vitality and deserved to be ignored.

"Its stamping out was, in their minds, a long-accomplished fact – the war was over and Christianity had lost."

Dembski contends that much has changed in our culture in the last 20 years. He insists that the intelligent design movement has grown internationally and that "Western intellectuals" have begun to take seriously the claim that life and the cosmos are the product of intelligence.

Dembski professes that atheistic materialism is being held in question and that Christianity is no longer being ignored, but "on the table for discussion."

"This is not to say that the discussion is friendly or that Christianity is about to find widespread acceptance at places like MIT," Dembski asserts.

"Instead of routinely ignoring Christianity as they did 20 years ago, many Western intellectuals now treat it with open contempt, expending a great many words to denounce it. But this is progress. The dead are ignored and forgotten. The living are scorned and reviled."

Perhaps we should be encouraged that federal judges want to strip away the National Day of Prayer. Maybe we should be buoyed by the fact that Christianity is under assault in America today.

Maybe we should take heart that atheist Richard Dawkins in his book "The God Delusion" portrays the Judeo-Christian God as "arguably the most unpleasant character in all of fiction. Jealous and proud of it; a petty, unjust unforgiving control-freak; a vindictive, bloodthirsty ethnic-cleanser; a misogynistic homophobic racist, infanticidal, genocidal, filicidal, pestilential, megalomaniacal, sadomasochistic, capriciously malevolent bully."

I deplore Dawkins' characterization of God, but, at least, the Almighty and Christianity are not being ignored. Maybe we are not as Laodicea-like as we have thought. Maybe the potshots at Christianity will arouse us, stir us, challenge us, and motivate us to greater faith and decisive action.

Maybe we will fight to keep the National Day of Prayer a part of the American way of life. But better yet, maybe we will recommit our lives to "pray without ceasing" as the Apostle Paul admonished us to do.

Here is my prayer for the nation: Our Father which art in heaven. Holy is Your name. You alone are worthy of honor and glory. We come before You today to ask for Your forgiveness for our sins of pride, idolatry, apathy, selfishness, greed, and hypocrisy. We have misappropriated Your values and like the people in Isaiah's day we have "called evil good, and good evil, and put darkness for light and light for darkness." Forgive us, Oh Lord.

We have broken Your laws, desecrated Your holy day, protected pornographers, abortionists, and those who have exploited people made in Your image. We have taken the government that You created for good and abused it. We have taken what You have made to be holy and perverted it. We have taken what You designed to be special and made it sordid.

Forgive us, Lord. Do not give us what we deserve, but grant us mercy and grace, Your undeserved favor. Grant our president the wisdom and faith to lead our nation in ways that are pleasing to You. Instill in the members of Congress the knowledge and understanding to enact laws that protect the sanctity of life from the unborn to the elderly and help them to promote the good of all people. Grant wisdom and faith to all those who have authority over us. Protect our military and watch over them with Your loving care.

Most of all, send Your Holy Spirit upon our beloved country. Grant that we might be worthy of another spiritual awakening. Make us a people of faith in a time of uncertainty. Help us to trust and obey the one true God, who is our Creator, our Sustainer, and our Redeemer through Jesus Christ, our Lord. For it is His name that we pray. Amen.

What are you Substituting for the Great Commission?

Much has been said in recent days about the Great Commission. When I give to my church I am supporting the Great Commission, but I must also openly, vocally, deliberately become a personal soul winner in my Jerusalem. I am afraid many Christians are no longer engaged in personal evangelism.

Unfortunately, we have substituted other things for being personally engaged in winning people to faith in Christ. First of all, we have substituted theological discussions for personal evangelism.

The Apostle James wrote about those who have forsaken some of the great marks of the Christian faith and have "turned aside unto vain jangling." The New American Standard Bible calls it "fruitless discussion."

There are many pastors and church members who like to hang out at Starbucks, drink lattes, and pursue the latest theological and philosophical fads. Endless papers, countless blogs, and tortured studies are issued constantly to defend this or that aspect of theology.

Even if the discussions are stimulating and enlightening, they are problematic if we do not act on what we learn about God's truth.

In fact, we are responsible for what we know. James 4:17 declares "Therefore to him that knoweth to do good and doeth it not, to him it is sin." When we know truth and refuse to act on it we simply heap judgment upon ourselves.

We must never substitute theological discussions for personal evangelism.

Secondly, I fear that we have substituted the social gospel for personal evangelism. Historically, the social gospel movement was most prominent in the late 19th century and the early 20th century. The movement became prominent through the leadership of men like Richard Ely, Washington Gladden, and Walter Rauschenbusch. These leaders were primarily post-millennial and believed that the Second Coming could not happen until humankind rids itself of social evils by human effort.

"In His Steps," a book published by Charles M. Sheldon in 1897, was one of the most influential books in the Social Gospel movement. According to Sheldon, American society would experience a dramatic transformation if only people would base their public and private actions on the answer to the simple question of "What would Jesus do?"

The social gospel worked to enhance social justice and equality for all people, sought to alleviate the suffering and poverty that plagued the planet, and was manifested in good works and helpful deeds.

Today it seems to me that we have the social gospel creeping back into faith. Many of our mission trips include building churches, renovating houses, landscaping, feeding the poor, clothing the needy, providing medical and dental service, and serving the physical and material needs of certain communities.

While all that is commended by Jesus, it is nothing more than the social gospel if it does not ultimately issue forth in a personal witness. It is not always easy to present the Gospel in certain situations, so in many cases we have begun to substitute the social gospel for personal evangelism.

Steve Sjogren calls this social gospel "servant evangelism" in his book "Conspiracy of Kindness." Sometimes these methods of evangelism that are strong in kindness are weak in the kind of confrontation that is necessary to win the lost.

In the July 2 issue of the Wall Street Journal Brad Greenberg writes: "Christians today typically travel abroad to serve others, but not necessarily to spread the gospel."

Greenberg adds, "Today, Christian missionaries need to balance both actions and words. The overwhelming majority of American missionaries today are 'vacationaries.' Joining mission trips of two weeks or less, they serve in locales where Christianity already predominates.

"This is especially apparent in the surge of American Christians now working for African orphanages or fighting the child-sex trade in Thailand. Although no hard numbers are available, missions experts note rising interest in strictly social justice and humanitarian work, even on short-term visits."

Whether we are ministering at home or abroad, we must never substitute the social gospel for personal evangelism.

Thirdly, some folks substitute political activism for sharing the glorious Gospel. I believe God's people need to be involved in the political process. In fact, I think we need to get involved at the precinct level. If we fail to get involved at that level so often when the general election comes our only choice is between the devil and a witch.

However, our salvation is not going to come from the Gold Dome in Atlanta or the nation's capital in Washington. Our salvation is from Jesus Christ alone and we must share Him at every opportunity. Political activism is no substitute for personal evangelism.

Fourthly, serving the church is no substitute for telling the good news that Jesus saves. However, so many Christians have become keepers of the aquarium instead of fishers of men. We do a lot of church work, but neglect the work of the church – evangelism.

We can oil the organizational machinery, form multiple committees, restructure this and that, massage the programs, tweak the worship services, plan, and strategize, but if the programs and ministries of the church are not ultimately designed to lead people to faith in Christ we are just cumbering the ground with things that are tertiary in nature.

I once had a Sunday School secretary who was faithful to get the report of all the classes. He prided himself on being precise in his mathematical calculations. He claimed that because of the meticulous work his position required that he could not attend a Bible study class and even worked through the worship hour. He was committed to his task, but he never once shared his faith so far as I know even though he vehemently claimed to be a child of God.

Serving the church is no substitute for personal evangelism.

Finally, Christian fellowship is no substitute for proclaiming the unsearchable riches of Christ. Some churches focus on fellowship. They seem to be more like a travel agency, planning trips, or a country club, having social activities, or a sports entity, organizing athletic events.

I agree that "the fellowship of kindred minds is like to that above," but the truth is that we will have all eternity to enjoy fellowship with the saints of God. No one likes fellowship, fun, and communion with the saints more than I, but Christian fellowship is no substitute for personal evangelism.

If you are substituting anything for personal evangelism you are substituting brass for gold.

An Oversimplification
That Cannot be Denied

As a child, I remember reading a book about Hans Brinker and The Silver Skates. Tucked away within the novel is a story about a Dutch boy who saved his country by putting his finger in a leaking dike. The boy stayed there all night, in spite of the cold, until the adults of the village found him and made the necessary repairs.

There are many versions of this story. One version told by Dr. Boli reveals that although the heroic young lad plugged the leak it was only the first of many leaks that developed over a period of time. The city fathers visited the schools of Holland and managed to persuade other young boys to use their fingers to plug the additional leaks with the promise of awarding them a Certificate of Good Citizenship.

Over the course of time the old, disintegrating dike sprung so many leaks that there were no more boys available to plug the holes.

Have you ever felt like your life was springing so many leaks that you didn't know where to start plugging the holes? Sometimes we experience financial loss, relational disappointments, vocational setbacks, emotional challenges, physical struggles, and spiritual trials. It becomes hard to know where to start plugging the leaks and putting the pieces together.

And what about the church? The pastors and lay leaders decide to evaluate the health of their church and discover that there are multiple problems. The difficulties include poor signage, inadequate parking, a cool reception to guests, unattractive facilities, ill-equipped Sunday School teachers, an unacceptable worship style, and uninspiring worship services. Where do you start when there are so many leaks to plug? So many problems to solve?

Finally, what do you do when the whole nation is in crisis, when the government, like a Holland dike, is springing leaks just about everywhere?

Recent headlines from newspapers across the nation announced that the recession is officially over, but most find that difficult to believe. The announcement sounds rather hollow to those who have had foreclosures on their homes, to those who have lost their jobs, to those who have heard empty campaign promises.

Winston Churchill said, "So they (the government) go on in a strange paradox, decided only to be undecided, resolved to be irresolute, adamant for drift, solid for fluidity, all-powerful to be impotent."

Perhaps it was Churchill's assessment of the government that inspired Ken Huber to say, "If we lie to Congress, it's a felony, but if the Congress lies to us it's just politics."

Huber didn't stop there. He added, "The government spends millions to rehabilitate criminals and they do almost nothing for the victims. You can kill an unborn child, but it's wrong to execute a mass murderer.

"We don't burn books in America, now we rewrite them. We got rid of the communist and socialist threat by renaming them progressives. We are unable to close our border with Mexico, but have no problem protecting the 38th parallel in Korea.

"You can have pornography on TV or the Internet, but you better not put a nativity scene in a public park during Christmas. We can use a human fetus for medical research, but it's wrong to use an animal.

"We take money from those who work hard for it and give it to those who don't want to work. We all support the Constitution, but only when it supports our political ideology. We still have freedom of speech, but only if we are being politically correct.

"Parenting has been replaced with Ritalin and video games. The land of opportunity is now the land of handouts. The similarity between Hurricane Katrina and the Gulf oil spill is that neither president did anything to help."

So, how do we handle a major crisis today? The government appoints a committee to determine who's at fault, then threatens them, passes a law, raises our taxes, and tells us the problem is solved so they can get back to their re-election campaign.

It may seem like an oversimplification, but the only answer to the leaks in our personal dikes, our church dikes, and our national dikes is Jesus Christ, the Son of God. That Christ is the answer to our problems and crises is so evident than even an atheist has admitted it.

Matthew Parris is an avowed atheist. He recently traveled to Nyasaland (modern day Malawi), the country he knew as a boy. In Malawi Parris viewed the work of a small British charity that had been at work in the African country.

Parris admitted, "It inspired me, renewing my flagging faith in development charities. But traveling in Malawi refreshed another belief, too, one I've been trying to banish all my life, but an observation I've been unable to avoid since my African childhood. It confounds my ideological beliefs, stubbornly refuses to fit my worldview, and has embarrassed my growing belief that there is no God.

"Now a confirmed atheist, I've become convinced of the enormous contribution that Christian evangelism makes in Africa; sharply distinct from the work of secular NGOs, government projects, and international aid efforts. These alone will not do. Education and training alone will not do. In Africa Christianity changes people's hearts. It brings a spiritual transformation. The rebirth is real. The change is good."

The Christianity Parris encountered in Africa is the kind of Christianity we need in America – not a diluted, cultural Christianity but a vital, authentic Christianity that is dynamic in nature. That kind of Christianity would quell much of the criticism being hurled at the Church.

It would help restore the consensus that Christianity has lost in this nation. That kind of Christianity would impact the educational system, entertainment industry, press, politicians, and every major area of our society.

Unfortunately, what we have parading around as Christianity today is such a poor imitation of the real thing that atheists are confirmed in their godless ideology. Let's live in such a way that atheists question their foolish worldview and Christ is revealed as the answer to our most adverse circumstances.

The Reality of the Resurrection

In college and seminary, I studied neo-orthodox theologians like Rudolph Bultmann, who would never assert that the resurrection is a historical reality. He purported that it was the believer's subjective experience.

Bultmann's view was that we can't know any historical details about the Resurrection, but we only know that the early church kept believing and proclaiming Jesus after his crucifixion.

Peter Jennings was a Canadian-American journalist, news anchor and the sole anchor of ABC's World News Tonight from 1983 until his death in 2005. He died from complications of lung cancer.

Jennings said, "I was raised with the notion that it was okay to ask questions, and it was okay to say, 'I'm not sure.' I believe, but I'm not quite so certain about the resurrection."

Bultmann sidestepped the resurrection and Jennings doubted it, but you must believe it to be saved. Paul said, "That if thou shalt confess with thy mouth the Lord Jesus, and shalt believe in thine heart that God hath raised him from the dead, thou shalt be saved" (Rom. 10:9).

There is no salvation without believing in the resurrection of Christ.

Martin Luther said, "Our Lord has written the promise of resurrection, not in books alone, but in every leaf in springtime."

Consider some of the proofs of the resurrection.

First, there was the empty tomb where Jesus had been interred and the grave clothes left in the tomb, both of which verify the resurrection of Christ. If those who opposed Christ wished to silence His disciples all they had to do was produce a body, but they could not (John 20:3-9).

Second, the infallible Word of God speaks often of the resurrection of Jesus Christ. It is foretold by the Psalms (16:10), announced by Christ (Mark 9:9-10; John 2:19-22) and proclaimed by the apostles (Acts 2:32; 3:15). The Gospel writers, Matthew, Mark, Luke and John, each gave their own eyewitness account of the risen Son of God.

The Bible validates the resurrection in many ways, including: the empty tomb (John 20:1-9), the testimony of the angels (Matt. 28:5-7), the knowledge of His enemies (Matt. 28:1-15), many infallible proofs (John 20: 20,27; Acts 1:3), and His multiple appearances after the resurrection – even to five hundred people at one time (I Cor. 15:6).

Third, a convincing argument for the resurrection is the unswerving commitment of the disciples of Christ who saw, heard, touched and ate with the Lord after his resurrection and dared to proclaim the message of the risen Savior.

At Jesus' death they were dejected and fearful but soon they were radically different. They risked their lives repeatedly to preach about Jesus. People don't put their lives on the line for things they don't believe. The disciples never wavered in their belief in Jesus' resurrection. None of them ever changed their story under the pain of persecution.

In fact, when Peter and the other disciples were brought before the council for preaching about the resurrection, Peter declared, "We ought to obey God rather than men. The God of our fathers raised up Jesus, whom ye slew and hanged on a tree" (Acts 5: 29-30).

After Peter's comments he and the other disciples were beaten and threatened, but left the council "rejoicing that they were counted worthy to suffer shame for his name."

A fourth proof of the resurrection is the changed lives of those who have called upon His name. There are millions across the globe who can say, "I serve a risen Savior. He's in the world today. I know that He is living whatever men say... You ask me how I know he lives? He lives within my heart."

Fifth, there were thousands upon thousands of people who were instantly and immediately converted after Christ was raised from the dead. The disciples preached to many who didn't really want to believe the Gospel, but in view of the testimony of the witnesses to the resurrection and the power of the Holy Spirit even hostile audiences repented and believed on Jesus.

A perfect illustration of this truth is the conversion of Saul of Tarsus. He traveled to Damascus to persecute the church, but was dramatically converted before arriving in the city. Logically, if Jesus had not been raised from the dead, Saul would have carried out his mission and exposed Jesus as a fraud who couldn't conquer death.

Sixth, there are also many historical, non-biblical accounts of the resurrection of Christ. Titus Flavius Josephus was a first century Roman-Jewish historian, who recorded Jewish history with a special emphasis on first century and the First Jewish-Roman War, which resulted in the destruction of Jerusalem in 70 AD. He has been credited with recording some of the earliest history of Jesus Christ outside the gospels. His insights into first century Judaism and the background of Christianity are extremely valuable and reliable.

Josephus wrote, "About this time appeared Jesus, a wise man (if indeed it is right to call him a man; for He was a worker of astonishing deeds, a teacher of such men as receive the truth with joy), and He drew to Himself many Jews (many also of Greeks). This was the Christ. And when Pilate, at the denunciation of those that are foremost among us, had condemned Him to the cross, those who had first loved Him did not abandon him (for He appeared to them alive again on the third day, the holy prophets having foretold this and countless other marvels about Him.) The tribe of Christians named after Him did not cease to this day."

Pliny the Younger, Suetonius and Tacitus, Roman authors and historians, all give first century accounts of the reality of Christ and the advancement of Christianity to Rome.

By observing these Roman and Jewish historians who inscribed their chronicles outside the New Testament canon, it seems implausible to suppose that Jesus' existence was the product of fiction. In fact, their works seem to corroborate the historicity of Christ and his resurrection. They were men who were basically unsympathetic to the messages of Jesus and proponents of animosity toward the Christian cause, yet their writings seem to verify the biblical record of the reality of the resurrection.

Neither holy Scripture or secular history answers every question about the resurrection, but they do help us to understand and when our understanding is fueled by faith we stand ready to celebrate Easter and all the victories and promises it affords.

Osama Bin Laden's Confession
of Christ is Forthcoming

I had just gotten home from having preached at Liberty Baptist Church in Dalton on Sunday evening. I had changed clothes and sat down to relax for an hour or so before retiring for the evening when the message came across the bottom of our television screen stating that a breaking news story was about to be released from the White House.

My wife and I began to speculate as to what kind of breaking news story we might anticipate. Were more tornadoes headed for Georgia? Had there been an attempt on the president's life? Had there been another terrorist attack? Had Iran or North Korea launched a nuclear missile?

Then we heard that the president would be making an announcement relative to Osama bin Laden. We waited and waited. Finally, the president walked down the red carpet in the East Room of the White House to announce that bin Laden had been killed by the American military's Special Forces and that "justice has been done."

The President stated, "For over two decades, bin Laden has been Al Qaeda's leader and symbol. The death of bin Laden marks the most significant achievement to date in our nation's effort to defeat Al Qaeda. But his death does not mark the end of our effort. There's no doubt that

Al Qaeda will continue to pursue attacks against us. We must and we will remain vigilant at home and abroad."

The next morning The Wall Street Journal reported, "The development capped a manhunt of almost a decade for the architect of the September 11, 2001 attacks that left 3,000 people dead and dramatically altered U. S. foreign policy and the nation's sense of security."

A US official indicated bin Laden's body has been buried at sea and was handled in accordance with Islamic tradition that a Muslim should be buried within 24 hours of death.

Finding a country willing to accept the remains of the world's most wanted terrorist would have been difficult, the official said. Even Saudi Arabia, bin Laden's country of birth, refused to accept the body of the arch-terrorist for burial. So, the US decided that a burial at sea would be both logical and appropriate.

The news of bin Laden's death ignited an outpouring of emotion as crowds gathered outside the White House shouting

"USA! USA!"

At the Ground Zero site jubilant crowds were waving American flags, cheering, shouting, and singing the Star-Spangled Banner. Throughout downtown Washington, drivers honked their horns deep into the night.

Morning newspapers from coast to coast had headlines that emblazoned the news of bin Laden's death. Consider some of those headlines:

"Americans Kill bin Laden" - The Houston Chronicle

"U.S. kills bin Laden a decade after 9/11" – The Charlotte Observer

"Bin Laden is Dead" – The New York Times

"Osama bin Laden Killed: 'Justice Has Been Done'" – The Washington Post

Osama bin Laden, Terror Mastermind, Is Reported Dead" – The Wall Street Journal

"Rot in Hell" - New York Daily News

"The Butcher of 9/11 is DEAD – The San Francisco Examiner"

"Got Him (Shot Him)" - The Saint Petersburg Times

CNN reported the comments of former Arkansas Governor Mike Huckabee, who stated, "It is unusual to celebrate a death, but today Americans and decent people the world over cheer the news that madman, murderer and terrorist Osama bin Laden is dead. Welcome to hell, bin Laden. Let us all hope that his demise will serve notice to Islamic radicals the world over that the United States will be relentless in tracking down and terminating those who would inflict terror, mayhem and death on any of our citizens."

However, not everyone was cheering the death of the mass murder. On Monday, Hamas condemned the killing by US forces of Osama bin Laden and mourned him as an "Arab holy warrior"

Radical Islamic websites praised bin Laden as a "shaheed" or martyr. One headline asserted, "The Lion of Jihad was killed in a fierce battle." One poster proclaimed, "Teary eyes and sad hearts go out to you, the dearest and most noble of people."

But how should we feel about bin Laden's death? First of all, I agree with President Obama and echo his words, "Justice has been done." Proverbs 28:4-5 states, "They that forsake the law praise the wicked: but such as keep the law contend with them. Evil men understand not judgment: but they that seek the Lord understand all things." Only lawless men would praise the kingpin of Al Qaeda. And only the wicked would think he should be given a free pass for his evil deeds.

But should we, as followers of Christ, rejoice over the death of this diabolical villian? Consider Ezekiel 33:11: "Say unto them, as I live, saith the Lord God, I have no pleasure in the death of the wicked: but that the wicked turn from his way and live." If God takes no pleasure in the death of the wicked (and bin Laden would certainly be numbered among the wicked), should we?

Furthermore, Jesus said, "Ye have heard that it hath been said, thou shalt love thy neighbor, and hate thine enemy. But I say unto you, love your enemies, bless them that curse you, do good to them that hate you, and pray for them which despitefully use you, and persecute you" (Matt. 5:43-33).

Here is another consideration: There was a time when I was an enemy of God. Paul wrote, "For if, when we were enemies, we were reconciled to God by the death of his Son, much more, being reconciled, we shall be saved by his life" (Rom.5:10). Christ died for his enemies.

Although I am grateful that justice has been executed and that Osama's reign of terror has ended, it would be very hypocritical for me to rejoice over bin Laden's death when I was once in the same general category as him – an unredeemed sinner, an enemy of God.

It may be a fleshly thought, but I am quite certain that I will rejoice in the day that bin Laden bows before Christ and admits that Jesus is Lord. Sadly, his acknowledgement of Christ's Lordship will not be for salvation, but as a condemned, unredeemed sinner for eventually, "every knee (will) bow ... and every tongue (will) confess that Jesus Christ is Lord."

A Jack Kevorkian or a Hippocrates

On June 3 Raymond Zack, age 52, died in the waters off Crown Memorial Beach in Alameda County, CA while first responders watched. Zack, who was suicidal, walked into 54-degree water that was neck deep and died of hypothermia after being in the water for one hour.

Lt. Sean Lynch, APD Investigations Divisions commander, stated, "The victim was six-foot-three, three hundred pounds; and his going into the water was a deliberate act. This person didn't want to be rescued, and we can't allow other people to be endangered needlessly."

Interestingly, the Alameda County Fire Department, Oakland Fire Department, Alameda County Sheriff Department, Oakland Police and East Bay Regional Park Police were on the scene, but no one tried to rescue the distressed man.

The Oakland Tribune reported, "Firefighters say they could not enter the water because budget cuts two years ago did not allow the department to recertify in land-based water rescues. A rescue attempt would have opened the city to liability. Police said they did not know if Zach was violent, armed or had drugs in his system."

The Coast Guard dispatched a 25-foot propeller-drive rescue vessel, but Zack stood in water too shallow for the boat to reach. The Coast Guard also sent a helicopter, but it was involved in another mission and could not rescue the man because it had to return to the Air Station in San Francisco to refuel.

When Zach lost consciousness and drifted to within 50 yards of the shore an unidentified woman, whom police called a Good Samaritan, went into the water to help bring him to land. The Alameda Fire Department transported the victim to Alameda Hospital where he was pronounced dead.

This tragic story reminds me of three things. First, it reminds me of church members who idly stand by and watch their churches die. In some ways they resemble Dr. Jack Kevorkian, who was known for championing a terminal patient's right to die via physician-assisted suicides.

When resident church members of anemic churches become apathetic and indifferent in their church attendance, service and stewardship they actually contribute to the death of their churches. Most churches have enough resident church members to enable their church to be strong, viable and dynamic, but alas, countless churches have Jack Kevorkian members who are doing more to contribute to the death of their churches than to their life and vibrancy.

Church members who have abandoned the church or are members in absentia need to consider what the world would be like without the church. The contribution that the church has made to education, wellness, the welfare of children and the home, disaster relief, missions and the common good of mankind is unfathomable.

Secondly, the story about Raymond Zack reminds me of Christians who never share their faith with the lost. People are not just tall and short, rich and poor, educated and unlearned, Republicans and Democrats, conservatives and liberals, refined and ill mannered, healthy and infirmed. Ultimately, they are either saved or lost. Yet so many of us seem to be content to let those who are lost continue their descent into hell without offering them the solution to their dreadful dilemma.

Like the first responders in Alameda County who watched as Raymond Zack died of hypothermia, most Christians seem to be content to watch friends, neighbors, even relatives go out into a Christless eternity without a witness.

What would we say of a watchman who went to sleep and thus failed to warn his city of the enemy army surrounding the city with the intent to kill and destroy? What would we think of the mother who failed to rescue her baby from the rattlesnake that had stealthily crawled into the baby's crib? What would we think of the doctor who had the ability to perform the surgery necessary to save a man's life and refused to do so?

And what must God think of those of us who have experienced His redeeming love and forgiveness but keep our salvation as a hidden treasure just like a miser would hoard his wealth while others around him are dying of starvation?

Thirdly, the story of Raymond Zack is painfully reminiscent of Americans who watch the nation sink into secularism and socialism and do nothing to reverse the downward trend.

Consider the following quote attributed to Alexander Tytler, Scottish jurist and professor at the University of Edinburgh: "A democracy cannot exist as a permanent form of government. It can only exist until the voters discover that they can vote themselves largesse (money/charity) from the public treasury. From that moment on, the majority always votes for the candidates promising the most benefits from the public treasury with the result that a democracy always collapses over loose fiscal policy, always followed by a dictatorship. The average age of the world's greatest civilizations has been 200 years.

"Great nations rise and fall. The people go from bondage to spiritual truth, from spiritual truth to great courage, from courage to liberty, from liberty to abundance, from abundance to selfishness, from selfishness to complacency, from complacency to apathy, from apathy to dependence, from dependence back again to bondage."

I would surmise that on the above compendium of the stages of a democracy that America may be somewhere between complacency to apathy and apathy to dependence. Based on that assumption, we are on a fast track to bondage. Apathy must be put to death. It is time for Christians to be assertive, involved, active, vigilant, and engaged in fervent prayer.

Our first response is not to march on Washington, write our representative in Congress, sign a petition, pass a resolution or join the "Tea Party." Our first response is to live and serve in such a way that God can smile upon us with His loving favor.

Hippocrates, often called the father of Western medicine, said, "Make a habit of two things: to help; or at lease to do no harm."

Decide if you want to be a Kevorkian or a Hippocrates.

Extreme Christianity

Back in February I saw an advertisement in a magazine hawking extreme Valentine gifts. The primary gift was a "decadent basket of two buttery and crisp caramel corns – traditional and chocolate drizzled, dark chocolate covered roasted almonds, rich and crunchy peanut brittle, creamy caramel filled Ghirardelli Chocolate squares, crunchy chocolate English toffee all tied up with a red ribbon for Valentine giving."

The extreme Valentine's Day gift looked like nothing more than an industrial-sized box of calorie laden "goodies" for the little lady in your life.

I cut the ad out of the magazine and put it in my briefcase, thinking I would get that gift for my wife, but I ended up getting her a weed eater instead.

No, I am kidding. If I got her a weed eater I would probably be wearing it as a necktie. I guess that would be an extreme necktie.

But we live in a day of extremes – extreme sports, extreme personal makeovers, extreme home makeovers, extreme couponing, extreme fitness, extreme science, extreme music, extreme engineering, etc.

In extreme sports skateboarders look for the most dangerous and hazardous obstacles to traverse, surfers look for the most intimidating and ferocious waves, hang gliders look for the most precipitous cliffs and the most blustery conditions and snow skiers look for the most formidable slopes with some even jumping out of helicopters to heighten the thrill of the descent.

Those who engage in extreme sports live by the motto: "If you are not living on the edge you are just taking up space." They believe that life is an adventure book waiting to be written, that they are the authors and their goal is to make their story rich and colorful.

There was a time when climbing Mount Everest would have been considered an extreme venture. I remember when the world celebrated Sir Edmund Percival Hillary's successful ascent to the summit of the world's tallest mountain on May 29, 1953.

However, today there are scores of people who climb the 29,028 ft. mountain every year and many of them look for even more daunting challenges.

There is an extreme sport today called BASE-jumping. It is an activity that employs an initially packed parachute to jump from fixed objects. "B.A.S.E." is an acronym that stands for four categories of fixed objects from which one can jump: buildings, antennae, spans (bridges), and earth (cliffs).

B.A.S.E. jumpers typically have a goal of jumping off each of the four fixed objects. This sport is incredibly dangerous, and a website has been established to list the names and circumstances of the extreme sports enthusiasts who have jumped to their death. The website I visited listed 161 fatalities.

Every year West Virginia has what they call a Bridge Day. As many as 200,000 people have gathered at the New River Bridge to watch hundreds of people jump off the bridge into the river 876 feet below. On Bridge day in 2006 one of the jumpers, Brian Lee Schubert, fell to his death, because his parachute failed to open.

While most of us would think taking such risks is foolish, there is something within the human spirit that longs to achieve greater, nobler, higher goals. The motto for the Olympic games is "Citius, Altius, Fortius." These three Latin words mean "swifter, higher, stronger."

Leo Buscaglia, well known professor and author, once said, "The person who risks nothing, does nothing, has nothing, is nothing and becomes nothing. He may avoid suffering and sorrow, but he simply cannot learn, feel, change, grow or love."

It would be interesting to observe the transformation that would occur in the whole of our society if the guiding principles of the Olympic athletes, the daring spirit of those who engage in extreme sports and those who refuse to risk nothing could be transferred to every segment of our culture. Excellence would become the norm, boredom would be eliminated, everyone would have a passion to succeed.

I would particularly like to see more extreme Christians in our society – Christians who go the second mile, take up their cross, deny self, sacrifice for the cause of Christ, scorn the values of this world, boldly share their faith, embrace the concept of Jesus as Lord, and who truly "press toward the mark for the prize of the high calling of God in Christ Jesus."

But alas, Vance Havner said, "Most Christians are so subnormal, that if they ever became normal, many would think they are abnormal."

A.W. Tozer said, "The complacency of Christians is the scandal of Christianity."

If athletes can earnestly compete for a corruptible crown and extreme adventurers can risk life and limb for the thrill of the sport, why are Christians so reluctant to stand for truth, so hesitant to launch out into the deep, too fearful to own His cause and too lukewarm to ignite the fires of revival?

Resting upon the laurels of past victories is not sufficient for the challenges we are facing today. Refining the church's organizational structure is not going to change much of anything. Business as usual is not going to get the job done today.

The complacent church must become the committed church. The defeated church must become the dynamic church. The ordinary church must become the extraordinary church. The mediocre church must become militant church. The social church must become the Spirit-filled church. The anemic church must become the aggressive church. The beleaguered church must become the bold church. The placid church must become the passionate church.

In order for that to happen we simply need some extreme Christians.

How to Criticize your Pastor

It has been said that the only way to avoid criticism is to say nothing, do nothing and be nothing.

Randy Garner, an author and professor in behavioral sciences, writes, "Not surprisingly, members of the clergy are not immune from the difficulties or stresses associated with criticism and criticism-prone situations. Most pastors struggle with criticism. Criticism and conflict 'go with the territory' in professional ministry."

Having been the object of criticism as a pastor and newspaper editor I can sympathize with pastors, Christian workers and others who have been critiqued, evaluated, appraised, analyzed and judged.

However, let it be known that there are three kinds of criticism.

First, there is benevolent criticism. The purpose of this criticism is to help the one criticized; the critique takes the side of the person, is more positive than negative, and its aim is to improve, to protect, to warn and to help succeed.

Benevolent criticism is expressed in your presence and normally in private. It works for you and may be considered a gift of prudence. This kind of criticism brings new ideas, a wider perspective, provides a spring of courage and improves your life.

When I was in seminary I served as an interim youth pastor for a church that was also seeking a pastor, but the interim pastor, Dr. Norfleet Gardner, was an elderly gentleman who became a mentor to me. He would let me preach about once a month at the early Sunday morning service or on Sunday evening. After each sermon he would give me an evaluation, sometimes correcting my grammar, sometimes questioning my sermon construction and sometimes challenging my interpretation of a text.

Dr. Gardner was also extremely encouraging and won the right to criticize because of his frequent expressions of love and compassion. I know his criticism was benevolent. I knew he was interested in my greater good. When those who love you cannot tell you when something needs correction, trouble is close at hand.

Second, there is neutral or balanced criticism. This kind of criticism is indifferent or impartial to the person being criticized. This kind of criticism is simply meant to correct, to perfect, to remedy, to provide objectivity and to facilitate accuracy, precision and effectiveness.

I had a teacher in the fourth grade, Lila Belle Cox, who was larger than life both pedagogically and physically. Her handwriting was impeccable, and she wanted her students to write in cursive with meticulous care. She was no respecter of persons when it came to offering corrective criticism. She just simply wanted her students to write with a precise flowing style that was not only readable, but also elegant.

I didn't particularly appreciate Miss Cox when I was a fourth grader, but she gave me a desire to write with style and grace. In fact, if everyone had been under her tutelage we would not have to sign documents by both printing and writing our signatures. The cursive signature would be quite sufficient, because it could be easily read.

Thirdly, there is belligerent criticism. This kind of criticism is likely to come from those who are not interested in helping you, but who are out to get you. It focuses on judgment and blame. Quite often this kind of criticism comes from a mere evil disposition and deserves no retaliation. Just let the flame of belligerence consume itself.

When I editorialize on certain topics I know that I can expect some of this venomous criticism, but even when the criticism seems to be belligerent I try to examine it to see if there is some element of truth in the seemingly unwarranted diatribe that will provide some needed counsel or correction.

Garner's research and observation had led him to conclude that harsh, persistent criticism, is the leading reason for pastors leaving the ministry.

If you feel the need to criticize, what approach will you take? Will you become a benevolent, balanced or belligerent critic? Frank A. Clark stated, "Criticism, like rain, should be gentle enough to nourish a man's growth without destroying his roots."

Most people do not realize that pastors have to walk a tightrope to keep peace in the flock of God. They must satisfy people marked by generational gaps, polity preferences, methodological predilections, philosophical inclinations, theological differences and a variety of ideas about how long, loud and loving his sermons should be.

There are some pastors who give little evidence of a divine calling and are either using the ministry to promote their own personal agenda or have found a congregation as lukewarm as they are and that require nothing more than the little he is willing to give.

Most pastors, however, are under extreme pressure. They live in a glass house with their wife and children's lives being put under constant scrutiny. They have three sermons to prepare each week. They have hospital visits to make and counseling sessions with members who have a variety of problems. There are endless meetings pastors are required to attend. There are shut-ins who need to be visited and souls that need to be saved. The list of duties is endless.

Instead of hurling barbs, slings and arrows in the direction of the pastor, try love, kindness and grace. Pray for him and determine to give him your support so that your response to his ministry will insure his success. If criticism is necessary, try the benevolent kind.

We might all do well to remember the words of Theodore Roosevelt, 26th president of the United States, who said, "It is not the critic who counts; not the man who points out how the strong man stumbles, or where the doer of deeds could have done them better.

"The credit belongs to the man who is actually in the arena, whose face is marred by dust and sweat and blood, who strives valiantly; who errs and comes short again and again; because there is not effort without error and shortcomings; but who does actually strive to do the deed; who knows the great enthusiasm, the great devotion, who spends himself in a worthy cause, who at the best knows in the end the triumph of high achievement and who at the worst, if he fails, at least he fails while daring greatly. So that his place shall never be with those cold and timid souls who know neither victory or defeat."

Is Atheism Reasonable?

O n March 24 the atheist/agnostics/humanists had what they called the "largest gathering of the secular movement in world history." The so-called "Reason Rally" was held on the Washington Mall in the nation's capital.

Non-believers referred to the rally as their "coming-out party" and claim that in America their ranks outnumber all Jews, Muslims, Hindus, and Buddhists combined. Many contend that the fastest-growing religious group in America is this group with no religion.

The estimated crowd of 10,000, undeterred by the overcast skies and constant drizzle of rain, gathered to listen to speakers like Richard Dawkins, the British author of "The God Delusion." Dawkins proclaimed, "There are too many people in this country who have been cowed into fear of coming out as theists, secularists or agnostics."

In the midst of the crowd rose a crucifix with an affixed sign that declared, "Banish the Ten Commandments to the dustbin of history."

David Silverman, the head organizer of the event, stated, "We will never be closeted again." Other posters read, "Good without a god" and "Hi Mom! I'm an atheist."

Annie Laurie Gaylor of the Freedom From Religion Foundation, declared, "God fixation won't fix our nation, because nothing fails like prayer." Self-defined skeptic and columnist for Scientific American magazine Michael Shermer remarked, "This country was not built on religion and God. It was built on reason."

Thomas Paine, American Revolutionary, wrote the three parts to "Age of Reason" at the turn of the 19th century and stated, "I do not believe in the creed professed by the Jewish Church, by the Roman Church, by the Greek Church, by the Turkish Church, by the Protestant Church or by any church that I know of. My own mind is my own church."

What about those who deny that this country was built on religion and God? What about those who claim that their own mind is their church or that atheism is based on reason? What about those who say that religion is the antithesis of reason?

Atheists and secularists not only insist that their philosophy of life is based on reason, but suggest that the Christian worldview is based on irrationality and ignorance. Consider the following arguments against atheism. The only rational and reasonable conclusion is that an eternal Creator is the one responsible for reality as we know it.

Former atheist Lee Strobel commented, "Essentially, I realized that to stay an atheist, I would have to believe that nothing produces everything; non-life produces life; randomness produces fine-tuning; chaos produces information; unconsciousness produces consciousness; and non-reason produces reason.

"Those leaps of faith were simply too big for me to take, especially in light of the affirmative case for God's existence … In other words, in my assessment the Christian worldview accounted for the totality of the evidence much better than the atheistic worldview."

But let us consider not only the Designer; next, let us also consider the design. Living things are extremely complex. Ken Ham, founder and president of Answers in Genesis, states, "Evolutionary theory rests upon the premise that all biological systems could have evolved from progressively simpler systems."

The truth is that nature manifests a certain irreducible complexity. The eye is a prime example of an irreducible complex structure, due to its many elaborate and interlocking parts, seemingly all dependent upon one another. Creationist Jonathan Sarfati has described the eye as evolutionary biologists' greatest challenge as a superb example of irreducible complexity in God's creation.

So, atheists claim they have a corner on reason, but their explanation for cause and effect or Designer and design is incredibly irrational and unreasonable.

In Ecclesiastes 3:11 the Bible says, "He (God) has also set eternity in the hearts of men."

In every man there is an emptiness that only God can fill. When I was in college I took a course in anthropology and wrote a term paper on four aboriginal tribes in different parts of the world. Each tribe had some kind of inner longing for a supreme being, for some kind of religion.

Then, there is also the truth that morality exists. We were made in the image of God and therefore instinctively have a moral conscious. Romans 2:14-15 tells us that moral law is written in the hearts of men. In other words, men intuitively know right from wrong even without God's special revelation in Scripture or in Jesus Christ. If objective moral values exist, then God exists.

Everyone has some level of mental obligation to do good and avoid evil. Why else do we have laws, government, military, prisons, and self-improvement books? The atheistic view is incompatible with real moral obligation. Therefore, the theistic view, which is compatible with real moral obligation, must be correct.

Furthermore, atheists live in a world that is without any significant purpose. According to Sharefaith, an apologetics website, atheists must believe that "the things that resemble design are not designed, merely an appearance of such. Suffering has absolutely no meaning, mankind has no free will, and love is not love, simply the appearance of love.

Man is reduced to an animalistic nature where existence is boiled down to eating food and procreation; a place where asking the question, 'God, do you truly love me?' will never produce an answer. Never.

However, according to Sharefaith, Christians believe that, "Humans are fortunate creatures who do live in a world where God truly exists. There is tremendous suffering in the world, but mankind also experiences the thrills of joy and the comfort of love. Humans are not illusions of design, but according to the Bible, are 'fearfully and wonderfully made' by a loving and passionate God."

Christianity offers joy in the midst of sorrow, comfort in the midst of pain, significant answers in a world of questions, hope in a world of despair and a future that is brighter than the noonday sun.

Is atheism reasonable? It is about as reasonable as an aspirin dispensary in a leper colony, giving humming- bird wings to a skydiver, or throwing an anvil to a drowning man.

God said, "The fool has said in his heart, there is no God" (Psalm 14:1). The dictionary defines "fool" as "a person who lacks judgment or sense; a person who has been tricked or deceived into appearing stupid; a weak-minded or idiotic person."

So, is atheism reasonable? I think not. The "Reason Rally" was a gathering of fools. However, the ten thousand who gathered in Washington were no more fools than any of us before Christ came to rule in our hearts.

A Nation of Fools is Surely Doomed'

Dietrich Bonhoeffer, a German Lutheran pastor and theologian, was vehemently opposed to the Nazi dictatorship and set himself against the euthanasia programs and genocide Hitler foisted upon the Jews and others.

When I was in college I read Dietrich Bonhoeffer's book "The Cost of Discipleship" and was greatly impacted by its message. Several years ago, while on a mission trip to Germany at the invitation of IMB missionaries Wayne and Pam Jenkins (Wayne is now the associational missionary for Western Baptist Association) I had the privilege of going to Flossenberg, where Bonhoeffer was imprisoned and eventually executed on April 9, 1945 at 39 years of age.

Hitler's execution of Bonhoeffer, six million Jews, Romani leftists, Soviet prisoners of war, Polish and Soviet civilians, homosexuals, people with disabilities, Jehovah's Witnesses and other political and religious opponents is estimated to be upwards of 11 million people.

Andy Andrews, in his latest New York Times bestseller, "How Do You Kill 11 Million People?" addresses the Holocaust and the mass destructions wrought by the Nazi regime and answers the question he poses in his title.

So, "How Do You Kill 11 Million People?" The answer is simple. "You lie to them!"

Andrews points out that Nazi Germany is not the only government that has institutionally killed its own citizens. It happened in the Soviet Union, where 61,911,000 were murdered by the Marxist government. It happened in Turkey during World War I and in other countries like Cambodia, North Korea, Mexico, Pakistan and the Baltic States.

Andrews does not concern himself with the method a government employs to do the actual killing or the mind-set of those deranged persons who conceive and carry out the slaughter of innocents.

"What we need to understand," Andrews explains, "is how eleven million people allow themselves to be killed"

Adolf Eichmann was selected as the operational manager of the Nazi genocide. By means of a carefully organized method of deceptions and prevarications Eichmann led millions down a primrose path to destruction.

First, barbed-wire fences were erected, encircling entire neighborhoods. These physical restrictions, according to Eichmann, were only temporary necessities of war constructed for the purpose of offering protection and safety.

Andrews explained, "Second, bribes were taken from the Jews with the promise of better living conditions. The bribes convinced the Jews that the situation was indeed temporary and that no further harm would befall them. After all, they reasoned, why would the Nazis accept bribes if they only intend to kill us and take everything away."

Then Eichmann eventually came to these cordoned off areas to tell the people that the Russians were advancing on the eastern front, that time was of the essence, that they were going to be transported to a beautiful place where they could have a home, find gainful employment, and live peaceful lives.

The railcars designed to accommodate eight cows would suddenly be packed with 100 human beings and padlocked.

Andrews reports, "At that moment they were lost. The trains rarely stopped until well inside the gates of Auschwitz" (or some concentration camp).

"Hitler was a man of the common people," Andrews writes, "and his speeches were exciting and passionate. He promised more and better and new and different. He vowed rapid change and swift action."

Hitler said, "How fortunate for leaders, that men do not think. Make the lie big, make it simple, keep saying it, and eventually they will believe it."

Andrews asks, "With all we know, does anyone believe that telling the truth will solve all a nation's problems? Of course not. But it is a beginning. In fact, speaking the truth should be the least we require of our elected leaders! After all, what are our standards for being led?

"You see, the danger to America is not a single politician with ill intent. Or even a group of them. The most dangerous thing any nation faces is a citizenry capable of trusting a liar to lead them.

"In the long run, it is much easier to undo the policies of crooked leadership than to restore common sense and wisdom to a deceived population willing to elect such a leader in the first place.

"Any country can survive having chosen a fool as their leader. But history has shown time and again that a nation of fools is surely doomed." Andrews specifies, "There are 545 human beings who are directly, legally, morally, and individually responsible for every problem America faces" – one president, nine Supreme Court justices, one hundred senators and 435 members of the House of Representatives.

Andrews observes, "By the way, have you noticed that if any one of us lies to them, it is a felony? But if any one of them lies to us, it is considered politics."

Andrews specifies that his book is not about Republicans or Democrats, conservatives or liberals. He exclaims, "I am not an 'us or them' kind of person. Actually, I am more of a 'we' person.

"Frankly," Andrews asserts, "I believe candidates from both parties have lied to the American people. Furthermore, I believe that many are slipping dangerously close to creating a habit of lying and rationalizing that their purpose in doing so is 'for our own good.'

"It has become standard operating procedure for many politicians to say whatever is needed in order to get elected. This must stop. History's list is deep and wide and filled with the names of tragic governments whose citizens did not stop it.

"Our nation is at a tipping point. Regardless of our political views, people everywhere can sense it. If we don't demand honesty and integrity from America's leadership now – and reward that integrity with our votes – our leaders will lack the fortitude to make the hard decisions that must be made to change course."

In Andrews book, "The Final Summit," he creates a supposed conversation between Abraham Lincoln and Joan of Arc where Lincoln asks, "Does adversity build character?"

Joan of Arc responds, "It does not. Almost all people can stand adversity of one sort or another. If you want to test a person's character, give him power."

Andrews concludes his argument by saying, "Great leadership is a product of great character. And this is why character matters."

David Brin stated, "It is said that power corrupts, but actually it's more true that power attracts the corruptible. The sane are usually attracted by other things than power."

Perhaps that is why we rarely have really good choices for most elective offices in our government, but let's vote for the most honest, honorable people that are available.

Nietzsche's Philosophy
Won't Change Me

Friedrich Nietzsche (1844-1900), the German philosopher, is considered one of the most important and original thinkers in the history of Western civilization. He grew up as the son of a Lutheran pastor and attended some of the most prestigious schools in Germany.

In 1841 Ralph Waldo Emerson wrote, "Beware when the great God lets loose a thinker on this planet. Then all things are at risk. It is as when a conflagration has broken out in a great city and no man knows what is safe or where it will end."

Some have contended that those words spoke prophetically of Nietzsche, who actually quoted them later in his autobiographical essay on Schopenhauer. Nietzsche, who was actually greatly influenced by Emerson, was a great thinker, but many of his ideas have actually put humanity at risk.

At the age of 20, Nietzsche wrote a poem to "the unknown God" saying, "I want to know you – even to serve you." But he later turned his back on the unknown one and became one of the most significant critics of religion in general and Christianity in particular. In fact, he decried Christianity and referred to it as "a crime against life."

Nietzsche is perhaps best known for his pronouncement, "God is dead," in his 1882 book, The Gay Science. He also said, "I can't believe in a God who wants to be praised all the time."

Well, Mr. Nietzsche, I am of the well-founded and accurate opinion that God is alive and you, sir, are dead, but that is a discussion for another time.

In another book by Nietzsche, Beyond Good and Evil, published four years after The Gay Science, he argues that men are driven by an amoral "will to power," and that superior men will sweep aside religiously inspired moral rules, which he deemed as artificial as any other moral rules, to craft whatever rules would help them dominate the world around them. This dangerous ideology, added to his anti-Semitism, made his philosophy very popular with the Nazis in Germany.

In addition to rejecting biblical morality, Nietzsche spurned the concept of absolute truth. He said, "You have your way. I have my way. As for the right way, the correct way, and the only way, it does not exist."

In case you are wondering about his amorality, the German thinker also wrote, "It is human passion, not rationality, that drives human knowledge, and such knowledge is subject to the changing tastes of culture. Since biased passion is all humans can hope for, no belief is ever absolute and all beliefs – especially in the realm of morals – are subject to change. Monday's taboo might be Friday's indulgence."

Then he added, "The reason for a constant flux in knowledge is because passions, being irrational, are constantly changing with every situation. A society will determine morality based upon what it feels is right at that moment and will be biased in doing so."

Last year Jennifer Ratner-Rosenhagen published a book entitled American Nietzsche: A History of an Icon and His Ideas. She explains in the book that Nietzsche's philosophies first burst onto the American scene at the turn of the 20th century and how his ideas about truth, Christian morality, theology, nihilism, democracy, and human equality have continued alternately to invigorate and shock Americans ever since.

One writer said, "If you were looking for a philosopher likely to appeal to Americans, Friedrich Nietzsche would be far from your first choice. After all, in his blazing career Nietzsche took aim at nearly all the foundations of modern American life … and for more than a century Nietzsche has been hugely popular – a surprisingly influential figure in American thought and culture.

Unfortunately, we see the handprint of Nietzsche in our political system, in many of America's mainline denominations, in our economic structure, and in our moral (or amoral) standards.

Nietzsche and others of his ideological bent have promoted the ideal of religious relativism, cultural diversity, tolerance, and philosophical pluralism to the great detriment of our society in America. I wish we would just get back to the ideals of our heritage and founding fathers.

I admire Nietzsche's mental prowess, and, we too, must aspire to be thinkers, but always remember that while we need to develop our mental capacity, exercise our minds, and study to show ourselves approved unto God, it is not intellectual suicide to believe the Bible and embrace the absolute truths contained therein.

I recently read the blog of some distressed soul who lamented the plight of our nation. He exclaimed, "Prices are going up, Iran is pounding the war drums and threatening to close off the Strait of Hormuz and that means oil and gasoline will be so high none of us will be able to pay or go anywhere (and) the good old American buck is worthless."

His tirade actually gets worse and he concludes his diatribe by saying, "I don't know what to do and I don't know what to tell you to do. The darkness is too great and we are all just little rats in their maze with no hope of deliverance. So, I guess we just hide in our little holes and hope that the darkness doesn't smash us too much.... I just can't take it anymore and have to let it all out, because I am sick of living in a world that has gone CRAZY."

Nietzsche's foolish proclamation about the death of God leads to nothing but this kind of hopelessness. We must remember that without Christ and His precious Word we are all helpless and hopeless, but with Him there is both deliverance (salvation) and genuine peace – the kind of peace that can sustain us in the midst of a storm.

Folks occasionally ask me why I use the editorial page as a soapbox to bash folks like Nietzsche and propagate my narrow views. They say, "Why bother, you won't ever change anybody with your vehement protestations."

I will respond like the old preacher who said, "I realize that my preaching against sin may not change anybody in this church, but I am going to keep on screaming and shouting against sin, so they won't change me."

Looking for Truth in a World of Prevaricators

I listened to the first presidential debate and looked for the candidate who was most assuredly standing on the truth. While the majority seemed to think Republican Mitt Romney won the debate and was perhaps the most believable, Calvin Woodward of the Associated Press wrote, "President Barack Obama and Republican rival Mitt Romney spun one-sided stories in their first presidential debate, not necessarily bogus, but not the whole truth. They made some flat-out flubs, too."

At one point, Romney rebutted an argument by saying, "You're entitled, Mr. President, as the president to your own airplane and your own house, but not to your own facts."

When the debate had ended I felt that my search for truth had collided with a series of pivots, spins, and political doubletalk. I concluded that if one is looking for absolute truth, don't look in the political arena.

In fact, anyone in America who launches out to search for truth may come to the realization that the truth is hard to find. We live in a land of dissemblers and prevaricators and many people actually seem to be more willing to believe a lie than the truth.

The mainstream media seems to be far from "fair and balanced." In fact, six huge corporations collectively own most of the major mainstream media outlets in this country and the news departments seem to be more concerned about catering to those who provide them paychecks than presenting the news in an unbiased fashion. Instead of communicating the absolute truth the media gives us the version of "reality" that their owners want us to have.

Additionally, many politicians have not been known to be paragons of honesty and truthfulness.

Richard Nixon said, "I'm not a crook."

Bill Clinton said, "I did not have sexual relations with that woman (Monica Lewinsky)."

Marion Barry said, "It's all made up. I don't know what happened."

John Edwards commented, "The story is false. It's completely untrue, ridiculous."

In each case these politicians' comments were proved to be untrue.

On another front, America's educational system has attempted to revise our history as a nation. For example, when I was growing up I was taught that as a lad George Washington cut down a cherry tree against his parents' wishes. When his father confronted him about the hewn-down tree young George admitted to his transgression and confessed to axing the tree.

Today, students are told that Washington did no such thing, because archaeologists have discovered that there were no cherry trees on the site of Washington's boyhood home. Teachers suggest that the story was fabricated to bolster the first president's heroic image.

While fact checking is appropriate to correct the record of past events, it is also true that some revisionism is an intentional effort to falsify or skew past events for specific motives. Christen Conger writes, "In popular culture, revisionist history has become synonymous with telling lies or embellishing the truth."

In addition to the media spinning the truth, politicians' fabrications, and the educational system revising our history, sometimes you can't even believe what you hear from certain pulpits. Today it seems many churches are founded on pragmatism (whatever works) instead of sound biblical theology or cotton candy sermons that lack real substance.

Some mainline denominations are losing their leaders to secularism or finding out that their priests are pedophiles or that their pastor has misappropriated funds or worse. These sincere believers feel like they have been betrayed, lied to, and belittled.

In other words, the truth is so hidden, perverted, diluted, obscured, and elusive that it is very hard for most people to develop strong convictions about anything or even believe anything. We have become a society of people without principle, passion, or purpose.

So, if you can't believe the media, if you can't believe the politicians, if you can't believe written history, and if you can't believe the pulpit, what can you believe?

Peggy Noonan, writing in the Wall Street Journal, states, "We are becoming a nation that believes nothing. Not in nothing, but nothing we're told by anyone in supposed authority."

Noonan continued, "Everyone knows what the word 'spin' means; people use it in normal conversation. Everyone knows what going negative is; they talk about it on Real Housewives. Political technicians always think they're magicians whose genius few apprehend, but Americans now always know where the magician hid the rabbit.

"And we shouldn't be so proud of our skepticism, which has become our cynicism. Someday we'll be told something true that we need to know, and we won't believe that, either."

Hopefully, we have not reached that perilous time the Apostle Paul predicted would come when he wrote, "Because they received not the love of the truth, that they might be saved. For this cause God shall send them strong delusion, that they should believe a lie" (II Thess. 2:10b-11).

There is only one ultimate truth, but like Pontius Pilate, most folks don't ever embrace it.

Jesus said, "To this end I was born and for this came I into the world, to bear witness unto the truth. Every one that is of the truth hears my voice. Pilate then said unto him, 'What is truth'?" (John 18:37-38)

Amazingly, Pilate was standing in front of the Truth and didn't comprehend it. Pilate's response, "What is truth?" is a quintessential modern response in a world of relativity. In a world dominated by pragmatic realities, ideological loyalties, political manipulation, and religious hypocrisy what, indeed, is truth?

It is important to know the truth, because the Bible says, "The truth will set you free." That being the case, the opposite must also be true. Lies and deceitfulness will put us in bondage.

Therefore, the pursuit of the truth is absolutely essential if there is to be liberty and freedom from oppression and servitude. We need to pray for God to give us and the people of America the spirit of discernment lest we be duped by the media, the school system, the politicians, and even by those who preach a false doctrine.

Truth and stability seem to be in short supply today. I like the way the old Irishman sang the hymn, "The Solid Rock." He sang, "On Christ the solid rock I stand; all other rocks are shamrocks."

Chasing Rabbits
or Fatal Distractions

Alexander Hunter, in his short story "A Christmas Fox-Hunt in Old Virginia," writes about the exciting hunting experiences in Colonial America.

Hunter explains, "To hunt the fox here was no child's play; it meant that those who followed the hounds must ride hard and ride far, over the sedge fields, through the dim woods, across the many streams, in the marshy swamps, with the cry, 'The devil takes the hindermost and the boldest rider wins!'"

But occasionally, to the dismay of the hunters the hounds would spot a rabbit and forget about the fox. They started chasing the rabbit much to the dismay of the hunters whose horses had been jumping fences and hurdling chasms and creeks at a rattling pace to catch the fox.

Now, chasing rabbits is commonplace, in fact, child's play. But fox hunting has been a sport for the daring and spirited hunter. I suppose the phrase "chasing rabbits" originated with a foxhunt that deteriorated into a hare hunt when the dogs were distracted by the scent or sight of some furry little bunny.

Preachers are notorious for chasing rabbits in their sermons; and although sometimes they are blessed detours, such unintended pursuits can also be detrimental to a well-constructed, riveting homiletical discourse.

The truth is that all of us are beleaguered by the temptation to chase rabbits. Unfortunately, we all succumb to distractions that keep us from being on task, that take us down side streets, that prompt compromise and militate against our highest calling.

My grandfather, Reverend M.I. Harris, was my first pastor. He was known as a man of prayer and faith. He always prayed that he would die in the pulpit. He prayer was almost answered. He died just after the Sunday morning worship service while eating lunch in the parsonage.

He once told a story about two of his sons, my dad, John, and my uncle, Parks, who also became a pastor. When John and Parks were boys my grandfather had prepared a field for the planting of corn.

The boys were given a large sack of corn and instructed to go down the rows and plant the kernels of corn about ten inches apart and cover the kernels with an inch or two of dirt and fertilizer.

My dad and his brother didn't want to plant corn that day. They wanted to go fishing instead. So, they struck a bargain with my grandfather, who agreed to let them go fishing when they finished planting the corn.

The boys worked for hours, stopped for a few minutes to eat the sandwiches they brought for lunch, and continued planting the corn. By mid-afternoon they came to the stark realization that they were nowhere close to finishing their assigned task.

The allurement of the fishing pond grew more appealing with every passing moment, so they decided to do a very foolish thing. They dug a hole in the middle of the field and poured the remaining kernels of corn they were supposed to plant in that one large hole. Having disposed of the corn, they got their fishing poles and headed for the pond (I guess chasing fish is somewhat like chasing rabbits.).

Everything went well for almost two weeks – until my grandfather decided to go to the cornfield to see if the tender corn stalks were beginning to emerge from the soil. As he walked down the rows he was pleased to see that for almost 20 rows the corn was coming up as expected, but then he came to the spot where the boys had buried half a sack of the seeds. Corn sprouts were coming up in concentrated abundance in that one spot. It was obvious what had happened.

My dad and my uncle had their sin exposed in vivid fashion. They had become weary of the work. Their attention had been diverted to something peripheral rather than the essential. The contrived distraction was too much to resist. Their sin found them out, the evidence was irrefutable, the verdict was pronounced and retribution followed.

Martha, the sister of Lazarus and Mary, got distracted. When Jesus came to their home in Bethany Martha graciously welcomed the Master into her home. Mary was also there that day and she sat at Jesus' feet and listened to what the Lord was saying.

Martha was "distracted by her many tasks," according to Luke 10:40. We can imagine what those "distractions" were – cooking the dinner, setting the table, polishing the candlesticks, running down to the local bakery to get some tasty delicacy for dessert.

The demanding and important work of a gracious hostess took a toll, frayed Martha's nerves, and caused her to burst into the room where Jesus and Mary were and interrupted the conversation with a shout, "Lord, don't you care that my sister has left me to do all the work by myself. Tell her to help me!" Martha had a momentary meltdown.

Jesus was put on the spot, but he responded with grace and truth: "Martha you are worried and distracted about many things. There is only one thing that is necessary, and Mary has made the right choice."

Hobbies and habits, television and travel, food and friends, shopping and sports, or any number of things can easily distract us from our high calling in Christ Jesus, but none of those things gives life meaning, purpose, hope, significance, or salvation. We as individuals and as churches must find out what is the most important thing – the one necessary thing – and commit ourselves anew to that one thing.

Jesus said, "Seek ye first the kingdom of God and His righteousness, and all these things shall be added unto you."

Churches can also get off task as a result of trivial pursuits and nonessential matters that stymie spiritual growth and evangelistic fervor. We must not be allured by the devil's distractions or prompted to chase rabbits.

Many of our churches are declining. Revivals seem to be mostly a thing of the past. Our world is hurtling toward godlessness; and 150,000 people die every day – most of whom are not saved.

Sometimes we are like the alcoholic who resorts to his liquor to forget his problems. We contrive distractions to forget how far we have fallen from the will, the way, and the Word of God.

My Wife Could Probably do my Job Better

Our daughter, Miriam, recently called our home on a Saturday afternoon. She had been to the University of Georgia to see our granddaughter, who is a freshman at UGA. I answered the phone.

Miriam was returning to her home in Douglasville and driving through Atlanta traffic. Her question to me was, "Do you have to possess some kind of special permission to drive on the HOV (High Occupancy Vehicle) lane or can you drive on it if there are two people in the car?"

I replied, "You must possess a Peach Pass to drive on the HOV lane."

Miriam responded to my answer to her question and mentioned that Harris, her son and our grandson, had arrived in Orlando. Harris, who plays a trombone in the Alexander High School band, was traveling with his band to Disney World where they were scheduled to perform during their school's Winter Break.

Miriam stated, "Harris just called and said the highway patrol had stopped the bus he was on and performed a random drug check with police dogs that 'sniffed' out their luggage."

When we had concluded our brief phone conversation my dear wife, Martha Jean, asked, "What did Miriam say?"

I gave my typical answer, "Nothing in particular." I, being an insensitive male, often give that sort of answer. When I come home from the GBC Missions and Ministry Center at the end of the day, Martha Jean will typically ask, "What happened at your office today?"

My patented answer is: "Not much."

One day she responded by saying, "I don't know how you manage to keep your job if your account of what happens there each day is accurate." (For those of you on my Board of Directors I actually have a more definitive answer.)

In response to Martha Jean's question on that Saturday afternoon I did manage to add, "She did say that Harris' bus was stopped by the highway patrol on the way to Orlando."

Then she proceeded to ask …

Why did they stop the bus?

Was the driver speeding?

Was the driver suspected of some felony or misdemeanor?

Were the students in danger?

Did they conduct a search?

If so, why did they search the bus?

How many patrolmen were there to search the bus? Where was the bus stopped?

What were the students doing while the bus was being searched?

Did they have those "drug dogs" sniffing for drugs?

If so, how many dogs did they have?

What kind of dogs did they have?

Did the search cause Harris any anxiety?

Did they find any drugs?

How long were they stopped?

Did the students have to get off the bus?

Why did they select the bus Harris was on?

How many adult chaperones did they have on the bus?

Have they arrived in Orlando yet?

Where did they stop to eat lunch?

Did Harris have enough spending money?

Then there was another barrage of questions about Miriam's trip to Athens to see Hayley.

I explained to Martha Jean that the conversation lasted less than a minute and I didn't get the information she was inquiring about. It was then that I concluded she would be a far better reporter than me, because she knows how to ask questions.

When I was a pastor I would frequently come home after having visited a new mother with her baby in the hospital and Martha Jean would ask me, "Tell me all about the baby."

My typical response was, "Well, it was a really nice baby.'

She would then ask …

Was it a boy or girl?

How long was the mother in labor?

Did she have an epidural?

How far were her contractions apart before she decided to go to the hospital?

How much did the baby weigh?

How long was the baby?

Did it have any hair?

How much hair did the baby have?

What color was the baby's hair?

Who did the baby look like?

What is the baby's name?

Are they going to call the baby by the first name or the middle name?

Did you take any pictures of the baby?

I generally had less information about the baby than Hillary Clinton had about the assault on the United States Embassy in Benghazi.

When I became the editor of The Christian Index I started reading books and articles on writing and journalism. I wouldn't have had to read all that material if I had just paid more attention to Martha Jean and her incredible ability to ask personal, pertinent, and penetrating questions.

One article I read stated, "The interviewing process can be quite challenging, but the journalist must remember that there is, for the most part, only one shot to get the story and when they are there speaking to the interviewee in person, they must be on the ball."

The following statement haunts me.

"There are few things that indicate amateur status more blatantly in the world of journalism than a reporter who runs out of things to say before the interviewee does."

So, I think my wife would be a great interviewer or reporter. But then E.J. Dionne, writing in The Washington Post, thinks the Catholics should consider a nun to be the next Pope. So, I hope to keep my job for a while longer.

Where is the Accountability?

Years ago, many Baptist churches had a church covenant. In my home church in North Carolina we had it posted in the church vestibule and in the back of our Baptist Hymnal. We would read it out loud every time we observed the Lord's Supper. In the covenant we promised to "maintain family and sacred devotions; to religiously educate our children; to seek the salvation of our kindred and acquaintances; to walk circumspectly in the world."

We also promised "to be exemplary in our deportment; to avoid all tattling, backbiting, and excessive anger; to abstain from the sale and use of intoxicating drinks as a beverage; and to be zealous in our efforts to advance the kingdom of our Savior."

There were other important aspects of the covenant we were urged to faithfully maintain. But today that covenant is regarded as antiquated, passé, and too legalistic for most churches.

In those days the church offering envelope had an eight-point record system whereby members could give an account of their faithfulness. The eight-points included: Sunday School Attendance, Brought Bible, Lesson Studied, Giving, Worship Attendance, Daily Bible Reading, Visits made, Other Contacts.

Churches also gave out attendance pins for those with perfect Sunday School attendance for the entire year. Some people had perfect attendance for 10, 20, 30 years. The church would have a special ceremony to award attendance pins to those who had not missed a Sunday in Bible Study all year.

We also had high attendance days for Sunday School and every Sunday School member was asked to sign their name on a strip of colored construction paper. The strips of paper were forged into a chain and the people were challenged – sometimes dared – not to break the chain on high attendance day.

During revivals we had the members "Pack a Pew." One night the women were assigned pews. On another night the men were responsible for filling their pew. The youth also had a night to be pew-packers. Prizes were given to those with the most people present.

We also had an every member stewardship canvas when all the church members were visited in their homes and asked to sign a pledge card to tithe or at least give a certain amount of money to the church in the coming year.

While there are some churches that still emphasize a church covenant, eight-point record systems, Sunday School attendance pins, pack pews for revival and have an every member stewardship canvas, it is mostly a thing of the past.

Many today would say those ideas are worn-out, legalistic, even foolish attempts to manipulate people. Those who employ those old- fashioned ideas are scorned and ridiculed. They are called old school, narrow-minded and out of touch with the times.

But did not those old methods provide some accountability that was good and that we have lost? And have we not tried to justify our casual and compromising brand of Christianity with a kind of hyper-grace that is unbiblical, detrimental to the cause of Christ, and similar to the world's cry for "tolerance?"

Our weekend trips, Sunday morning soccer games and travel ball schedules, our late Saturday night excursions into the world, our desire to sleep in on the Lord's Day, our lackadaisical attitude toward church attendance is all covered by a self-serving view of grace that doesn't seem to fit the plaintive call of Christ who has asked us to deny ourselves, take up our cross, and follow Him.

Obviously, legalism is terrible and antithetical to God's Word when it becomes a system to seek God's acceptance or blessings through personal effort. When an individual places his focus on his own ability to control himself and conform his behavior, he is a legalist; and the fruit of legalism is pride, hypocrisy, and condescension.

However, if a person is motivated by God's Spirit to set goals and press toward the mark of the high calling of God in Christ Jesus, is he being a legalist? Can eight-point record systems and high attendance goals and following church covenants not offer the accountability some people need within the realm of what is good and godly?

Surely, the biblical message of grace is wonderful, glorious, and life-transforming. It is essential to salvation, spiritual health, and life itself. But in recent years we have been introduced to this "hyper-grace."

It may be that this term is derived from I Timothy 1:14 where we find the Greek word "hyperpleonazo" which actually means "hyper-plentiful" or "overwhelming." Indeed, God's grace is not only sufficient or even plentiful, but it is overly plentiful and super- abundant. When God condescends to redeem imperfect and sinful people it is always an expression of amazing, marvelous grace.

But there are those today who have interpreted this hyper, super-abundant grace to not only signify that our sins are covered by grace and completely forgiven, but also that our daily walk as a child of God is also covered by grace; and we don't have to ask forgiveness for sin on a regular basis as a believer.

The Bible strictly warns against "turning the grace of God into lasciviousness" (Jude 4). There is the danger of taking grace to the extreme just like the Pharisees took legalism to the extreme. While the number who actually embrace this theological position may be small there are multitudes that reckon on God's grace to somehow cover both their sins of commission and omission.

Many of them talk about being a part of the Kingdom of God, but through their sins of omission place little emphasis on the local church. They claim an allegiance to the invisible, transcendent Kingdom of God, but minimize the importance of the local church. This is patently wrong.

The church is the centerpiece of God's work in this world. I would suggest that service to God in the local assembly is every believer's primary service in life. Your work is subservient to your walk with the Lord and your witness for Christ. Both your walk and your witness are integrally related to the local assembly.

Should we become more legalistic? Should we minimize the doctrine of grace? No. We should have an understanding of God's grace that fosters and inspires accountability. We need to become accustomed to accountability because there is a great day of accountability coming. See II Corinthians 5:10.

Truth, Trust and Testimony
in a Time of Tension

On February 9, 2012 The Christian Index published my editorial entitled, "The Calvinists are here." The editorial received considerably more attention than I anticipated – or wanted. The reviews were mixed, but I received plenty of counsel, commendations, and criticism.

I stated, "The Conservative Resurgence and the Great Com-mission Resurgence have been joined by a Reformed Resurgence. The Calvinists are here. Their presence is evident in many phases and places in Southern Baptist life."

In the weeks leading up to the 2012 Southern Baptist Convention annual meeting in New Orleans, LifeWay Research released a study that showed nearly equal numbers of pastors in the SBC consider their churches as Calvinists/Reformed as do Arminian/Wesleyan, and that more than 60 percent were somewhat or strongly concerned about the effect of Calvinism in the Southern Baptist family.

Most Southern Baptists would have to agree that Calvinism, or Reformed theology, has been a frequent topic of conversation at many coffee klatsches or when fellow Baptists gather to "chew the fat."

SBC Executive Committee President Frank Page addressed the issue of Calvinism during the Executive Committee report at the 2012 SBC annual meeting.

"Friends, I'm concerned because there seems to be some non-Calvinists who are more concerned about rooting out Calvinists than they are about winning the lost for Christ," he said. "Some Calvinists seem to think that if we do not believe the same thing about soteriology that they believe somehow we are less intelligent or ignorant at best.

"I simply say to you today that it's time to realize that a Great Commission Advance needs everyone," he said. "Calvinists and non-Calvinists have worked together for decade upon decade upon decade in this Convention."

Baptists' frequent discussions and recurrent preoccupation with Calvinism prompted Page to appoint an advisory team to help him craft a strategic plan to bring together various groups within the convention who hold different opinions on the issue of Calvinism. Baptist Press announced the first 16 members of the advisory team on August 15, 2012. Eventually, three more members were appointed to make a 19-member team.

The purpose of the advisory team was to produce a written report on how we as Southern Baptists can find a way to cooperate together in our common commitment to the Great Commission despite our theological differences on the subject of Calvinism.

Obviously, there is only so much an advisory team can do, but this team, composed of a balanced and respected collection of Baptist leaders, proceeded to pray, pool their intellectual and theological assets, and produce a document that would aid Page and the SBC Executive Committee in fulfilling their responsibility of "encouraging the cooperation and confidence of the churches, associations and state conventions and facilitating maximum support for worldwide missions and ministries."

The statement from the aforementioned team has been entitled "Truth, Trust, and Testimony in a Time of Tension." Overall, it is an outstanding and conciliatory document. It seems to address all issues of concern to those who have felt like the future of our denominational unity is in jeopardy.

First of all, it specifies, "We are a doctrinal people … who stand together upon the doctrines most vital to us all, confessed together in The Baptist Faith and Message." To me it would appear that the BF&M surpasses all other confessions of faith including the Abstract of Principles, the Chicago Statement on Biblical Inerrancy, The New Hampshire Confession, etc.

Another critical issue that was addressed pertains to pastors who gradually and surreptitiously introduce reformed theology or church polity and perhaps in some cases Arminian theology and church polity into unwary churches, ultimately leading to tension and division. Or as Adam Harwood, who was assistant professor of Christian Studies at Truett-McConnell College before accepting a position at New Orleans Seminary, explained, "It denounces partisan and hidden theological agendas."

The document effectively addresses this issue, stating, "We expect all candidates for ministry positions in the local church to be fully candid and forthcoming about all matters of faith and doctrine, even as we call upon all pulpit and staff search committees to be fully candid and forthcoming about their congregation and its expectations."

I thought it was also prudent to state, "No entity should be promoting Calvinism or non-Calvinism to the exclusion of the other."

The advisory team affirmed that there is nothing lacking in the atonement of Christ to provide for the salvation of anyone and that no believer can be obedient without telling others about Jesus.

There were a few areas that I viewed as somewhat curious, such as the statement on the destiny of children who have not reached the age of accountability. Rather than making a statement about that issue the report simply says, "We agree that most Southern Baptists believe that those who die before they are capable of moral action go to heaven through the grace of God and the atonement of Christ, even as they differ as to why this is so." That appears to be more like the result of a survey than a statement or confession of faith.

In reflecting on the aforementioned statement in question, Harwood asks, "Most? What Southern Baptist will make the case that some who die as infants may suffer in hell?"

However, I was extremely pleased with the bold statement expressing a strong conviction that our purpose is not to reduce our theological rhetoric to the winning of a debate, but to elevate our biblical knowledge to the winning of souls.

Regarding that issue the report says, "We deny that the main purpose of the Southern Baptist Convention is theological debate. We further deny that theological discussion can be healthy if our primary aim is to win an argument, to triumph in a debate, or to draw every denominational meeting into a conversation over conflicted issues. Of more significance to our life together than any allegiance to Calvinism or non-Calvinism should be our shared identity as Southern Baptists."

Overall, the report is exceptionally helpful and should prove to be an effective guideline for pastors, churches, denominational entities, and all Southern Baptists. We certainly need to heed the report of the advisory team, focus on those tremendous tenets of the faith we hold dear, and get on with the business of pushing back the darkness lest the darkness overtake us all.

When Sin has a Face

O n June 26 The United States Supreme Court announced its ruling on the Defense of Marriage Act (DOMA) and Proposition 8. The high court decided to overturn provisions in DOMA signed in 1996 by President Bill Clinton protecting traditional marriage between one man and one woman as husband and wife. The decision not only allows, but encourages same-sex marriage in our country.

The Supreme Court also announced its decision to reverse the voter-approved Proposition 8 in California, making it legal for same-sex couples to wed in the state. In making this landmark decision the court ruled against the democratic, or majority, vote of the people of California, saying that state bans on gay marriage would also be unconstitutional.

Regarding these decisions, the leadership of Traditional Values Coalitions released a statement explaining, "Some days our civilization erodes slightly in feet and inches, other days it drops a mile at a time. Today is one of those days when our culture's decline is widely felt."

When the Court decides what is legal and appropriate for a secular, civil government and when comparative changes take place in our own personal environment how should we respond?

Many conservative Christians have knee-jerk reactions to such decisions and are quick to pass judgment. We have been programmed to view divorce, abortion, homosexuality, and other sins with condemnation and vehemently declare that they are among those transgressions that are symptoms of our moral decline and crippling our culture. We sometimes even dare to paint the transgressor with a "scarlet letter" and isolate them or keep them at arm's length.

But what happens when the Supreme Court rules against our biblical principles or what happens if those sins suddenly have a face?

Senator Rob Portman of Ohio reversed his stance on same-sex marriage two years after learning that his son is gay.

In a review with reporters in his senate office earlier this year Portman said that his son, Will, announced to his mother and him in February of 2011 that he was gay. Portman added, "It allowed me to think of this issue from a new perspective, and that's the perspective of a dad who loves his son a lot and wants him to have the same opportunities that his brother and sister would have – to have a relationship like [my wife] Jane and I have had for over 26 years."

Portman said that his son, who is now a junior at Yale University, inspired him to reasses his position on same-sex unions. The senator also consulted clergy on the matter, as well as friends such as former Vice President Dick Cheney, whose daughter, Mary, is openly gay. According to Portman, Cheney told the senator to "follow [his] heart" on the matter.

Portman explained, "The overriding message of love and compassion that I take from the Bible, and certainly from the Golden Rule, and the fact that I believe we are all created by our Maker, that has all influenced me in terms of my change on this issue."

In John 8 we are told that the religious leaders in Israel brought to Jesus a woman taken in adultery and said, "Moses in the law commended us, that such should be stoned; but what sayest thou?"

Those scribes and Pharisees were prepared to pelt her with rocks. I can imagine that throughout the horrible ordeal she had her head hung down in shame, perhaps with her long, flowing hair hiding her face, concealing her identity. They were all ready to stone her because they saw her as a fallen woman and they were committed to meticulously keeping the law.

But what if when she turned her face upward to look at Jesus her hair fell away from her face and her identity was exposed for all to see? And what if one of the Pharisees suddenly recognized the woman to be his daughter, niece, or sister? Do you think he would have been as eager to stone her once he saw her face?

Should our convictions about adultery change when the adulterer is a family member? Should our view of homosexuality be altered when we discover that our son announces that he is gay, or our daughter comes out of the closet to admit that she is a lesbian? Should our condemnation of abortion be modified when we discover that a loved one has terminated the life of her unborn child?

Should we alter our convictions when sin suddenly has a face?

Portman may have followed his heart and may have found some passages of Scripture that supported his conclusion, but most of us could find proof texts to justify our beliefs or behaviors.

The pleasingly plump person could cite Nehemiah 8:10 as his/her justification for gluttony – "Go your way, eat the fat, and drink the sweet, and send portions unto them for whom nothing is prepared: for this day is holy unto the Lord: neither be ye sorry; for the joy of the Lord is your strength."

Through the years men have used the account of Jesus turning the water into wine at the wedding feast in Cana of Galilee as a justification for imbibing strong drink. However, "oinos," the Greek word for "wine" in that context, can mean "grape juice" that is not fermented. Anyone who understands Jesus Christ would find it completely out of character for him to be in the business of making any kind of alcoholic beverage.

In the 19th century both the North and South in this country used the Bible to justify their views on the issue of slavery, illustrating that there are "proof texts" in the Bible for just about anything.

So, Portman was wrong to use a few verses of Scripture to satiate his desire to appease his son and condone his lifestyle. Real love involves correction and chastening. God's Word tells us that He chastens those whom He loves.

It is because He doesn't want us to disobey Him, because He loves us and understands the damage that sin does to us.

If we love our children, we discipline them in order to protect them from the dangers of this world. We get that entire attitude from our Heavenly Father, because He will do whatever is necessary to conform His children into the likeness of Christ inasmuch as He predestined us for this very reason.

It is absolutely true that we are most protected in close proximity to Him. Therefore, since sin separates us from Him, then sin places us in an unprotected position.

So, how can we say that we love someone then stand by and say nothing knowing that they are practicing sin and carrying on as though it is okay? When we continually shield loved ones from the consequences of their errors we often deprive them of the opportunity for the growth and maturity that could possibly eradicate problematic behavior. In what has come to be known as "tough love," the chastening hand is always controlled by a loving heart.

So, when sin has a face we do not change our view of sin, but we demonstrate an unconditional love for the sinner – a love that prays for them, a love that tells them the truth, a love that warns them of the consequences of sin, a love that points them to Christ, a love that doesn't waver even if is rejected or fails to produce a change, a love like the father had for the prodigal son, and a love that continues to love even if the prodigal chooses not to come home.

Don't Forget to Express
your Gratitude

Have you ever met a leper? I have. His name was Johnny Cline. I met him when I was pastor of Flint Groves Baptist Church in Gastonia, NC years ago. Johnny was 14 years old when I first met him. He probably weighed 55 pounds, maybe less.

Johnny was confined to his home – a rather dilapidated shanty that had the stench of death about it. He had no feet nor hands. Most of his hair had fallen out. He was covered with sores. He was a sad, pitiable sight with practically no hope of improving his lot in this life.

I prayed for God to bless Johnny, to communicate His love to him, to give him strength, but I didn't pray for God to heal him.

I am not sure why I didn't. Maybe I was too young in the ministry to know how to pray in that seemingly hopeless situation. Maybe I somehow thought he was beyond the help of the Almighty. Maybe I didn't want to risk the embarrassment of my prayer being unanswered.

But what if God had healed Johnny? It would have been a miracle of biblical proportions. I am sure Johnny would have been incredibly, exceedingly, and eternally grateful if such an amazing miracle had been wrought in his life.

That is why I have often wondered why only one of the ten lepers Jesus healed in Luke 17 came back to return thanks to the One who healed him. It seems unconscionable for nine lepers to experience such a miraculous healing, such marvelous grace, and not express gratitude for it.

In my opinion, ingratitude is one of the most inexcusable sins there is, and thanksgiving is one of the most beautiful virtues I know. Webster's Dictionary defines "ingratitude" as "forgetfulness of, or poor return for kindness received." It can also be defined as not appreciating or valuing what you have or have been given. In fact, unexpressed gratitude is ingratitude.

We live in an entitlement conscious society. Many think the government, or some benevolent society owes them a living. Self- interest and self-centeredness militate against gratitude.

In Romans 1:21 Paul characterizes the unbelief of the heathen by writing, "Because, when they knew God, they glorified him not as God, neither were thankful, but became vain in their imaginations, and their foolish heart was darkened."

Each season has its own divine signature of beauty as often captured in the photographs of my 13-year-old granddaughter, Brinley Harris.

Furthermore, Paul said that in the last days, "Men shall be lovers of their own selves, covetous, boasters, proud, blasphemers, disobedient to parents, unthankful, unholy" (II Tim. 3:2).

Someone said, "If you want to find gratitude, look for it in the dictionary. The reward for giving comes from the good feeling it gives the giver. Don't expect any other returns."

But during this Thanksgiving season, let's resolve to be more grateful and also more expressive of our appreciation for all things.

The Psalmist said, "Thou hast turned for me my mourning into dancing; thou hast put off my sackcloth, and girded me with gladness to the end that my glory may sing praise to thee, and not be silent. O Lord, my God, I will give thanks unto thee forever" (Ps. 30: 11-12).

There are many things that concern me about what is going on in our land, but we are still the most blessed people on the planet. This Thanksgiving season is a good time to count your blessings and name them one by one. It may surprise you what the Lord has done. Hmmm. Sounds like the words to a hymn, doesn't it?

Spurgeon said, "When we bless God for mercies, we prolong them. When we bless God for miseries, we usually end them. Praise is the honey of life, which a devout heart extracts from every bloom of providence and grace."

A recent autumn trip to the Biltmore Estate in Asheville and to the Billy Graham retreat center, the Cove, reminded me of God's creative genius. The morning air was crisp outside our balcony window. Autumn's cold brush had repainted the treetops with festive fall colors. The spruce trees glistened with their emerald green branches. They stood in glorious stately splendor above the more numerous deciduous trees cloaked in blinding splashes of garnet and gold.

The scene described above was almost like a church altar call inviting me to be more grateful for our blessed Creator and the beautiful world He has provided for us. The blood-red leaves scattered nearby also reminded me of my glorious Redeemer who shed His precious blood to pay the ransom price for my sins.

In the days ahead try seasoning your words with expressions of thanksgiving and sprinkling your actions with demonstrations of kindness.

Snowmageddon

I got caught in Snowmageddon, but found it to be an unusual blessing. Plummeting temperatures, traffic snarls, and stranded motorists created problems for many and some people even encountered frightening traveling experiences – car crashes, broken bones from slipping on ice, and other formidable hardships. On the contrary, I found the experience to be challenging, but delightful in many ways.

Snow fell on the Atlanta metro area and much of Georgia on Jan. 28, 2014. Although meteorologists had prognosticated winter weather, they also had a record of making similar predictions that never materialized. Maybe their prediction of snow was received with the same sense of urgency as the people in Aesop's fable responded to *The Boy Who Cried Wolf.*

Governor Nathan Deal and Atlanta Mayor Kasim Reed blamed the resulting traffic gridlocks on decisions by schools, businesses, and the government agencies to send people home at the same hour, thus overwhelming the roads with vehicles.

The Governor explained the delay in urging businesses to close earlier, saying, "If we close the city of Atlanta and our interstate system based on maybes (maybe the storm will be severe, maybe not), then we would not be a very productive [state or city]."

I started my usual trek to my home in Smyrna from Duluth at about 2:30 p.m., which at that time of day would usually take about 35 minutes. As I traveled down I-85 toward I-285 I soon realized that the three right lanes were moving at a snail's pace.

The digital sign over the Interstate indicated that the westbound traffic on I-285 was moving at 5 mph. The excessive traffic in those three right lanes and the information provided by the digital sign was all I needed to alter my route and head into the city and connect with I-75 north near Atlantic Station.

Although the snow was falling in a near-blinding flurry I was moving at a reasonable clip toward downtown Atlanta. However, suddenly the car in front of me began to spin out of control and slammed into the concrete barrier in the median of the road.

Then, no more than 150 yards in front of me I saw an 18-wheeler jack-knife, creating havoc in all of the southbound lanes. I knew the careening tractor-trailer truck would create a horrific impasse, so I exited at Lennox Road and began to inch my way toward Peachtree Road and over to West Paces Ferry Road. It took about eight hours to travel less than five miles. I was hoping to connect with I-75 North from West Paces Ferry, but didn't know the entrance to the interstate was blocked.

Throughout the afternoon, into the evening, and all the way to midnight I amused myself in the stalled traffic by talking on my cellphone to Danny Watters and Marcus Merritt, who spent most of the night sitting on I-20 near Six Flags. Scott Barkley, our production editor who lives in Cartersville, had his commute come to a grinding stop and ended up spending the night in Woodstock with some perfect (emphasis on perfect) strangers who opened their home to him.

Phone conversations continued with family members, folks from Maysville Baptist Church where I served as interim pastor, GBC's Kevin Smith, and my dear friend and GBC Executive Director Bob White.

During the night Sandy Springs police delivered a baby (named Grace) in an automobile on I-285. Great stories of graciousness and helpfulness emerged from many sources. I saw people coming out of their houses offering food and water to stranded motorists. Pedestrians were helping push cars that were out of gasoline to a safe place.

Good Samaritans seemed to be in abundance. Police officers and a variety of public servants were extremely helpful. Publix and Kroger grocery stores, Home Depots, and other businesses opened for people who needed a place to spend the night.

Near midnight when I had resigned myself to spending the night in my car I got a call from my son-in-law, Billy Godwin, who calculated my location on West Paces Ferry and said he had a former Baylor University friend who lived nearby. He arranged for me to spend the night with him and his family.

I was reluctant to accept hospitality from someone I did not know, but Billy insisted. When he called back to let me know that his old Baylor buddy would welcome me in their home I was only .2 miles from his home. It took almost an hour to get to his street, but he was waiting for me when I arrived.

So, I spent the night with Mr. and Mrs. Robert Spiotta and their ninth-grade daughter, Marianna. The Spiottas are among the most gracious and hospitable people I have ever met. When I got to their house, Yvonne, Robert's wife, welcomed me with a splendid turkey sandwich, fruit, and cookies. I slept in a comfy, warm bed and woke up the next morning to a breakfast of bacon, eggs, fruit, and English muffins.

The Spiottas also opened up their home to two other stranded motorists. The "Bed and Breakfast" experience at the home of these new friends was superlative.

What did I learn from Snowmegaddon? I learned that if you enter a storm make sure your automobile is filled with gasoline. You don't want to run out of gas and the warmth it provides on a wintry night when you are marooned on some lonely stretch of road or stranded on some congested highway.

You also want to make sure you visit a restroom before you drive into the face of a storm. I am very glad I did. Those who failed to do so found that the solutions to their problems were extremely limited and uninviting.

It would also be advisable to have a stash of granola bars and some bottles of water handy in your auto. Put a blanket in the trunk in case you find yourself in such a precarious position. Also make sure you have a charger for your cellphone in your car.

I also learned that there are still a lot of good, benevolent people in this world. I am so glad I got connected with the Spiottas. They were unselfish angels of mercy. I think I could have made it through the night if I had remained in the car, but they translated what could have been a negative experience into a most positive one.

I also discovered how much I love my wife. It ultimately took 22 hours to complete my 30-mile journey, but it seemed like an eternity. I was headed home on Tuesday with the full expectation of enjoying a snowy evening in our cozy sitting room with the woman of my dreams and not getting there before evening was disappointing, but hearing her voice and being reassured of her love and prayers along the way was worth the experience of being trapped in Snowmageddon.

Humor in the Pulpit

I find myself often painting a picture of gloom and doom as I editorialize on some of the religious, social, and political issues of our day.

It is not pleasant. In fact, it's often painful to write about our declining and plateaued churches, the plummeting baptismal rates in the Southern Baptist Convention, the rising tide of anti-denominationalism, the socialist agenda being foisted upon our nation, the tragedy being wrought by activists judges, the devaluation of life as our personhood is under assault, the dismantling of the sanctity of marriage as we begin to slouch toward Sodom, and a variety of other things.

So, in this editorial I would like to do something rather out of the ordinary and address the value of humor. Josh Billings once said, "There ain't much fun in medicine, but there's a h_ _k of a lot of medicine in fun."

The Bible says the same thing and with more decorum and propriety in Proverbs 17:22: "A merry heart doeth good like a medicine: but a broken spirit drieth the bones." Henry Ward Beecher added, "Mirth is God's medicine. Everybody ought to bathe in it."

I think many of us take ourselves far too seriously. I have always loved evangelist Junior Hill not only because of his godly character, but also because of his self-deprecating humor. He has deliberately set himself up as the brunt of his own jokes and in doing so he has won the appreciation of many.

It was said of Charles Spurgeon that he glided from laughter to prayer with the naturalness of one who lived in both elements.

Spurgeon's friends and even casual acquaintances remarked on his hearty laughter. His humor also found expression in his sermons and writings, for which he was sometimes criticized. Spurgeon responded that if his critics only knew how much humor he suppressed they would keep silent.

Neil Wyrick, writing for Preaching Magazine, comments, "It is not necessary, on a Sunday morning, to become a comedian for Christ. Yet neither is there a scriptural reference that claims, 'blessed are the bored.' No less a preacher than Spurgeon spoke of the mistake of thinking that virtue lays in gravity and that smiles are a symptom of depravity. Humor can grab attention that might otherwise be drifting away."

For example, in a sermon I have occasionally illustrated our failure to face up to our sins by telling a true humorous story from my experience as president of the Georgia Baptist Convention. I was presiding over our annual meeting in Macon in 1999 when we were in a heated discussion about two churches in our convention that were seemingly endorsing a homosexual lifestyle.

It was an extremely stressful moment and the convention had increased security to prevent or minimize any possible demonstrations that some had anticipated. In the midst of all that tension I was told that an alarm had sounded in another part of the coliseum and that the law enforcement authorities had been called and the convention proceedings could potentially be suspended.

I immediately looked for my wife, who had been sitting with our four-year-old grandson and noticed they were not in their place. That concerned me, because I wanted to be able to keep an eye on them.

The afternoon session was not suspended, and we finished our business and adjourned the meeting at the appropriate time. We had supper in the Green Room of the Convention Center, had the evening session, and went to Tabernacle Baptist Church downtown to the reception for the new president. Martha Jean and I got to our hotel very late that night.

It was the first time we had a chance to really talk privately that day. I asked her how her day had gone, and she said, "You won't believe what happened today. I left the afternoon session in the heat of the discussion about the homosexual issue to take (our grandson) Harris to the restroom. The corridors were empty, because everyone wanted to be in that business discussion. As we walked down the hall Harris saw a fire alarm that he could reach and before I could get to him, he pulled the fire alarm."

Harris was the loveable culprit who nearly caused that afternoon session to be suspended by his mischievous deed. I asked Martha Jean, "What did you do when that happened?"

She said, "We ran."

This kind of humorous story can capture the attention of the congregation and illustrates that we must not run from our misdeeds, but face them and deal with them redemptively.

Obviously, humor injected at certain points in a sermon can serve the preacher's purpose exceedingly well when used with spiritual discernment, but pastors need to be careful about using the pulpit as the place for a comedy routine.

In fact, the pulpit should be a place for both laughter and weeping. To have one without the other would foster an imbalanced preaching ministry. It has been said that the problem in our day is that we have a dry-eyed church in a hell-bent world.

I have heard that George W. Truett was an amazingly effective pulpiteer, because he preached with a tear in his voice. His voice of pathos and feeling would make his congregation weep and never be ashamed of it.

In Acts 20:31 the Apostle Paul said to the Ephesian Christians, "I ceased not to warn everyone night and day with tears."

Of course, a preacher must not weep and cry in the pulpit unless God Himself moves him to do so. George Whitefield was often moved to tears when he preached. But he preached with tears only because he was moved to do so by God. Speaking of those who tried to copy Whitefield, and cry whenever they preached, D. Lloyd-Jones said, "Of course, a man who tries to produce an effect (by weeping in the pulpit) becomes an actor and is an abominable imposter."

Most of our weeping and praying should be done in private, or sometimes in the services before the preaching. However, it is unlikely that there can be real revival and genuine individual conversions, unless people are brought to tears over their sinful condition.

I believe there is a place for both laughter and weeping in the church.

Sarah Huckabee's Question

I recently had the privilege of meeting Governor Mike Huckabee at the Bailey Smith Real Evangelism Conference in Corinth, MS.

Six years as a media host on the Fox News channel have not impaired what columnist Nora Caplan-Bricker calls "his folksy charisma and self-depreciating wit." He is as smart as they come, has incredible appeal as an American statesman, and is as convictional as any Baptist preacher I know.

The former Arkansas governor and 2008 presidential candidate addressed a full house in the spacious worship center of Wheeler Grove Baptist Church. He spoke of the importance of standing up for truth and righteousness even if it becomes necessary to stand all alone against formidable odds.

Huckabee exhorted his hearers to stand up for liberty and the values we as Christians hold dear. He cited the tragedy of apathy in the nation and the church. His message brought to mind two quotes that seemed appropriate for the occasion.

The first quote pertains to apathy in the nation. Charles de Montesquieu once stated, "Thy tyranny of a prince in an oligarchy is not so dangerous to the public welfare as the apathy of citizens in a democracy."

The second quote relates to apathy in the church. Vance Havner said, "We have anarchy in the world, apostasy in the professing church, and apathy in the true church. This answer is in an awakening. The religion that used to put our fathers to shouting in the aisles has put us to sleep in the pews."

I know this – the slums and inner cities may be the breeding place for drugs, debauchery, and crime, but middle-class suburbia has become the incubator of self-satisfaction, indifference, and unconcern.

The Governor's message shook all modicums of complacency in his audience; and he drove his point home with exact precision by telling about a trip he took to Israel with his family.

One of the places he intended to visit was the Yad Vashem. The Yad Vashem located on Har Hazikaron, the Mount of Remembrance, is a vast, sprawling complex of tree-studded walkways leading to museums that memorialize the victims of the Holocaust.

The Governor's daughter, Sarah, was ten years old at the time and he wanted her to see the museum, but at the same time was concerned about how the heart-rending photos and graphic displays would affect his impressionable young daughter.

In the museum the survivors and the dead tell their stories through scribbled notes, vivid paintings, children's games, family photographs, and concentration camp uniforms.

The Holocaust was the murder by Hitler and Nazi Germany of six million Jews. While the Nazi persecution of the Jews began in 1933, the mass murder was committed during World War II. It took the Germans and their accomplices four-and-a-half years to murder six million Jews. In one 250-day period in 1942 they murdered some two-and-a-half million Jews. The Nazis never showed any restraint and only slowed down when they no longer had any Jews to kill.

Huckabee stated, "You must remember that this mass murdering of people did not come from some hostile tribal people from some remote, uncivilized part of the world, but the Holocaust came from a highly educated society. The German people were the most technologically advanced people on earth at the time of this atrocity. They had some of the greatest universities in the world. Their theologians were world-renown. Multitudes of their people professed to adhere to the Christian faith.

"However, Dietrich Bonheoffer, a Lutheran pastor and modern-day martyr, stood up against the Nazi regime, but on September 9, 1940 he was forbidden to publish or speak in Germany. On April 5, 1943 the Gestapo arrested him and three months later he was indicted on the charge of subversion by the armed forces. He spent 18 months in prison before he was taken to the concentration camp at Flossenburg where he was hung with a piano wire on the morning of April 9, 1945."

The Buchenwald Report described the ghastly events at another concentration camp, Auschwitz-Birkenau, thusly: "The elderly were loaded onto dump trucks and then dumped into burning trenches while still alive. The remainder was led into the gas chambers. Meanwhile new transports were arriving all the time.

"In front of the gas chambers was a dressing room. On its walls was written in all languages: 'Put shoes into the cubbyholes and tie them together so you will not lose them. After showers you will receive hot coffee.'

"Here the poor victims undressed themselves and went into the chamber. There were three columns for the ventilators, through which the gas poured in. A special work detail with truncheons drove the people into the chamber.

"When the room was full, small children were thrown in through a window. (SS Sergeant) Moll grabbed infants by their little legs and smashed their skulls against the wall. Then the gas was let into the chamber. The lungs of the victims slowly burst, and after three minutes a loud clamoring could be heard. Then the chamber was opened, and those who still showed signs of life were beaten to death."

Other Holocaust atrocities were equally disturbing or even worse. How would a ten-year-old girl respond to the revelation of such a harrowing, disturbing experience?

Huckabee recalled, "When we had finished going through Yad Vashem there was a place for those who had visited the Holocaust museum to register their names and addresses and comments.

"I had not gotten any indication from Sarah as to how she had processed the information she had gathered from the experience. However, I had noticed that she had observed the recounting of the 'Holocaust' with a keen interest and deep concern.

"When we got to the registration book, I noted that Sarah wanted to write down her information. I wondered what she would write. I looked over her shoulder and noted that she signed her name and provided her address. However, there was also a place for comments. 'Will she write something there?' I wondered. 'And if she does, what will she write?'

"She paused for a moment, assessed the horrors of the Holocaust depicted at Yad Vashem and then carefully wrote, 'Why didn't somebody do something?'"

The Light: Rejected, Neglected, and Feared

*T*he *Atlanta Journal Constitution* recently published an online article entitle "Bible losing influence in America." The AJC article cited another article in *The Washington Times* bearing the unbiased headline "Going to hell in a handbasket."

The Times reported, "For the first time, the number of Americans skeptical of the Bible is equal to the number who believe the words are inspired directly by God and contain no errors except for maybe a few of the tricky passages."

The American Bible Society, in their 2014 "State of the Bible" report, said that the number of Americans skeptical of the Bible has increased 10% since 2011.

The AJC article explained, "Young people, the so-called 'Millennial Generation' (who range in age from 18-29) must be too busy taking 'selfies' or copying-and-pasting links to Reddit to heed the book last updated some 2,000 years ago."

The Bible is losing its influence in American life because truth is under attack in our culture. Vodie Baucham, Jr., in his book *The Ever-Loving Truth*, writes, "The person who believes in ideas, concepts, values, or facts that are true for all people in all places for all times is rare, indeed."

Two of the philosophies that lend themselves to this depreciation of absolute truth are relativism and subjectivism. Relativism is the view that truth is always changing. However, truth is immortal. It does not change. The grass withereth, the flower fadeth, but the Word of our God shall stand forever" (Is. 40: 8).

Relativism rules in situations like political races when candidates lick their forefinger, hold it in the air to see which way the wind is blowing, and develop their "stump" speeches accordingly.

For example, in a 2001 Gallup Poll 53% of Americans considered gay relations to be "morally wrong." By 2011, these numbers had changed radically with 56% calling gay relations "morally acceptable" and only 39% saying they were "morally wrong."

Had God's Word changed? Did heaven all of a sudden give license to homosexuality? Did truth change when Barack Obama, Bill and Hillary Clinton, and Rob Portman abandon their commitment to traditional marriage and voice their support of gay marriages? Absolutely not!

On the other hand, subjectivism is the philosophy that suggests something may be true for you, but not for me. It is more of a "live and let live" view of life. This philosophy purports that truth is subjective, not objective. It is the incorrect notion that truth is relative to individuals.

Remember the words of James Russell Lowell, who in the 19th century wrote the poem, *The Present Crisis*. He penned, "In regards to subjectivism 'Truth forever on the scaffold, wrong forever on the throne.'"

Today it appears that truth is on the scaffold and tolerance on the throne, but Lowell adds these lines: "Yet the scaffold sways the future, and, behind the dim unknown, standeth God within the shadow, keeping watch above his own."

Relativism and subjectivism and all the other "isms" may seem to prevail in our day, but ultimately truth will triumph. And I had rather lose a battle in a cause that will ultimately win than to win a battle in a cause that will ultimately lose.

All the cynics and skeptics may devise alternative philosophies, because, in fact, they are afraid of the truth. Plato said, "We can easily forgive a child who is afraid of the dark; the real tragedy of life is when men are afraid of the light."

But in addition to the skeptics are the unknowing or illiterate. The Bible is by far the best-selling book in the world, but probably purchased by many as a good luck charm rather than something to be cherished and read daily.

Al Mohler, president of Southern Seminary in Louisville, KY, states, "While America's evangelical Christians are rightly concerned about the secular worldview's rejection of biblical Christianity, we ought to give some urgent attention to a problem much closer to home – biblical literacy in the church. This scandalous problem is our own, and it's up to us to fix it."

And the nation may have rejected the notion of absolute truth, because they are simply not acquainted with it.

Jay Leno, former host of *The Tonight Show* on NBC television, made sport of Americans' inability to answer simple questions about the Bible. He would randomly interview people on the streets of New York and ask them Bible questions. The answers he got were most telling.

He said to a young lady from Louisville, KY, "On the first day of creation God said, 'Let there be _____.'"

Instead of saying "light" she said, "peace."

Then Leno said, "Finish this quote. 'Blessed are the meek for they shall _____.'"

The young woman responded, "Eat." The correct answer is: "They shall inherit the earth."

When he asked her, "How many commandments are there?" She said, "Twelve."

One man said Jesus was born 400 years ago and a young woman said Christ was born 250 million years ago.

This generation has been called the unseeded generation. *Time* magazine, in a 2007 cover story, reported that only half of U.S. adults could name one of the four Gospels. Fewer than half could identify the first book of the Bible.

There are three fundamental things we must do if we are to reverse the trend of biblical illiteracy. (1) Parents must diligently teach their own children the Word of God (Dt. 6:4-9). (2) Our pulpits must vigorously preach expository sermons that are anointed by the Holy Spirit. (3) Christians must become faithful witnesses of God's redeeming grace and inerrant truths.

Finally, we have the responsibility to make the Word of God and Christianity attractive. We are to live in such a way that people will want what we possess.

Edgar Guest said, "I'd rather see a sermon than hear one any day; I'd rather one should walk with me than merely tell the way: The eye's a better pupil and more willing than the ear, fine counsel is confusing, but example's always clear."

If we have found the Bible to be a rich treasure, we must live it, share it, proclaim it, teach it, broadcast it, and shout it from the rooftops. Those of us who were a part of the Conservative Resurgence didn't seek to win a victory for the cause of inerrancy so that we could keep our Bibles in a pristine condition as one would keep some treasure under lock and key.

The best Bible is one that is worn, well-marked, and lived out in daily life. We must neither reject the light, neglect it, nor be afraid of it.

One Opinion on why our
Baptisms are Plummeting

A recent news release from LifeWay Christian Resources indicated that in 2013 Southern Baptist Convention churches experienced another decline in the number of baptisms reported. Although the percentage of decline was not as severe as last year the reported baptisms have declined seven of the last nine years.

Thom Rainer, president and CEO of LifeWay, stated, "I am grieved we are clearly losing our evangelistic effectiveness."

Commenting on the statistical report, Frank S. Page, president and CEO of the SBC Executive Committee, cited the Old Testament prophet Amos: "Woe to you who are at ease in Zion" (Amos 6:1).

He added, "That warning in the Book of Amos is a clear call to the people of God who have lowered their guard, relaxed their vigilance, and reduced their commitment and passion for the things of God. That very same thing can be said of our modern-day churches as we yet again see a disappointing decline in our ability to reach our continent for Christ."

Surely, there are many things that have contributed to this decline in baptisms. Many of them are obvious: fewer churches with soul-winning ministries, fewer churches having revival meetings, fewer altar calls, fewer evangelistic sermons, fewer dollars being allocated for evangelistic outreach – and the list goes on.

However, there is something else I have noticed in recent years. I am hearing fewer confessional prayers and songs in our worship services.

We are well aware of David's confessional prayer in Psalm 32 where he beseeches God, "I acknowledge my sin unto thee, and mine iniquity have I not hidden. I said, I will confess my transgressions unto the Lord, and thou forgavest the iniquity of my sin."

In Psalm 51 David's plaintive plea is: "Wash me thoroughly from mind iniquity, and cleanse me from my sin. For I acknowledge my transgressions, and my sin is ever before me."

In Daniel, the great prophet of God cries out, "We have sinned, and have committed iniquity, and have done wickedly, and have rebelled, even by departing from thy precepts and from thine ordinances … Neither have we obeyed the voice of the Lord, our God, to walk in his laws, which he set before us by his servants, the prophets."

And in Luke 18:13 the tax collector humbled himself and prayed, "Lord, be merciful to me a sinner." Because this man honestly confessed his sin, he was justified by God.

Martin Luther prayed confessional prayers. He cried out to God, "I am a sinner; You are upright. With me there is an abundance of sin; in You is the fullness of righteousness."

Charles Spurgeon prayed, "Our Father, we are very weak. Worst of all we are very wicked if left to ourselves, and we soon fall a prey to the enemy … We hear of oppression and robbery and murder and men seem let loose against each other. Lord have mercy upon this great and wicked city … As Abraham pled for Sodom; we plead for London."

George W. Truett prayed, "Little do we know of this blessed, glorious privilege and duty, and poor has been our behavior with reference to prayer. Forgive us, we pray thee, for our neglect, our ignorance, and our disobedience. Help us to be repentant on account of every evil way, and cleanse us from all unrighteousness. Turn us away from every wrong course."

In a recent conversation with Jon Duncan, GBC state missionary who provides leadership in our convention's music and worship ministry, he reminded me that confession of sin is necessary if we are to clearly understand God's Word and will for our lives.

He cited Isaiah as an example. In Isaiah chapter five the prophet lamented over Israel's six woeful sins, but in chapter six he offered his own prayer of confession: "Woe is me! for I am undone; because I am a man of unclean lips, and I dwell in the midst of a people of unclean lips: ..."

Not until he had confessed his sin did he hear the voice of God and respond to God's call to ministry. Obviously, confession of sin paves the way to understanding God's truth, knowing God's will, having God's favor, and being able to worship in spirit and truth.

However, today much of our praying in public is directed toward thanksgiving and adoration and little attention seems to be given to prayers of confession and repentance. If public prayers have little to do with contrition and sorrow for sin, isn't it likely that private prayers follow the same pathway?

Likewise, most churches seldom sing choruses or songs that make any mention of sin. Today many look with scorn upon what has been called "worm theology." The term is derived from a line in Isaac Watts' hymn "Alas! And Did My Savior Bleed," which says, "Would he devote that sacred head for such a worm as I?"

I think that hymn was written when people had a higher view of God. Now we seem to have a higher view of man and choose not to dwell on the ugliness of sin. Hymns like "Out of my bondage, sorrow and night … [and] out of my shameful failure and loss, Jesus, I come, Jesus, I come" are not as palatable to the sophisticated American churchgoer.

Dr. Cornelius Plantinga, senior research fellow at the Calvin Institute of Christian Worship, recently stated, "In very many evangelical and confessionally Reformed churches these days, sin is a rare topic."

Plantinga added, "Over 158,000 churches in North America get the music for their worship services from Christian Copyright Licensing International; [and they] provide a valuable service to churches by streamlining the process of obtaining licenses for their worship music."

Looking at the content of CCLI songs, Plantinga observed that there are "very few penitential songs." The biblical tradition of lament, which is all through the prophets and the Psalms, is gone. It's just not there.

"Mindful that seekers come to church in an American no-fault culture in which tolerance is a big virtue and intolerance a big vice, worship finders in evangelical churches often want nothing in the service that sounds judgmental," he said. And for that reason "lots of evangelical churches these days are unrelievedly cheerful."

Dr. David Wells, distinguished senior research professor at Gordon Conwell Theological Seminary, explained, "Leaving sin out of worship is consistent with the theology of many evangelical churches in which 'God is on easy terms with modernity and mostly concerned with church growth and psychological wholeness.'"

The Apostle Paul would not feel welcome in many evangelical churches today, he added. "Where is [Paul's] easy smile? Why does he want to discipline people? Why is he so doggone dogmatic? Where are the stories in his sermons? And where does he get off implying that the woman singing special music in church should not do so while also lying on top of the church piano?"

So, what does all this have to do with our decline in baptisms? If we are not praying penitential prayers and if we are not singing songs that reprove the soul it is also likely that our sermons will tend to be more suited to appeasing the conscience than bringing about conviction of sin. The bottom line is there can be no salvation of the soul until there is an awareness of sin. There is only one thing we can bring to the equation in the search for salvation and that is our own wretched, shameful, sinful nature.

An awareness of sin + God's amazing Grace = salvation … and ultimately more baptisms.

The Lies Versus the Truth

In order to find the first falsehood to disgrace the earth you have to go all the way back to the Garden of Eden. Lying on this earth started when Satan, as a sly, subtle, slithering snake, said to Eve, "Ye shall not surely die."

With those condemning words Lucifer attempted to negate what God had said about eating the forbidden fruit. In essence he insisted that he was telling the truth and that the Almighty was lying when He said, "Ye shall not eat of it, neither shall ye touch it, lest ye die."

Jesus said of Satan, "for he is a liar and the Father of it" (John 8:44). Satan not only lied to Eve at the dawn of creation, but he has inspired falsehoods and fabrications in every generation since his first appearance on Earth.

The Oxford English Dictionary defines lying as "telling an intentional falsehood, which indicates a manipulation." Sir Walter Scott exclaimed, "Oh, what a tangled web we weave … when first we practice to deceive." Leo Tolstoy stated, "Anything is better than lies and deceit."

The Bible says, "Lying lips are an abomination to the Lord" (Pr. 12:22). For example, evolution is a big lie. Genesis 1:27 declares, "So God created man in his own image, in the image of God created he him; male and female created he them." Mankind is created in God's own image.

Psalm 8:5 says, "For thou hast made him a little lower than the angels, and hast crowned him with glory and honour." In fact, it takes far more faith to believe that man evolved from some amoeba than it does to believe that God created him.

While Richard Dawkins has insisted that his discovery of evolution has enabled him to be an "intellectually fulfilled atheist" it has really done nothing more than express a dismally inadequate view of the Creator God of the Bible who is the author of all that exists and "in whom all things hold together" (Col. 1:17). Dawkins' misunderstanding or denial of creation theology and his embracing of the big lie of evolution is his way of justifying his atheism.

Another big lie is universalism, the philosophy that all roads lead to God and eternal life. It sounds so tolerant and loving to proclaim that all religions are equally valid and that they all ultimately lead to heaven. The exclusivity of the Gospel and the belief that Jesus Christ is the only way to heaven is considered politically incorrect and too narrow a view for today's sophisticated society.

One universalist pastor, Scott Alexander, proclaimed, "Every human being is a child of God – quite naturally possessing their divine parent's inclination toward goodness and right, and therefore unavoidably drawn toward heaven and health by God's all-powerful and encompassing love."

That sounds good, but it is a big lie. The Bible says, "Enter in at the narrow gate; for wide is the gate, and broad is the way, that leadeth to destruction, and many there be who go in that way. But narrow is the gate and hard is the way, which leadeth unto life, and few there be that find it" (Matt. 7: 13-14).

There is scarcely anything more wicked than a preacher who would lead his hearers away from the truth with a heretical message. The Bible speaks of "ungodly men [who] turn the grace of God into lasciviousness, and deny the only Lord God, and our Lord Jesus Christ" (Jude 4).

Unfortunately, many politicians have been known for being purveyors of prevarication. There is the old question: "How can you tell when a politician is lying? When his (or her) lips move." That is a tired old cliché, but it may be more accurate than we want to admit.

We know that Richard Nixon lied about his involvement in the Watergate scandal. We know that Bill Clinton lied about his tryst with Monica Lewinsky. We know that George H. W. Bush lied when he said, "Read my lips. No new taxes."

Some have said that President Obama is a weak leader, but I think he is a smart leader who is managing to impose his questionable agenda upon the American people with incredible success. The promises about affordability of the president's health care program, the mixed messages about the attack on the embassy in Benghazi, the campaign promises about transparency in his administration seem empty and void of reality to many. So, his Pinocchio moniker may have been assigned to him with good reason.

In his 1925 autobiography Mein Kampf, Adolph Hitler advocated the "big lie." He wrote, "… in the big lie there is always a certain force of credibility; because the broad masses of a nation are always more easily corrupted in the deeper strata of their emotional nature than consciously or voluntarily; and thus in the primitive simplicity of their minds they more readily fall victims to the big lie than the small lie, since they themselves often tell small lies in little matters, but would be ashamed to resort to large-scale falsehoods.

"It would never come into their heads to fabricate colossal untruths, and they would not believe that others could have the impudence to distort the truth so infamously. Even though the facts which prove this to be so may be brought clearly to their minds, they will still doubt and waver and will continue to think that there may be some other explanation."

Joseph Goebbels, the minister of propaganda in Nazi Germany, expanded Hitler's comment by adding, "The big lie can be maintained only for such time as the State can shield the people from the political, economic and/or military consequences of the lie. It thus becomes vitally important for the State to use all of its powers to repress dissent, for the truth is the mortal enemy of the lie, and thus by extension, the truth is the greatest enemy of the State."

But here is the primary point of the editorial. Because of the rapid descent of our nation it is apparent that the world knows how to lie better than the church knows how to tell the truth.

'Don't Mess with the
Pulpits of America!'

The United States of America was established with freedom of religion as the cornerstone of its foundation. David Barton of Wall Builders stated, "Thomas Jefferson had no intention of allowing the government to limit, restrict, regulate, or interfere with public religious practices."

In fact, Jefferson wrote a letter to Benjamin Rush, a fellow-signer of the Declaration of Independence, saying: "The clause of the Constitution which, while it secured the freedom of the press, covered also the freedom of religion."

Jefferson also declared, "And can the liberties of a nation be thought secure if we have lost the only firm basis, a conviction in the minds of the people that these liberties are the gift of God? That they are not to be violated but with His wrath."

Yet, in recent years we have seen the erosion of our religious liberties. The first severe blow came in 1962 when the Supreme Court ruled on the Engel v. Vitale Case that it was unconstitutional for state officials to compose a school prayer and encourage its recitation in public schools.

The prayer in question was: "Almighty God, we acknowledge our dependence upon Thee, and we beg Thy blessings upon us, our parents, our teachers and our country. Amen."

The prayer seems innocuous enough, but the Court's ruling articulated by Justice Hugo Black stated that the prayer was an unconstitutional violation of the Establishment Clause.

The ruling in the Engel v. Vitale Case became the basis for subsequent decisions banning clergy-led prayer at graduation ceremonies and student-led prayer at high school football games.

Several factors in Justice Black's background arguably influenced him to rule unfavorably against religion. He had been a member of the Ku Klux Klan, an organization that was known to be particularly bigoted against Catholics. Also, at the time he wrote his opinion he was not a practicing Christian, was prejudiced against religion, and was engaged in judicial activism.

Since Justice Black's opinion was written, the American Civil Liberties Union, various atheist groups, and activist judges have wreaked havoc with America's religious freedoms.

The Liberty Institute and the Family Research Council have published the 2014 edition of their survey on Hostility to Religion in America. Here are some of their findings.

In the Van Orden v. Perry case and the McCreary County v. ACLU case the displaying of the Ten Commandments at the Texas capitol and in a Kentucky courthouse was challenged.

The United States Congress has opened with prayer since the founding of the United States and Congress hired a chaplain to give these opening prayers the same week it passed the First Amendment, but threats and lawsuits challenging these prayers are growing more frequent.

In Balch Springs, TX city officials told senior citizens at a senior center that they could not pray before their meals, listen to religious messages, or sing gospel songs because religion is banned in public buildings. After senior citizens filed a lawsuit, government officials told the senior citizens that if they won the lawsuit their meals would be taken away, because praying over government-funded meals violates the "separation of church and state."

In Kountze, TX the high school cheerleaders wanted to display encouraging messages to the football players of both KHS's team and the opposing teams. The cheerleaders decided that the best way to encourage the players was to write Bible verses on the "run-through" banners that the football players run though at the beginning of each game.

The Freedom From Religion Foundation discovered that the cheerleaders were writing Bible verses and sent a letter to the Kountze Independent School District demanding the school district stop the cheerleaders. The superintendent of Kountze I.S.D. then banned any student group, including the cheerleaders, from bringing signs with religious messages to sporting events.

Minneapolis hosts a gay pride festival in a public park each year. Subject to city approval, vendors of all kinds are allowed to set up booths in order to sell their wares to the public. However, when Brian Johnson, an evangelical Christian, requested a booth to distribute Bibles, the city denied his application and proceeded to pass an ordinance that limited the distribution of such materials.

The United States Navy has been required to remove all Bibles from guest rooms of lodges and hotels on U.S. Navy bases. The Air Force Academy has removed a Bible verse written on a cadet's whiteboard after it determined the posting had offended other cadets.

The family of a second-grade student at a Texas elementary school says their daughter's teacher took her Bible away during a "read-to-myself" session. The teacher reportedly said the Bible is inappropriate reading material.

On Oct. 14 Fox News reported that Houston's lesbian mayor, Annise Parker, had issued subpoenas demanding five pastors turn over sermons dealing negatively with homosexuality, gender identity, or the Houston Equal Rights Ordinance (H.E.R.O.). The news reported that ministers who failed to comply could be held in contempt of court.

The public outcry against Parker was notable. More than 1,000 Bibles were sent to Parker's office in protest of her subpoenas. Governor Mike Huckabee, Duck Dynasty's Phil Robertson, and Edwin Young, pastor of Houston's Second Baptist Church, spoke at a rally on Nov. 2 to sound the alarm on "the abuse of government power."

At the rally Young fervently declared, "Let me speak in words that any Texan should understand: 'Don't mess with the pulpits of America!'"

Russell Moore, the president of the ERLC, responded by saying, "I am stunned by the sheer audacity of [these reports]. The preaching of sermons in the pulpits of churches is of no concern to any government bureaucrat at all. A government has no business using subpoena power to intimidate or bully the preaching and instruction of any church, any synagogue, any mosque, or any other place of worship."

The examples of our religious liberties being challenged are innumerable and extend into almost every area of life in America. The question is this: Where will it all end?

Todd Starnes has written a book called *God Less America*. In the book he gives countless examples of our religious liberties being attacked. He explains, "We are facing uncertain times. America's values are under assault.

Religious liberty has been undermined. Radical Islam is on the rise. We live in a day when right is now wrong and wrong is now right."

One story that stands out in Starnes' mind is a lesson Ronald Reagan gave during a radio address in the 1970s. Reagan told the story about Germany's invasion of Ukraine when the Germans told Ukrainians they could not sing religious songs. The Germans rewrote the lyrics to "Silent Night" and took out all references to Christ and Mary.

"The reason why that story is so interesting now is because we are starting to mirror it. Just last Christmas in Long Island a school had taken out references to Jesus and Mary in 'Silent Night' for their Christmas production," Starnes explained.

Franklin Graham once said, "I believe that a time is fast-approaching – I think it will be in my lifetime – when the preaching of the Gospel is referred to as hate speech."

The answer to our threatened religious freedom is found in Galatians 5:1 where Paul exhorts us: "Christ has liberated us to be free. Stand firm then and don't submit again to a yoke of slavery."

We Aren't Moving to
the Back of the Bus

Christmas is all about an innocent child who was born over two thousand years ago into abject poverty to homeless refugees on the outskirts of a brutal empire. A host of angels appeared in the sky to impoverished shepherds singing, "Glory to God in the highest, and on earth peace, good will toward men."

That innocent child, conceived by the Holy Spirit and born of a virgin, grew up to live a sinless life, performed miraculous deeds of kindness and love, died a vicarious death as our Savior and Lord, rose victoriously from the dead, and defying the law of gravity ascended back to heaven where he ever lives to make intercession for us.

Yet, while He was on this earth He made people so angry they wanted to kill Him. He challenged their superficial religion. He exposed their greed and materialism. They despised and rejected Him, because He didn't keep all the laws they had devised regarding the Sabbath.

They viewed with disdain and derision His claim to be God. They were jealous of the followers He amassed. Yet, they struggled in vain to find any real blemish in His character.

I have often wondered what would happen if Jesus were to be born in our day. Would his parents have to escape to some foreign land, because of the death threats of some modern day "Herod"? Would He mystify the religious leaders with His wisdom as an adolescent? Would He have reason to expose the religious (Christian) church for its compromise and indifference? Would he incur the same kind of wrath He did when He came 2,000 years ago? Would He be executed in some cruel and shameless way?

I believe He would garner the same kind of reception He did when He came to this earth 21 centuries ago. In fact, I'm confident that the false charges and animosity would be hurled at Him more rapidly and with even greater hostility. I am not sure it would take 33 years for Him to be crucified if He were born in America this Christmas.

I am beginning to see shades of Christian persecution here in our beloved land. Based on what has happened throughout history we can only expect it to increase. Jesus said, "And you shall be hated of all men for my name's sake" (Matt. 10:22).

In Proverbs 29:27 the Bible says, "He that is upright in the way is an abomination unto the wicked."

Jesus said, "If the world hate you, ye know that it hated me before it hated you. If ye were of the world, the world would love its own; but because ye are not of the world, but I have chosen you out of the world, therefore the world hateth you" (John 15:18-19).

I recently had the privilege of speaking at the Centennial Celebration of Kilpatrick Association at First Baptist Church in Thompson. I stated, "Ten years ago I feared that the persecution of Christians may come in the lifetime of my grandchildren. Five years ago I feared that it might come in the lives of my children. Today I fear that it may come even in my lifetime."

I have changed my criterion of success in the church. Once I thought success depended on how many were in attendance in Sunday School or worship, how many baptisms the church could report on its Annual Church Profile, and how much money was coming into the coffers. That is no longer true. I believe a successful church today is that church that is adequately preparing its members for the coming persecution.

Last year the Bulloch Board of Education cracked down on religious expression in their schools by censoring Christmas cards. For years the teachers at Brooklet Elementary School posted Christmas cards in the hallways outside their classrooms, but last year the school board put an end to that.

It was reported, "They took down the cards so the kids can't see them. Some of the cards had the word Christmas and some had Nativity scenes."

Teachers have been ordered to remove any religious icons or items from their classrooms – ranging from Bibles to Christian music.

Two years ago, the American Atheists placed a billboard in Times Square that showed a picture of Santa Clause and a picture of the crucified Christ, with the caption "Keep the Merry! Dump the Myth!"

What do you think would happen if anyone dared to put up a billboard of Mohammed with the word "myth" under his picture? There would no doubt be blood in the streets and denunciations from the White House and Congress.

I just don't understand the thought process of those who want to suppress the true meaning of Christmas or ban religious freedom. There is a hue and cry for equality, but those who insist on equality are enthusiastic about celebrating the announcement that Michael Sam is the first openly gay football player drafted into the NFL. Yet, they vilify Tim Tebow for unashamedly taking a stand for Christ.

There is ample information available to indicate that Marxist indoctrination is ongoing in certain public-school systems in America; but some schools would be threatened with lawsuits if they dared to teach that America was founded upon Christian principles.

Evolution is taught as common fare in most public schools, but one of the American Civil Liberties Union's top lawyers says that teaching creationism in science classes violates the U.S. Constitution and invites legal challenges.

Nineteen Minutes is a racy novel that 14-year-old English students in New Hampshire have been assigned to read at a local high school, but they can only read the Bible at their own risk and peril.

New York City Mayor Bill de Blasio recently announced that he is moving toward closing the public schools of the city for Eid al-Fitr and Eid al-Adha, significant days on the Islamic calendar, to honor the Muslim religion. However, in the same city students will get out of school for the last week in December for what they are calling, not Christmas holidays, but the winter recess.

Christianity has been relegated to the back of the bus in our day. We need someone with the determination and courage of Rosa Parks, who will say, "We have had enough of your intimidation. We are not moving to the back of the bus. We are holding our ground for the sake of Biblical equality."

Chief Kelvin Cochran Suspended for Telling the Truth

Atlanta Mayor Kasim Reed has suspended the city's fire chief, Kelvin Cochran, from his position. It is a month's suspension without pay. I know Chief Cochran. He is a Georgia Baptist – one of us. Chief Cochran is a member of Elizabeth Baptist Church in Noonday Association. He serves there as a deacon and Sunday School teacher. He is a humble, dedicated, faithful servant of God.

However, Chief Cochran has been suspended without pay for one month because he authored a Christian book in which he describes homosexuality as a "perversion." The Atlanta Journal-Constitution reported, "Mayor Kasim Reed's spokeswoman Anne Torres said the administration didn't know about (Cochran's book) *Who Told You That You Are Naked?* until employees came forward with complaints. In addition to suspending Cochran, Reed's office has now opened an investigation to determine whether the chief discriminated against employees.

"Cochran has been ordered to undergo sensitivity training and barred from distributing copies of the book on city property after a number of firefighters said they received them in the workplace," Torres said.

Kelvin Cochran was born in Shreveport, LA in 1960. He was the fourth of six children and his father died when he was five years old. After his father's death the family moved to a "shotgun" house on Rear Snow Street in an impoverished section of the city. His mother never remarried and struggled to make sure her children were fed and clothed.

One Sunday after church Kelvin and his family heard fire trucks headed down their street. The house across the street from where they lived had caught fire. Kelvin watched as the firefighters put on their equipment and got their fire hoses to extinguish the inferno. It was then, as a five-year-old boy, that Kelvin decided he wanted to become a firefighter.

He had been taught that if you put your faith in God, get a good education, respect your elders, and treat others as you would have them treat you your dreams will come true.

During those years there were no blacks in the Shreveport Fire Department, but Kelvin was never discouraged from dreaming his dream.

Kelvin grew up under the ministry of Rev. E. Edward Jones, who became the pastor of Galilee Baptist Church in Shreveport in 1958, and who continues to provide godly leadership for the church. Pastor Jones became a father figure and role model for Kelvin. He also observed the character of godly men with good families.

Upon graduating from high school Kelvin went to Louisiana Tech in Ruston but it was a short-lived academic endeavor. He left college and went back to Shreveport to fulfill his goal of becoming a firefighter. His dream was realized when he earned his place with the Shreveport Fire Department in 1981.

Within four years he was promoted to fire training officer and served in this capacity from 1985 to 1990, when he became assistant chief training officer and continued to earn promotions until he became the department's fire chief in August of 1999. That was also the year he received his bachelor's degree from Wiley College. Ultimately, he went back to Louisiana Tech, reversed his earlier academic misfortunes, and earned a master's degree.

On Jan. 2, 2008, Chief Cochran was selected by Atlanta Mayor Shirley Franklin to become the city's fire chief. He entered into a Daniel fast prior to making his decision and concluded that God was leading him to accept the position.

He served in that capacity until July 2009, when President Barack Obama appointed him as U.S. Fire Administrator for the United States Fire Administration in Washington, D.C. In that capacity, Chief Cochran was charged with overseeing, coordinating, and directing national efforts to prevent fires and improve fire responses.

On May 8, 2010 Chief Cochran returned to Atlanta to resume the position of fire chief. As the Atlanta's fire chief, Cochran has spent innumerable hours training his force of almost 1,200 people. He has shared the principles and values that he believes are essential to a caring and efficient department.

Among those principles, which he has called "The Fire Service Doctrines," is the value which he has called "Ism Free." He insists there is to be no discrimination regarding sexism, favoritism, racism, territorialism, or nepotism. Under Cochran's administration that has become the code for the Atlanta Fire and Rescue Department.

Kelvin's leadership as an Atlanta public servant roots back to his faith and commitment to Christ. Kelvin and his wife, Carolyn, are a part of Elizabeth Baptist Church and serve as an integral part of their fellowship.

Several months ago, the men of the church were engaged in a series of studies called "A Quest for Authentic Manhood" and when some of the men began to mention their struggles with condemnation, Cochran wondered how "saved" men could live under the dark cloud of guilt and condemnation. The question, "Who told you that you were naked?" gripped his heart and mind.

He began to study the word "naked" from a biblical perspective and concluded that the "naked" were spiritually dead. He thought, "The instigator of spiritual death is Satan. The progenitor of spiritual death is Adam. And when Adam and Eve succumbed to Satan's provocative temptation they realized that they were naked."

Cochran also studied the word "clothed" and realized that it was a reference to redemption. He surmised, "When a man is adequately covered, he is confident and accountable – that a redeemed man is no longer 'the naked', but with Christ he is 'the clothed.'"

The fire chief sensed that through his study the Lord was leading him to write a book that he chose to call *Who Told You That You Were Naked?*

Cochran has never tried to market his self-published book, but has shared the book with his church and given books to his colleagues at work. After work on Monday the Chief has hosted a Bible study for those who were interested. Other colleagues have frequently sought him out for spiritual counseling. He consistently provided counsel by sharing truths from the Word of God.

Even when he gave his books to colleagues he never signed the books as the fire chief, because he did not want to appear to use his position in an untoward way.

However, on page 82 of Cochran's book he wrote that uncleanness "is opposite of purity; including sodomy, homosexuality, lesbianism, pederasty, bestiality, and all other forms of sexual perversion."

Those words, which are consistent with the teaching of the Bible, are the ones that prompted Cochran's suspension. But this issue is bigger than the impact it has had on Kelvin Cochran. It impacts every Baptist and every person of faith in Georgia and in the nation.

I realize our churches are open and our religious institutions continue to function and everything on the religious front may look copacetic. But when you begin to look beneath the surface, acknowledge the threats, and analyze them, you begin to realize that our religious liberty is under an organized and concentrated assault.

Recently there have been multiple attempts to prevent Christians from speaking to the cultural issues of the day. *The Christian Index* has attempted to communicate to you, our readers, of some of the moves to silence believers, push activist agendas, stifle freedom, and intimidate our pulpits.

In Janet Folger Porter's book *The Criminalization of Christianity* she writes, "As a Christian in this country, you may be understandably reluctant to speak out on moral issues like abortion, homosexuality, or pornography. But while we have the right to remain silent, that's not what God calls us to do.

"Because if the world can silence the truth, it will silence the Gospel."

Code Blue

Several years ago, I was visiting a friend in the intensive care unit of Atlanta's Northside Hospital. My friend was recovering from an extensive surgical procedure and appeared to be making a successful recovery. His nurse came into the room to examine his incision and I stepped out of the room while she was caring for his needs.

While I was waiting to re-enter the room to conclude my visit I heard a distinct alarm-like sound that came from the nurses' station no more than 15 feet from where I was standing. One nurse said to another, "There's a code blue in Room 10."

The two nurses literally sprang from their seats and ran into Room 10. Within a matter of seconds a man with a stethoscope in his hand rushed past me into the same room. Then the nurse who had been serving my friend opened the door behind me and rushed to the room where the whole staff seemed to be gathering.

In less than a minute she came back to where I was standing and asked me to leave the intensive care unit. As I was exiting the ICU two men, presumably physicians, rushed toward the room that seemed to be the focus of everyone's attention.

I knew that there was a patient in distress. I went into the waiting room, bowed my head, and prayed. I waited for almost 30 minutes, because I had not concluded my visit with my friend. I had not even told him goodbye.

Finally, not knowing how long the ICU would be closed to guests, I stood up to make my way out of the hospital, but as I was turning down the hall to go to the elevator the same nurse who had been attending to my friend emerged from the intensive care unit, found me, and told me I could re-enter the ICU and finish my visit.

She told me that the patient in Room 10 had experienced a respiratory arrest, but as a result of the swift action of the medical staff he had been resuscitated. I knew that such a condition demanded immediate and decisive treatment and that a lack of oxygen to the brain could cause unconsciousness and result in irreparable damage, even death.

I believe we are living in a "code blue" world. The whole world is in chaos with war, famine, pestilence (Ebola), the march of the Muslims, and the crucifixion of Christians. The America that I have known for most of my life is disintegrating economically (with an astronomical debt), militarily, politically, morally, and spiritually.

Many churches are on life support and tottering on the brink of extinction. My home church in North Carolina is little more than a shell of the vibrant fellowship teaming with life I knew as a boy. Countless other churches have similar histories of decline. Furthermore, souls all around us are desperately lost and drifting aimlessly toward eternal retribution.

The preachers of America must sound the "code blue" alarm and "cry aloud and spare not." The pulpits of our churches must reverberate with the clarion sound of the trumpet, calling people to humility, repentance, and service (action).

Alex de Tocqueville (1805-1859), French political thinker and historian, reportedly wrote: "I sought for the greatness and genius of America in her commodious harbors and her ample rivers – and it was not there ... in her fertile fields and boundless forests and it was not there ... in her rich mines and her vast world commerce – and it was not there ... in her democratic Congress and her matchless Constitution – and it was not there.

"Not until I went into the churches of America and heard her pulpits aflame with righteousness did I understand the secret of her genius and power. America is great because she is good, and if America ever ceases to be good, she will cease to be great."

America's pulpits need to once again be set aflame with pastors calling their flocks to righteousness. Those of us who have been entrusted with the proclamation of the Word of God must preach with fire and passion.

Richard Baxter, a preacher, revivalist, and soul winner, exclaimed, "I preached as never sure to preach again, and as a dying man to dying men."

That must become the measure of our urgency in the pulpit – not preaching as a mere professional clergyman, but preaching as did Jeremiah who said, "[His Word] is in my mind and heart as if it were a burning fire shut up in my bones, and I am weary with enduring and holding it in; I cannot contain it longer" (Jer. 20: 9 Amplified Bible).

We must sound the alarm in order to awake the sleeping church. This is no time for mild homilies, insipid devotionals, or vesper services. It is time to ring the bell on sin and stir up the army of God into action. The Word of God is quick and powerful and sharper than any two-edged sword. It has the power to save souls, transform lives, lift burdens, mend broken homes, revive churches, and spare and deliver nations.

There is also a need for the church to wake up. A lackadaisical, lukewarm church in Laodicea prompted the Lord to call them "wretched, and miserable, and poor, and blind and naked." That same kind of apathy can also destroy a nation.

Robert M. Hutchins, president of the University of Chicago (1929-51), said, "The death of democracy is not likely to be an assassination from ambush. It will be a slow extinction from apathy, indifference, and undernourishment."

Cyril Connolly, English intellectual, literary critic, and writer, stated, "Slums may well be breeding grounds of crime, but middle-class suburbs are incubators of apathy and delirium."

I don't know when Christ will return, but I do know that much of the prophecy regarding the return of our Lord has been fulfilled and Jesus said, "And when these things begin to come to pass, then look up, and lift up your heads; for your redemption draweth nigh" (Luke 21:28).

I have never felt such a sense of urgency in my lifetime. Maybe that is because I am becoming more and more aware that my days are numbered. However, it could also be due to the fact that the Lord's return is near and "the night cometh, when no man can work" (John 9:4).

The second coming should never be an excuse to hide in a bunker and anxiously await His return, but it should be a remarkable incentive to right the wrong we have done, faithfully labor in the Lord's vineyard, and win the lost with a fervency never yet demonstrated on earth.

I believe "code blue" has been sounded for our churches and our nation, but very few seem to be responding to the call and rushing to the intensive care unit where the church is on life support and the nation is tottering on the brink of chaos.

Robert Moffatt, the Scottish Congregationalist missionary to Africa, said, "We'll have all eternity to celebrate our victories, but only one short hour before sunset to win them."

Price Tags

Pastor Stephan Brown gives the illustration about the creative crooks who broke into a department store. He stated, "They entered the store unnoticed and stayed long enough to accomplish their mission.

"You may wonder what they stole, but that's just the catch. They didn't take anything. Instead, these thieves switched the price tags. The tag on a $395 camera was removed and placed on a box of stationery. The $5.95 sticker off a paperback book was attached to an outboard motor. Everything was shuffled.

"When the store opened the next morning, you would have expected total chaos. Surprisingly, though, the store operated normally at first. Some customers literally got some steals while others felt the merchandise was overpriced. Incredibly, four hours slipped by before the hoax was discovered."

It appears to me that in America somebody has switched all the price tags. The socialization of values has turned right and wrong upside down. Our society is now guilty of promoting lies and evil and reproaching the truth and good.

In a 2008 interview with Pastor Rick Warren of Saddleback Church, then-presidential candidate Barack Obama was challenged to define marriage. Mr. Obama responded, "I believe marriage is a union between a man and a woman." On Nov. 1, 2008 he stated, "I am not in favor of gay marriage."

More recently in an exclusive interview on ABC television President Obama stated, "It is important for me to go ahead and affirm that I think same sex couples should get married."

Some have explained President Obama's more recent affirmation of gay marriage as an "evolution" of his philosophy of marriage.

My purpose in this editorial is not to discuss whether or not same sex marriage should be condoned, accepted, legalized, and celebrated. My position on the subject is well-documented. My concern is whether or not truth evolves.

My firm conviction is that truth does not evolve or change. There are objective, absolute truths that are immutable and unalterable. Such is the case with God's Word. The writer of Psalm 119:160 explains, "Thy word is true from the beginning, and every one of thy righteous judgments are true." I doubt the writer was employing hyperbole with the words, "true," "righteous" and "judgments."

Furthermore, truth is very narrow. Billy Graham once told about a flight he took from Korea to Japan. They ran through a snowstorm and as they were about to land in Tokyo, the ceiling and visibility were almost zero. The pilot had to make an instrument landing.

Dr. Graham said, "I sat up in the cockpit and watched him sweat it out as a man in the tower at the airport talked us to the appropriate runway. I did not want this man to be broadminded. I wanted him to be narrow-minded. I knew that our lives depended on it."

So, truth is very narrow and it does not evolve.

Furthermore, you cannot separate God's Word from himself. He is immutable. That means that He does not change. What God says is who He is. Doubting God's Word is akin to questioning His character.

Evangelist Steve Hale, in his book *Truth Decay*, states, "Truth is not a subjective matter of taste, but an objective matter of fact. Truth is truth no matter where you live on the planet."

Hale refers to Norm Geisler and Frank Turek's book, *I Don't Have Enough Faith to Be an Atheist*, and presents six unequivocal truths about absolute, objective truth. They are:

Truth is transcultural. If something is true, it is true for all people, in all places, at all times. (2+2=4 is for everyone, everywhere at every time.)

Truth is unchanging even though our beliefs about truth change. When we began to believe the earth was round instead of flat, the truth about the earth didn't change, only our belief about the earth changed.

Truth is not affected by the attitude of the one professing it. An arrogant person does not make the truth he professes false. A humble person does not make the error he professes true.

All truths are absolute truths. If there is final objective truth, it is still true even when everyone else disagrees and even when it is outlawed by man.

Beliefs cannot change the truth, no matter how sincerely they believe something to be true. Someone can sincerely believe the world is flat, but that only makes him or her sincerely mistaken.

Truth is discovered, not invented. It exists independent of anyone's knowledge of it. Gravity existed prior to Isaac Newton.

Some are of the opinion that Jesus' loving nature and inclusiveness means that he overlooked or accepted certain behaviors the Bible clearly specifies as prohibitive and against God's creative mandates. Jesus, indeed, loved everyone and associated with all kinds of people, but He was not "tolerant" of their sins and alternative lifestyles.

It is true that he forgave the woman taken in adultery in John 8, but He then told her to "go and sin no more." Jesus would not have forgiven her had she not repented, but even then there was the admonition to cease from the sin that had brought condemnation to her soul. He forgave her because He loved her, but He condemned her sin because He loathed it with a holy hatred.

God has always been intolerant toward sin! His Word says: "Wash yourselves, make yourselves clean, put away the evil of your doings from before My eyes. Cease to do evil…" (Is. 1:16).

Since truth is immortal and immutable why doesn't the media, Hollywood, and the leaders of our nation stand up for the kind of truth that saves and the kind of righteousness that exalts a nation? (Proverbs 14:34)

I will tell you why. The truth of God is like a mirror that "shows us up" for what we really are. It is a book of love and compassion, but it also condemns sin and calls the sinner to repentance.

Most folks don't want to be reminded of their sins. They want to cover their sins and the only way to do that is to keep the Bible out of the public square and prevent preachers from sharing their message outside their own pulpits.

We have lost our moral compass. We have perverted right and wrong to the extent that there are those who say adultery is acceptable, fornication is adventurous, marriage is prudish, abstinence is pedantic, imbibing alcohol is conventional, and homosexuality is just an alternate lifestyle.

Someone has changed all the price tags and worthless things have been given a false value and things of worth have been made to look cheap by a generation that has lost its way.

Does Doctrine Matter?

O n the evening of September 11, 2012 Islamic militants attacked the American diplomatic compound in Benghazi, Libya, killing U.S. Ambassador J. Christopher Stevens and three other Americans. The following January, Secretary of State Hillary Clinton appeared before the Senate Foreign Relations Committee to answer questions about the Benghazi attack.

Wisconsin Senator Ron Johnson was questioning Secretary Clinton in an attempt to ascertain whether the attack was the result of a public demonstration gone awry or an act of terrorism.

Clinton's emotional response was, "What difference at this point does it make?"

To carry this concept even further, there are those who are asking, "What difference does gender make?" For example, marriage is all about the complementarity of men and women. The etymology of the word "complementary" suggests the completion, or fulfillment, of something or someone. For example, God affords a measure of completion and fulfillment though a life-long, faithful sexual relationship. This is found in and through the particularity of the other person, in the unique and concrete interweaving of many similarities and differences.

Complementarity is central to any marriage. For centuries cultures around the world have believed that sexual difference is the foundation of that complementarity.

However, now there are those who are saying that sexual difference is not enough for us to know that two people complement each other and that in some cases same-sex couples complement each other better than heterosexual couples. So, they ask, "Does gender really matter?" or "What difference does it make?"

The World Health Organization speaks of gender fluidity and reports, "We do not accept the prevalence of two rigidly defined genders 'Female and Male': and believes in freedom to choose any kind of gender with no rules, no defined boundaries and no fulfilling of expectations associated with any particular gender." In other words, they say, "Gender is not determined by one's anatomy" or "What difference does it make?"

Recently, I was talking to a man not quite my age who is a member of one of our Baptist churches. He informed me that he would soon have his name taken off the church membership roll. I asked him, "Why would you do that?"

He said, "I am getting married in two weeks and my wife is a Catholic and I promised her I would become a Catholic."

I inquired, "How long have you been a Baptist?"

He replied, "I have been a Baptist all my life, but I have been visiting the Catholic church with her for several months and although it is a bit more formal, there is really not that much difference. Basically, we all believe the same thing."

I wanted to say, "Are you kidding me?"

Although he was probably in his late 60s, there is a growing population of church going folks who regard doctrinal issues as a bore and a bother. Pragmatism and rationalism seem to be surreptitiously creeping into many churches and diluting the doctrine.

Noted pastor and author John MacArthur stated, "Sound, biblical doctrine is a necessary aspect of true wisdom and authentic faith. The attitude that scorns doctrine while elevating feeling or blind trust cannot legitimately be called faith at all, even if it masquerades as Christianity. It is actually an irrational form of unbelief."

Many seem to be insensitive to the historic differences within the church: election and free will, infant vs. believers' baptism, the validity of charismatic gifts, the form of church government, Reformed vs. Dispensational theology, and the varying views of Scriptural authority. They don't really care about these differences, and they demonstrate their attitudes by easily moving from church to church with differing ideologies.

Any experienced pastor could certainly confirm the fact that many modern believers seem to have no penchant for doctrinal differences. And there are some pastors who carefully avoid addressing doctrinal issues for fear that would be too negative, confrontational, and divisive.

The Apostle Paul said, "For if the trumpet give an uncertain sound, who shall prepare himself to the battle?" (I Cor. 14:8). There are far too many "uncertain sounds" in the pulpits of the land. Pastors must remember that the writer of Hebrews has a word for pastors when he writes, "… for they watch for your souls, as they that must give account, that they may do it with joy, and not with grief; for that is unprofitable for you" (Heb. 13:17).

And the laity must remember that a nonchalant, lackadaisical, "what difference does it make" attitude about truth/doctrine may help one blend in with our pluralistic society, but it may not meet with God's approval nor correspond with His uncompromising precepts. God's Word is absolute truth. Some things are non-negotiable and there are some things that make a difference.

Yet, today's political correctness demands that those with uncompromising beliefs are urged to be more open-minded. Those with convictions are asked to be less dogmatic. Those with intestinal fortitude are advised to be less confrontational. Those with backbone are counseled to be less rigid or abrasive. Those with firm doctrinal positions are informed that cultural diversity and religious pluralism now rule the day and should be regarded with favor.

In every generation there is the temptation to homogenize our doctrine down to the lowest common denominator, jettison those doctrinal issues that appear to be controversial, and adjust our belief system to accommodate the culture. Some even contend that it doesn't matter what a person's "doctrine" is.

The Apostle Paul said, "Holding fast the faithful word as he has been taught, that he may be able, by sound doctrine, both to exhort and convict those who contradict" (Titus 1:9).

Paul, through the inspiration of the Holy Spirit, told Timothy in 1 Timothy 1:3-7 to "… charge some that they teach no other doctrine …." He also told Timothy in 2 Timothy 4:3 that "… the time will come when [people] will not endure sound doctrine, but according to their own desires, because they have itching ears, they will heap up for themselves teachers."

John said when a person abandons the doctrine of Jesus the Christ, in reality he/she abandons God: "Whoever transgresses and does not abide in the doctrine of Christ does not have God. He who abides in the doctrine of Christ has both the Father and the Son. If anyone comes to you and does not bring this doctrine, do not receive him into your house nor greet him; for he who greets him shares in his evil deeds" (2 John 1:9-11).

What difference does it make? Does doctrine matter? Absolutely! The Southern Baptist Conservative Resurgence won the battle for inerrancy, but we must be forever vigilant in contending for the faith once and for all delivered to the saints.

The Mind: A Battlefield

I am convinced the mind is the major battlefield in life. Whatever gets your mind gets you. Therefore, we need to guard, discipline, and renew our minds, because the battle for sin always starts in the mind.

The Apostle Paul declares: "For the weapons of our warfare are not carnal, but mighty through God to the pulling down of strongholds; Casting down imaginations, and every high thing that exalteth itself against the knowledge of God, and bringing into captivity every thought to the obedience of Christ" (II Corinthians 10:4-5).

The Greek word for "captivity" means "to control, to conquer, to bring into submission." We are to take control of every thought and make it obedient to Christ. That is not easy, because our minds are often disobedient and rebellious. When I want to think a certain way, my mind wants to go in a different direction.

Of course, our greatest asset is our minds and so Satan wants to captivate our minds, our thought processes. The battle for sin always starts in the mind, so Lucifer launches his most artful attacks against our minds. He will use any means available to impair our thought processes – to lead us into sin or to get us to believe a lie.

Years ago, I read Allan Bloom's book *The Closing of the American Mind*, in which he contends that the higher education of the 60s and 70s "failed democracy and impoverished the souls of today's students." In those days students' minds were indoctrinated with relativism, the philosophy that denigrates absolute truth. I was exposed to the concepts of relativism, neo-orthodoxy and situational ethics. My mind was under assault with spurious philosophies on a daily basis.

Interestingly, as a college student I was also required to read George Orwell's book 1984. I actually find the novel more fascinating today than I did 50 years ago. In Orwell's futuristic work he deals with government corruption and mind control.

The novel is about a society (Oceania) divided into three classes of people: the inner party members, the outer party members, and the probes. The inner party members control the information the other classes receive and live in luxury while the rest of the population lives a miserable life.

The inner party of Oceania has so much power over the minds of the people that they are able to convince them that their memories are false. The inner party is constantly changing documents and history to satisfy their needs and the great mass of people blindly acquiesce to the propaganda they are fed by the inner party.

It appears to me that the Common Core Standards in Advanced Placement United States History (APUSH) is designed to do just that. Common Core is the government's plan to nationalize public school education and is written to significantly alter the students understanding of U.S. History.

This new curriculum essentially revises our history and does not mention the sacrifices U.S. civilians and armed forces made to defeat fascism, but it does recommend teachers focus on wartime experiences, such as the internment of Japanese Americans, challenges to civil liberties, debates over race and segregation, and the decision to drop the atomic bomb, which raised questions about American values.

The human brain is an amazing mechanism, but it is also extremely susceptible and vulnerable to all kinds of ideas and philosophies. Our minds, amazingly, have the capacity to comprehend both the noble characteristics of divinity and the dark side of evil. It is incredible that someone's brain will respond favorably to social media requests to join ISIS. It is also astonishing that some are so gullible they will embrace the indefensible tenets of some bizarre cult.

I do not know how a thinking person can be a socialist and believe the distribution of wealth does not destroy initiative. I cannot grasp how giving Iran, the heart of radical Islam, $150 billion contributes to our wellbeing or the wellbeing of the world in general. I cannot comprehend how a person can treat another person as chattel or a second-class citizen regardless of his/her race or ethnicity. I have always had a problem with intelligent people who cannot accept that a child in the womb is a living person. I also have difficulty understanding how anyone can think of the union of two homosexuals as a marriage.

Arthur Milikh, assistant director of the B. Kenneth Simon Center for Principles and Politics at the Heritage Institute, asserts, "Despots of the past tyrannized through blood and iron. But the new breed of democratic despotism does not proceed in this way; it leaves the body and goes straight for the soul (mind)."

Through the biased reporting of the mainstream media the "inner party" seeks to reach into our minds and hearts. It seeks to break our will to resist, to quell any interest in questioning its authority, and to eliminate any propensity to think for ourselves. The inner circle's doctrine of tolerance and barrage of leftist propaganda is designed to intimidate and dare us to contradict them, essentially trying to silence us and ultimately this silencing could potentially culminate in a cessation of thinking.

We see this happening today as Christians are marginalized, threatened, and as their convictions are treated with scorn and derision. Conservative Christians are even ridiculed by other Christian churches for their adherence to biblical principles.

One church purchased a billboard strategically located alongside Billy Graham Parkway in Charlotte that said, "Missiongathering Christian Church IS SORRY for the narrow-minded, judgmental, deceptive, manipulative actions of THOSE WHO DENIED RIGHTS AND EQUALITY TO SO MANY IN THE NAME OF GOD."

Missiongathering describes itself as an "emerging" church. One has to wonder what they are emerging from and what they are emerging into.

David Brody, writing for CBN News, exclaims, "When it comes to the issue of same-sex marriage, are evangelical Christians actually the ones more ridiculed than homosexuals? In the media's narrative, you would think that homosexuals are the poor souls who have been banished by society like ugly stepchildren and are now rising to overcome incredible odds.

"The tables have been turned. Evangelicals are now the ugly stepchildren. In our American culture today, you can easily make the argument that it is harder to stand for biblical truth than to be a supporter of gay marriage in our society."

In 1835 Alexis de Tocqueville wrote his two-volume work entitled: Of Democracy in America. He foresaw an "immense tutelary power" – the modern state – which would degrade men rather than destroy their bodies.

Over time, he feared, the state would take away citizens' free will, their capacity to think and act, reducing them to "a herd of timid and industrious animals of which the government is the shepherd." Is it possible that we are on the brink of that becoming reality?

We must pray that God will give us a sound mind according to II Timothy 1:7.

Pale Pastels and Mixed Messages

I unequivocally prefer listening to preachers, politicians, and CEOs who say what they mean and mean what they say. I have a tremendous respect for people with deep, heartfelt convictions about biblical principles and immortal truth.

Howard Hendricks, former professor at Dallas Theological Seminary, once said, "A belief is something you will argue about, but a conviction is something you will die for." Our convictions determine our conduct. They motivate us to act in certain ways. Some of those convictions should represent hills upon which we are willing to die.

Today, because of the pervasive influence of political correctness we hear far too many mixed messages, ambiguous statements, vague promises, and uncertain sounds.

The Apostle Paul said, "For if the trumpet give an uncertain sound who shall prepare himself to the battle" (I Cor. 14:8). Uncertain sounds and mixed messages rarely resemble a reveille calling us to arise and prepare for the battle.

At the Sept. 15 meeting of the Georgia Baptist Convention Executive Committee concerns were expressed over comments made by Russell Moore, president of the Ethics and Religious Liberty Commission of the

Southern Baptist Convention. Moore has stated that while he would not go to a same-sex wedding, he would go to the couple's shower and reception.

J. Robert White, the GBC executive director, protested, "A reception is a celebration of the wedding. There is no way under the sun you will ever find me at such a reception."

I am appreciative of our Georgia Baptist Convention executive director's comments, because we need leaders to speak of moral and civic issues with clarity and convictions. Dr. White has proven himself to be a man of conviction and character.

On March 1, 1975, in the wake of the disastrous post-Watergate election, Ronald Reagan stood before a disheartened Conservative Political Action Conference and proclaimed, "A political party cannot be all things to all people. It must represent certain fundamental beliefs, which must not be compromised to political expediency, or simply to swell its numbers."

Here is what Ronald Reagan told the assembled delegates of CPAC that day: "I am impatient with those Republicans who after the last election rushed into print saying, 'We must broaden the base of our party' – when what they meant was to fuzz up and blur even more the differences between ourselves and our opponents.

"Our people look for a cause to believe in. Is it a third party we need, or is it a new and revitalized second party, raising a banner of no pale pastels, but bold colors which make it unmistakably clear where we stand on all of the issues troubling the people?"

Then Reagan added, "It is time to reassert our principles and raise them to full view. And if there are those who cannot subscribe to these principles, then let them go their way."

I was proud of SBC President Ronnie Floyd and the 16 former SBC presidents who came out with a bold statement on the sanctity of marriage at this summer's annual meeting in Columbus, OH.

They stated without any hint of compromise: "What the Bible says about marriage is clear, definitive, and unchanging. We affirm biblical, traditional, natural marriage as the uniting of one man and one woman in covenant commitment for a lifetime. The Scriptures' teaching on marriage is not negotiable. We stake our lives upon the Word of God and the testimony of Jesus."

Then they concluded their bold statement with these words: "We stake our very lives and future on the Truth of God's Word."

In this day of uncertain sounds this is the kind of gallant and intrepid language we need coming from our leadership and from the pulpits of our churches.

Rick Warren, pastor of Saddleback Church in Lake Forest, CA, commented, "Biblical convictions are essential for spiritual growth and maturity. What is ironic today is that people often have strong convictions about weak issues (football, fashions, etc.) while having weak convictions about major issues (what is right and what is wrong).

In the first chapter of the book of Daniel we read about Daniel and his three Hebrew friends, Shadrach, Meshach, and Abednego. First, they demonstrated their firm resolve not to defile themselves with the rich food and bubbly wine offered by the Babylonians.

In Daniel, chapter 2, we learn that Daniel interpreted King Nebuchadnezzar's dream and taught the king that it was God who gave him dominion and power and might and glory.

In Daniel 3, Daniel's three friends refused to fall down and worship the image of gold that King Nebuchadnezzar had set up. Their faith was tested. They stood on their conviction of faith not to bow down to the image of gold knowing that to refuse to do so meant being cast into the fiery furnace.

You know the story. They wouldn't bow. They wouldn't bend. They wouldn't burn.

Shadrach, Meshach, and Abednego declared their belief in God's sovereignty and revealed the power of God to the whole world.

In Daniel 6 King Darius issued a decree declaring that those who wished to pray were commanded to pray to him alone and no other. Daniel, who was the first of all the presidents and princes in the kingdom, refused to submit to the king's edict. Daniel 6:10 states: "Now when Daniel knew that the writing was signed, he went into his house; and his windows being open in his chamber toward Jerusalem, he kneeled upon his knees three times a day, and prayed, and gave thanks before his God, as he did aforetime."

Daniel's uncompromising devotion to God landed him in the lion's den, but he dared to obey his Creator and Sustainer.

With respect to Kim Davis, the Kentucky Clerk of Court who refused to grant marriage licenses to same sex couples in Rowan County, Russell Moore contends that since she holds a government position she is required to uphold or execute the law. He makes a distinction between an agent of the state and persons who are being coerced by the state in their private lives.

I know that we are to render to Caesar the things that are Caesar's and to God the things that are God's, but when there is a conflict between the two allegiance to God transcends allegiance to the state. Daniel clearly demonstrated that his preeminent allegiance was to God.

Abraham Kuyper stated, "When the principles that run against your deepest convictions begin to win the day, then the battle is your calling, and peace has become sin. You must at the price of dearest peace lay your convictions bare before friend and enemy with all the fire of your faith."

We live in a nation that has run amuck with political correctness and the doctrine of tolerance. May God bless us to have faith like Daniel and his three friends and the courage to speak and live in bold colors rather than pale pastels.

The Tragedy of a Spiritual Vacuum

It is a known fact that empty and under-utilized spaces are readily recognized and exploited by criminals.

My wife inherited a small tract of land near Sinton, TX almost 25 years ago. It is supposedly a few acres in a very remote area with no physical structures on the property. Five years ago, we were in San Antonio for a meeting and decided to drive to Sinton to see the property. We went to the county courthouse to find a map or directions to the property we had been paying taxes on for a quarter of a century.

When the person who helped us find the directions to the property realized the location of the land, she said, "I would advise you to stay as far away from that property as possible. There are immigrants in that area who would think nothing of shooting intruders." Martha Jean and I took a vote and the decision was unanimous to stay away from our inherited land and allow the appearance of the property to remain a mystery.

An empty house is a vacuum that invites occupants of the vilest sort. Drug addicts, prostitutes, and vile and unscrupulous people of all descriptions love to fill that kind of vacuum and generally do.

First of all, a vacuum does not discriminate. Empty and under-utilized spaces are neither particular nor selective. Since such abandoned places have no monitor or overseer it is very likely those places will be inhabited by people who need attention, counsel, correction, and love the most.

Second, a vacuum does not hesitate. Since an empty space is unlikely to have an overseer, those who wish to fill that vacuum do not have to fill out a form for occupancy. There is no protocol to adhere to as a requisite for occupancy. There are no waiting lists. The vacuum can be filled immediately.

Third, a vacuum does not cooperate. Those who fill up empty spaces or under-utilized areas make up their own agendas and their own rules. In fact, those who occupy once-empty spaces may be averse to rules and given to more of an antinomian society. They are not interested in developing a common moral consensus. They feel no need to cooperate.

I have presented this introduction to explain why I think we have a spiritual vacuum in America.

First, the majority of mainline protestant churches have become apostate. For many people their Christianity is cultural rather than biblical and the relationship they have with God is marked by superficiality rather than authenticity.

Many protestant churches have jettisoned the inspiration and authority of God's Word. They have put men under the authority of women contrary to Scripture. They have acquiesced to the Supreme Court's definition of marriage and given a secondary place to the Supreme Being's definition of marriage. They have compromised on the sanctity of human life. This is unconscionable in view of the fact that an unborn baby is murdered every 23 seconds; and five states have legalized assisted suicide.

They have substituted the social gospel for the Gospel of Jesus, the only begotten Son of God, who was crucified, buried, and raised from the dead. They have replaced the exclusivity of the Gospel wth the philosophy of universalism.

The list of compromises and accommodations is almost endless; and people are abandoning the mainline protestant churches by the millions.

Second, the Catholic Church has its own set of problems. Not only has the church been ravaged by priests who have diminished the influence of the church with their sexual perversions (protestants by no means have escaped the trauma of sexual scandals), but the church as an institution is mostly apostate.

Only each individual Catholic can truly know if he/she is trusting in Jesus as He is defined in the Bible for their salvation or if they are trusting in a false hope of following Catholic doctrine to save them. The doctrines of the Catholic Church are convoluted and their doctrine of salvation is contrary to New Testament teaching.

Consequently, people are leaving the Catholic Church by the millions. Dan Merica of CNN recently reported that one in ten Americans is an ex-Catholic. In fact, if it weren't for the infusion of Catholic immigrants from Latin America, the Catholic Church in America would be shrinking pretty fast.

According to a CNN report, Catholics are leaving the church because of the sex abuse crisis, dissatisfaction with the priests, uninspiring homilies, the status of women, etc.

Finally, the evangelical churches in America are ridden with apathy. Fewer and fewer church members are giving or serving with their time, talents, and treasures as compared to ten or 20 years ago, and it gets worse as one goes back to the giving and serving trends of generations past.

Not only are more and more evangelicals failing in faithfulness to their churches, but many are not even effectively involved in their own families. They have little interest in being involved in their local government and many of them don't even vote in national elections.

Dr. Richard J. Krejcir stated, "We can see this problem in most board-rooms of churches these days. People shift blame and become argumenta-tive. Yet, many of these do little to seek solutions or engage in real, authentic prayer. When we, as Christians, are not experiencing the wonders of the spiritual life and the Christian experience, we will stagnate. If you are a leader, your ineffectiveness can trickle down to the rest of the body and spread like a malignant cancer."

So, when people smell the stench of stagnation and experience the malignancy of cancer in churches they leave and it is difficult to blame them.

So, because of the apostasy of the mainline denominations, the abuses in the Catholic Church and the apathy in the evangelical churches people are departing the churches in America and leaving a vacuum; and a vacuum subtlety invites someone or something to occupy it and cares little who it is.

And have you noticed who is coming to fill that vacuum? It is the Muslims, Hindus, Buddhists, Mormons, Jehovah Witnesses, and a variety of false religions and cults. How are they managing to fill that vacuum? They are more zealous and passionate than we are. While we are giving "incentives" for our missionaries to come home because of a lack of funding, the General Conference of the Church of Latter Day Saints (Mormons) announced in April of 2014 that they had 83,035 missionaries serving in the United States and around the world. Southern Baptists have only a fraction of that.

Vance Havner said, "It is high time that something, persecution if necessary, broke up our complacency and made missionaries out of mere church members."

For the Sake of Freedom, it's Time to Resurrect the Black Robed Regiment

O ur religious liberty is under assault. We need to get the Religious Freedom Restoration Act passed in Georgia. Our state is among the minority of states that have not passed it. Every state contiguous to Georgia has already passed legislation to protect its citizens from religious discrimination.

The most recent assault on religious liberty comes from the state of Washington (a state that does not have the needed RFRA legislation) where Bremerton assistant football coach, Joe Kennedy, has been put on leave because he refused to comply with district directives to stop praying before and after games.

CBS News reported that Kennedy initially agreed to comply with the district's order, but then, with support from the Texas-based Liberty Institute, a religious-freedom organization, he resumed the postgame prayers.

CBS explained that Kennedy would silently take a knee for 15 to 20 seconds at midfield after shaking hands with the opposing coaches. His football team joined him as he prayed at times, as well as players from the opposing team and even fans. His lawyers insist he is not leading students in prayer, but just praying himself.

The school district passed their edict in response to the Seattle chapter of the Satanic Temple with 42 members who suggested that by allowing Kennedy to kneel and pray they were creating a forum for religious expression for all groups. So, the devil's disciples also requested permission to perform an invocation on the field after the game.

Satanic chapter head Lilith Starr described their style of prayer meeting by saying," It'll definitely be a theatrical production with robes and incense and a gong. There are a number of students," Starr insisted, "who don't feel like they're being represented on the field."

This is simply one isolated example of our religious liberty coming under attack, but the number of attacks is growing exponentially in every city and state, and particularly those states that do not have Religious Freedom Restoration legislation.

Our history records a time when America's pastors preached politics, resisted tyranny, and founded a nation on the Bible.

Dr. Joel McDurmon, author and resident scholar for American vision, states, "The problem is that our pulpits and preachers today have abandoned the fullness of what Christ commanded us: to disciple nations and to teach them all of His commandments.

"That Great Commission includes the call, which our forefathers ably demonstrated, to speak truth to the public realm: to call out rulers, government's laws, abuse, and to demand liberty and justice. In all our preaching today about iniquity and sin, we neglect to address inequity and tyranny.

"And worse: should one dare to mention that broader social and political scope of the Great Commission today they are likely to be harangued not only by humanists and leftists, but by a vast majority of Christians and clergy. The response will be almost unanimous, almost in perfect chorus: 'Christians should not preach politics! We should preach the 'Gospel' only!"

In Alice Baldwin's book, *The New England Pulpit and the American Revolution*, she writes, "No one can fully understand the American Revolution and the American constitutional system without a realization of the long history and religious associations which lie behind these words: without realizing that for a hundred years before the Revolution men were taught that these rights were protected by divine, inviolable law."

However, a recent Barna poll revealed that pastors know and believe that the Bible speaks to social and political issues, but they are not addressing them. In fact, a whopping 80% of pastors do not preach what they know they should be preaching – what they acknowledge to believe the Bible actually says.

Barna stated that there are five factors that the majority of pastors view as measures of success: attendance, giving, number of programs, number of staff, and square footage.

Barna commented, "What I'm suggesting is [those pastors] won't probably get involved in politics because it's very controversial. Controversy keeps people from being in the seats, controversy keeps people from giving money, from attending programs."

There may be Georgia Baptist pastors who fear that addressing social and political issues from the pulpit will produce controversy or result in a governmental reprimand or the church losing its tax-exempt status.

Preachers who are afraid of controversy need to get over it. We need to bring back the Black Robed Regiment. The Black Robed Regiment was the "patriot preachers" of the 18th century, who led their congregations to battle the abusive tyranny of the Redcoats.

If politics are corrupt today, and they are, it is because Christians have too often removed themselves from participation and preachers have failed to teach their congregations about the biblical principles of liberty and government so that their flock will have a template to use with politicians.

And, according to TheWordOut.net it is not likely that a church is going to lose its tax-exempt status when pastors address political and social issues. In fact, from the founding of the country until 1954, churches and other nonprofit organizations were permitted to expressly endorse or oppose candidates for political office. That changed when Lyndon Johnson ran for United States Senate. He was opposed by a nonprofit organization (not a church), and after he won the election, he proposed legislation to amend the Internal Revenue Code to prohibit nonprofit organizations, including churches, from endorsing or opposing political candidates. The Code was amended in 1954 without any debate regarding the impact of the bill.

The Internal Revenue Code now expressly prohibits churches and other nonprofit organizations from directly endorsing or opposing political candidates. From 1954 to the present, only one church has ever lost its IRS tax-exempt letter ruling, but even that church did not loose its tax-exempt status for opposing then-Governor Bill Clinton for President in 1992.

The Church at Pierce Creek, located in Binghamton, NY (a church where Operation Rescue founder Randall Terry attended at the time), took out full-page ads in the *USA Today*, and the *Washington Times* newspapers. The ads opposed Governor Clinton for president because of his position on abortion and homosexuality, and then the ads solicited 'tax-deductible donations' to defray the cost of the advertisements. The church received hundreds of contributions.

So, if the Church at Pierce Creek did not lose its tax-exempt status, it is unlikely that a church is going to do so if a pastor addresses political and social issues. In fact, last year 1,966 pastors preached politics from their pulpits on Pulpit Freedom Sunday, an annual event aimed at overturning the IRS rule that churches could lose their tax-exempt status if their pastors back or attack political candidates in their sermons.

The Arizona-based conservative group Alliance Defending Freedom declares that Pulpit Freedom Sunday is an event associated with the Pulpit Initiative, a legal effort designed to secure the free speech rights of pastors in the pulpit. They are always on call to defend pro bono (without cost) those pastors and churches that feel that their religious freedom is being infringed upon.

History proves that anointed preaching can result in spiritual revival and societal transformation like that seen in the First and Second Awakenings. Fearless preachers and uncompromising preaching are all the more necessary in these dangerous times.

The Southern Baptist Convention is Undergoing a Seismic Shift

Following the 1990 Southern Baptist Convention in New Orleans a host of conservative Baptists converged on the Café du Monde to celebrate another victory for the cause of Biblical inerrancy.

Paige Patterson, writing in the *Southwestern Journal of Theology* proclaimed, "The aroma of café au lait and powdered sugar-covered beignets was discernible several hundred feet from the famous coffee house.

"That night as the convention parliamentarian led the rejoicing conservatives in singing 'Victory in Jesus,' that coffee aroma was to conservatives the aroma of life unto life, but to scores of moderates who had tasted several years of defeat, it became the aroma of death unto death."

I have had over a month to process the events of the most recent Southern Baptist Convention in Dallas; and for me it was a Café du Monde experience. The only difference is that I felt like I smelled the aroma of death unto death – at least for the SBC I have known for a very long time.

The Southern Baptist Convention is not just changing; it has changed. Many will consider it a blessed conversion. Others will feel disenfranchised, marginalized, and excluded. This convention confirmed that my decision to retire at the end of this year is well founded, because I feel like a voice crying in the wilderness.

I grew up listening to the sermons of R. G. Lee and W. A. Criswell. Those men of God preached with great conviction, emotion and passion.

R. G. Lee with his distinctive southern drawl, command of the English language and masterful oratorical ability declared, "The Bible is a living Book. Book of the church militant is the Bible. Book of the church triumphant is the Bible. It's the Book our mothers stained with grateful tears, the Book our fathers touched with reverent hands, the Book that unrolls the panorama of creation, the Book that gives the lofty imagery of the prophets, the Book that gives the portrait of Christ, the Book that gives the philosophy of salvation."

W. A. Criswell was no less eloquent, but perhaps more direct in confronting liberalism when he declared, "There is some knot on a log, wart on a dill pickle who think that he's been to school and he knows more than God. . . We have professors who think theological hairsplitting will save the world. Not in a thousand years. It's a fervent heart and preaching for a verdict that saves the world."

Southern Baptists were all about evangelism and missions for many years, but in the last decade it seems that we have changed our focus; and the decline in baptisms at home and abroad have been precipitous.

Chuck Kelley, President of New Orleans Baptist Theological Seminary, has explained, "The true bad news is that when you put last year in the context of all previous years, it indicates the SBC is in the midst of a decline that shows no sign of either slowing down or turning around.

The new emphases subtly infiltrating Southern Baptist life seems to be social justice, the social gospel, feminism, tolerance and intolerance.

First, let us consider social justice. According to David C. Rose, social justice is a solution in search of a problem. I believe that we should show compassion for all people, but when social justice requires compromise on moral and spiritual issues it is desperately wrong. Rose says, "Social justice is both misguided and dangerous. It is misguided because it regards observed inequality as prima facie evidence of injustice because of insufficient understanding of how a free market economy actually works. It is dangerous because social justice advocates therefore attempt to solve a moral problem that doesn't exist and, in so doing, reduce a society's ability to solve moral problems that really do exist."

Second, Consider the social gospel, which has surreptitiously found its way back into our denomination. The social gospel embraces ministries that provide help to the needy – clothes closets, food banks, and health-clinics - almost anything that would contribute to the welfare of society.

Churches should be engaged in these social ministries, but these ministries should not be the primary objective. Every social ministry or act of kindness should create a bridge to share the Gospel.

When I was pastor of Eastside Baptist Church in Marietta I read Steve Sjogren's book, *Conspiracy of Kindness*. Sjogren gives his readers an almost unlimited list of unassuming acts of kindness that Christians can practice to communicate the love of Christ. I discovered that many of our folks were excited about giving out water on a hot summer day, painting house numbers on the edge of the sidewalk, shining people's shoes for free in the mall and even providing free gift wrapping for a department store at Christmas, but they never shared the Gospel.

Good deeds are important, but there are countless service organizations that help the public. Christians not only have the privilege of putting a man in a new suit, but putting a new man in a suit as a result of the change wrought by sharing the Gospel.

Third, Southern Baptists seem to be welcoming a feminist movement in the church. George Barna reports through his surveys that the majority of attendees in a typical church are women. He refers to women as "the backbone of the Christian congregations in America." He also reports that 93 percent of the senior pastors in America are men.

However, does that mean that we should seek equality for women and ordain them as pastors? It has been rumored that one of America's most notable Bible teachers, Beth Moore, should become the SBC president in 2020. If she did, she would be placed in a position of preaching the president's sermon.

The Bible does not support the practice of women serving as pastors or teaching men (I Timothy 2: 12), but the intrinsic value and extreme giftedness of women have throughout history fortified and enhanced the ministry of the Holy Spirit in the church.

Fourth, the menacing worldly view of tolerance has raised its ugly head in the Baptist church. There was a time when lifestyles embodied in the LGBTQ community were universally condemned.

Today because of the normalizing of this deviate behavior in the media, the propagandizing of students in the schools and the sensitivity training of corporate America we are getting too comfortable with sin and tolerant of aberrant lifestyles. The pulpit must not be silent in this day of tolerance lest our congregations become lukewarm. George Whitefield said, "Congregations are lifeless because dead men preach to them." Adrian Rogers said, "The sins we once hid in the back alleys, we now parade down Main Street."

Fifth, whereas tolerance abounds in some areas, intolerance abounds in others. It was good that we recognized our U. S. military and had a patriotic emphasis in the first session of our Convention in Dallas, but I could not believe the disrespect some messengers demonstrated regarding the invitation of Vice President Mike Pence to address our convention. Three motions were made to try to prevent him from speaking and when he did speak some walked out of the convention center obviously protesting his presence.

Have some Southern Baptists become like Jehovah Witnesses who refuse to salute the flag, do not rise in response to the playing of the national anthem and often choose not to vote in elections?

The New Testament gives us some broad principles on how we are to respond to our government. Romans 13 declares that the origin and institution of government is something that God has ordained. I Timothy 2 reminds us that we are to pray for those who have authority over us. If God has established the government for our good and asked us to pray for those who rule over us; and we are fortunate enough to have a Christian as Vice President is it right to protest his invitation to speak to SBC messengers?

In the late 1960s W. A. Criswell predicted that Christianity would be virtually extinct by 2000. He believed it would happen because so many preachers had "lost the conviction that the Bible is the Word of God."

Perhaps the Conservative Resurgence postponed what Criswell thought was inevitable. He said then and I believe he would say now, "I believe it is time for every pastor and church member to call upon God to intervene on behalf of his church" – and I believe we need His intervention in the life of our Convention.

Trust Publishers House,
the trusted name in quality Christian books.

Trust House Publishers
PO Box 3181
Taos, NM 87571

TrustHousePublishers.com